The Easiest Way to Learn and Teach English/Spanish

La Manera Más Fácil de Aprender y Enseñar Inglés/Español

MACKENZY JOSEPH

"If you're running after money for yourself not to help the world and others, you lose the real purpose of life."

If you wish to get the first free audio recording lessons or your
diploma after finishing this book email us at:
Yourlessons2day@gmail.com

Si desea obtener gratis la primera grabación de audio o su diploma después de
terminar este libro envíanos un mensaje al: Yourlessons2day@gmail.com

PROLOGUE

PRÓLOGO

WELCOME TO THE EASIEST WAY TO LEARN & TEACH ENGLISH/SPANISH
BIENVENIDO A LA MANERA MÁS FÁCIL DE APRENDER Y ENSEÑAR INGLÉS/ESPAÑOL

The Easiest Way to Learn & Teach English/Spanish is the beginning and intermediate level course created especially for people whose first language is English or Spanish. The levels are dividing in 3 Months for basic which started from greetings and end up with individual questions (VOCABULARY: U-V-W-X-Y-Z). However, the remaining nine months are for intermediate group. Within the three (3) Months is allowed by the teacher and students to use both languages (English and Spanish) to learn properly the basic, after three months no Spanish or English must be permitted in the classroom in order to help students in developing what they learned for the last three months. This book has been written to teach Spanish speakers how to speak English & as well English speakers how to learn Spanish.

La Manera Más Fácil de Aprender y Enseñar Inglés/Español es el comienzo de un curso b á s i c o e intermedio creado especialmente para las personas cuyo primer idioma es inglés o español. Los niveles se dividen en tres meses para el básico que iniciará a partir de saludos y terminan a las preguntas individuales (VOCABULARIO: U-V-W-X-Y-Z). Los 9 meses restantes son para el grupo intermedio. Dentro de los 3 meses está permitido al profesor y a los estudiantes de utilizar los dos idiomas (Inglés y Español) para aprender correctamente el nivel básico, después de 3 meses se prohíbe hablar Español o Inglés en el salón con el fin de ayudar a los estudiantes a desarrollar lo que aprendieron durante los últimos 3 meses. Este libro ha sido escrito para enseñar a los Hispanos a hablar Inglés y a la gente cuyo idioma nativo es Inglés a aprender Español.

WHOLE LEARNING APPROACH
ENFOQUE DE APRENDIZAJE TOTAL

The Easiest Way to Learn & Teach English/Spanish adopts many principles & applies them to the classroom.

La Manera Más Fácil de Aprender y Enseñar Inglés/Español adopta muchos principios y los aplica en el salón de clase.

As we know, students are partners with their teachers in the learning experience. Students and teachers are actively encouraged to express, integrate their previous knowledge and into a new learning approach.

Como sabemos, los estudiantes son socios con sus maestros en la experiencia de aprendizaje. Estudiantes y profesores están activamente estimulados a expresar, integrar sus conocimientos y experiencias en un nuevo enfoque de aprendizaje.

Learning is personalized so that students have many opportunities to learn by themselves & know the way to teach others.

El aprendizaje se personaliza para que los estudiantes tengan oportunidades para aprender por sí mismos y saber cómo enseñar a otros.

Students can learn English or Spanish as a communication tool.

Los estudiantes pueden aprender Inglés o Español como herramienta de comunicación.

In "The Easiest Way to Learn &Teach English/Spanish," students are given the opportunity to speak, listen, read and write.

En "La Manera Más Fácil de Aprender y Enseñar inglés/español" todos los estudiantes tienen la oportunidad de hablar, escuchar, leer y escribir.

Learning involves success. Believing that student who succeeds in dedicating some time every day to learn the lessons step by step will acquire the language more rapidly.

El aprendizaje implica éxito. Creemos que los estudiantes que toman unos minutos en dedicar un poco de tiempo cada día para aprender las lecciones paso a paso adquirirán el idioma más rápido.

Even though English or Spanish is not their native language, it's important to learn about the U.S or Mexico culture, for example, the holidays (Independence's Day etc.).

A pesar de que Inglés o Español no es su lengua maternal, es importante aprender acerca de la cultura de Estados Unidos o México, por ejemplo, los días festivos (Día de la Independencia etc).

STRUCTURE OF THE COURSE

ESTRUCTURA DEL CURSO

The beginning, and the intermediate levels of The Easiest Way to Learn and Teach English/Spanish consists of grammar, vocabulary, reading, pronunciation, phrases to build, phrases to translate and conversations.

El nivel básico e intermedio de La Manera Más Fácil de Aprender y Enseñar Inglés/Español consiste en gramática, vocabulario, lectura, pronunciación, construcción de frases, traducción de frases y conversaciones.

The themes have been selected for educational value. The task within each level generates a range of 100% to speak and understand English or Spanish. Each lesson is combined with listening activities.

Los temas se han seleccionado con valor educativo. La tarea de cada nivel genera un rango de 100 % para hablar y entender Inglés o Español. Cada lección contiene actividades de audio.

CONTENTS

CONTENIDOS

ACKNOWLEDGMENTS

AGRADECIMIENTOS

First, sincere thanks go to God for giving me the opportunity to write this book that may be useful to English speakers or Spanish speakers. Special thanks to my friend Ben Lepp, at "The Easiest Way to Learn & Teach English/Spanish Book Company," who agreed with me about the idea of sharing this book with people who really want to learn or improve their knowledge and skills whether in English or Spanish. I also want to thank him for his generosity in sharing information with me. This helped me quickly shape this book. Although I encountered some significant and unplanned obstacles in preparing this book, I hope it will benefit everyone who wants to learn English or Spanish.

En primer lugar, mi agradecimiento sincero a Dios por darme la oportunidad de escribir este libro que puede ser útil para personas que habla Inglés o Español. Un agradecimiento especial a Ben Lepp, mi compañero en La Manera Más Fácil de Aprender y Enseñar Inglés/Español, quien estuvo de acuerdo conmigo sobre la idea de compartir este libro con personas que realmente quieren aprender o mejorar sus conocimientos y habilidades en cualquiera de esos idiomas. También quiero darle las gracias por su generosidad en compartir información conmigo. Esto me ayudó a formar rápidamente este libro. Aunque he encontrado algunos obstáculos en la preparación de este libro, espero que beneficiara a todos los lectores que quieren aprender Inglés o Español.

This book comes together with the help of the Deputy Juan Manuel Alatorre Franco, Dr. Alberto Avila Mora and the Engineer Héctor Manuel Ortíz Delgado director of the University "Technologico de Ocotlan" and Gerardo Iñiguez Hernandez, the director of the recording station, who helped me to record the lessons for the education of the youths and adults.

Este libro viene junto con la ayuda del Diputado Juan Manuel Alatorre Franco, Dr. Alberto Ávila Mora y el Ingeniero Héctor Manuel Ortíz Delgado el director de la Universidad "Tecnológico de Ocotlán" y Gerardo Iñiguez Hernandez, el director de grabación, que me ayudó a grabar las lecciones para la educación de jóvenes y adultos.

Special thanks to my Grandparents, Mavelus Jeannis and Exalia Fleurima. My father, Jean Joseph, my mother, Mersedane Jeannis, my sister Guilaine Joseph, & my friends, Jose Flavio Sánchez, William Atkins Denton, Jason Elston, Jeffrey Chervil, Stacey Meika, Sam Sheridan Graves Jr., Celia Jeannis, Silvia Beatriz Duron Naranjo, Guillermina Martínez, Bertha Alicia Hernandez Arana, Brenda D. Moore, Joshua Littlefield, Cecilia Altamirano Contreras and Edwin Marlon Rodríguez Ortega for helping me find the opportunity to write this book, and for always believing in me.

Un agradecimiento especial a mis abuelos, Mavelus Jeannis y Exalia Fleurima. Mi padre, Jean Joseph, mi madre, Mersedane Jeannis, mi hermana Guilaine Joseph, y mis amigos, José Flavio Sánchez, William Atkins Denton, Jason Elston, Jeffrey Chervil, Stacey Meika, Sam Grave Sheridan Jr., Celia Jeannis, Silvia Beatriz Duron Naranjo, Guillermina Martínez, Bertha Alicia Hernández Arana, Brenda D. Moore, Cecilia Altamirano Contreras y Edwin Marlon Rodríguez Ortega por ayudarme a encontrar la oportunidad de escribir este libro, y por creer siempre en mí.

Heartfelt thanks to my friend; Dale Hudson for understanding what it takes to create a book like this and for recording the lessons. His time and effort in doing this helped me immeasurably in bringing this book to the people.

Un caloroso agradecimiento a mi amigo; Dale Hudson por entender todo el esfuerzo que se hizo para crear un libro como éste y por grabar las lecciones. Su tiempo y esfuerzo en hacer esto me ayudó inmensamente en llevar este libro a las personas.

Finally, thanks to Mr. John Heiskell, who gave me the passion for beginning my venture in writing a bilingual book for people who need to speak English or Spanish.

Finalmente, agradezco al veterano John Heiskell, quien despertó la pasión en mí en comenzar mi aventura escribiendo un libro bilingüe para la gente que necesita hablar Inglés o Español.

CONTENTS OF STUDENT'S BOOK
CONTENIDO DEL LIBRO DE ESTUDIANTE

INTRODUCTION

PRESENTACIÓN

Spelling and pronunciation/Ortografía y pronunciación

Success is one of the main keys of The Easiest Way to Learn & Teach English/Spanish. At the earlier stages, it encourages students to make their best guesses. Spelling and pronunciation will show them the differences about many words that begin with a,e,i,o,u and y which do not have the same pronunciation.

El éxito de La Manera Más Fácil de Aprender y Enseñar Inglés/Español es una de las principales claves. En las primeras etapas, se estimula a los estudiantes en adivinar, deletrear y pronunciar para mostrarles las diferencias de muchas palabras que comienzan con a, e, i, o, u, y que no tienen la misma pronunciación.

Vocabulary development/ Desarrollo de Vocabulario

In English/Spanish, a word can have many meanings. We use the same procedure to teach students. We carefully pick vocabulary examples from A to Z.

En Inglés/Español, una palabra puede tener muchos significados. Utilizamos el mismo procedimiento para enseñar a los estudiantes. Elegimos con cuidado los ejemplos de vocabulario A a Z.

Phrases to build/ Construcción de frases

Students will feel successful in making phrases that help them to be more comfortable in expressing themselves in English or in Spanish. In the beginning, it is normal to make some mistakes. However, they should not quit because one of the life's lesson is, if you fall down, you get back up.

Los estudiantes tendrán éxito en hacer frases que les ayudan a estar más cómodos en expresarse en Inglés o en Español. Al principio, es normal cometer algunos errores. Sin embargo, no deben de renunciar ya que la lección de vida es, si te caes, vuelva a levantarte.

Phrases to translate/ Traducción de frases

Reading & translation provide various opportunities. This helps the students learn from their mistakes. We train students who really want to learn English or Spanish.

Leyendo y traduciendo ofrecen muchas oportunidades. Esto ayuda a los estudiantes a aprender de sus errores. Enseñamos a estudiantes que realmente quieren aprender Inglés o Español.

Individual questions/ Preguntas individuales

Questioning students are part of the teaching; therefore, it is a procedure. Students need to be carefully taught how to make questions and how to answer them. These questions are repeated through previously learned vocabulary.

Hacer preguntas a estudiantes es parte de la enseñanza, por lo tanto, es un procedimiento. Los estudiantes necesitan ser capacitado cuidadosamente para saber cómo hacer preguntas y saber cómo contestarlas. Estas preguntas se repiten a través del vocabulario aprendido previamente.

Reading comprehension /Lectura de comprehensión

Our bodies, as well as our brains, need to be nourished by reading every day. We have selected different subjects for classroom usage, not only helping students' pronunciation but also with previously learned grammar and vocabulary.

Así como nuestros cuerpos, nuestros cerebros, tienen que ser alimentados por la lectura todos los días. Hemos seleccionado diferentes temas que pueden ser usados en el salón de clase, no solamente ayudando los estudiantes con sus pronunciaciones sino también con la gramática y el vocabulario que han aprendido previamente.

Teacher's part/ Parte del professor

After reading individual scripts, the class will take time analyze the reading comprehension. When finished, the teachers will ask direct questions to their students. The teacher's part is to test student's comprehension and give feedback.

Después de la lectura individual, la clase se tomará tiempo para analizar la lectura de comprensión. Cuando termina, los maestros harán preguntas directos a sus estudiantes. La parte del profesor es poner a prueba la comprensión del estudiante y retroalimentar el tema.

LESSON I

LECCIÓN I

Greetings and meetings/Saludos y encuentros

Hi! (Formal)/Hello! (Formal)/Hey! (Informal): Hola!
Good morning (Formal) or morning (Informal): Buenos días
Good afternoon: Buenas tardes
Good evening: Buenas noches

How to greet and answer in English/Cómo saludar y contestar en Inglés

¿Cómo está (s)?o **¿Cómo está ústed?** How are you? How do you do? How are you doing? How is it going? **How have you been?** ¿Cómo has estado? **How is everything?** ¿Cómo van las cosas? How are things with you? ¿Cómo van las cosas?	1- **Fine thanks, and you?** Bien gracias, y tú/y ústed? 2- **Pretty good thanks, and yourself?** Muy bien gracias, y tú/y ústed? 3- **Great thanks, how about you?** Muy bien gracias, y tú/y ústed? 4- **I am doing well, what about you?** Bien gracias, y tú/y ústed? 5- **More or less/not bad/not so good**: Más o menos – No muy bien **Four ways to say "y tú/y ústed" in English** 1) And you? 2) And yourself? 3) How about you? 4) What about you?

SAY GOOD BYE

DESPEDIRSE

Good bye/So long/Bye bye!	Adios!
See you later	Hasta luego
See you then	Hasta luego
See you soon	Hasta pronto
See you tomorrow	Hasta mañana
See you next week	Hasta la próxima semana
See you next time	Hasta la próxima
Take care of yourself	Cuidate!
Keep or stay in touch	Estamos en contacto
Good night or have a good night	Que tenga (s) buenas noches
Have a nice day	Que tenga (s) un buen día
Have a nice weekend	Que tenga un buen fin de semana
Have a good trip	Que tenga (s) un buen viaje
Have a good time	Que la pases bien

Three ways to say: "Gracias igualmente" in English

Tres formas de decir: "Gracias igualmente" en Inglés

1) Thank you, you too.   2) Thank you, same to you.   3) Thank you, likewise.

HOW TO INTRODUCE YOURSELF

CÓMO PRESENTARSE

Introduction I/Presentación I

Patricia: Hi, good morning.
Patricia: Hola, buenos días.
Peter: Good morning.
Peter: Buenos días
Patricia: How are you?
Patricia: ¿Cómo estás / Cómo está ústed?
Peter: Fine thanks, and you?
Peter: Bien gracias, y tú / y ústed?
Patricia: I'm doing great, <u>by the way</u> my name is Patricia. <u>What´s your name</u>?
Patricia: Muy bien, <u>por lo tanto</u> me llamo Patricia. <u>¿Cómo te llamas?</u>
Peter: I´m Peter or <u>my name is Peter.</u>
Peter: Me llamo Peter o <u>mi nombre es</u>
<u>Peter.</u> **Patricia: <u>Nice to meet you,</u> Peter.**
Patricia: <u>Mucho gusto,</u> Peter.
Peter: Nice to meet you too.
Peter: <u>Igualmente.</u>

Introduction II/Presentación II

Henry: Patricia **<u>I'd like you to meet</u>** John
Henry: Patricia **<u>me gustaría presentarte</u>** a John

Patricia: Hi, John **<u>it's great to meet you</u>** / Hi, John **<u>it's a pleasure to meet you.</u>**
Patricia: Hola, John <u>gusto conocerte</u> / Hola, John <u>es un placer conocerte</u>.

John: Hello, Patricia **it's great to meet you too** or **the pleasure is mine**.
John: Hola, Patricia <u>igualmente</u> / Hola, Patricia <u>el placer es mío</u>.

Introduction II other version/Presentación II otra versión

Henry: Patricia **this is** John, John **this is** Patricia.
Henry: Patricia <u>te presento</u> a John, John <u>te presento</u> a Patricia

Patricia: Hi, John **pleased to meet you**
Patricia: Hola, John <u>mucho gusto</u>.

John: **Pleased to meet you too.**
John: <u>Igualmente</u>.

How to introduce yourself at a meeting/Cómo presentarse en una reunión

Donald Smith: <u>**Hi, my name is**</u> Donald Smith, **I am** an Electronic Engineer and **I work at** General Electric Company **in** New York. **I'm from** the United Kingdom (UK).

Donald Smith: <u>Hola, mi nombre es</u> Donald Smith, <u>soy</u> Ingeniero Electronico y <u>trabajo en</u> la Compañía General Electric <u>en</u> Nueva York. <u>Soy de</u> Inglatera.

THREE WAYS TO SAY "MUCHO GUSTO O GUSTO CONOCERTE" IN ENGLISH

1- **Nice to meet you.**   Answer : Nice to meet you too.
2- **It's great to meet you.**   Answer : It's great to meet you too.
3- **Pleased to meet you.**   Answer : Pleased to meet you too.
4- **It's a pleasure to meet you.** Answer : The pleasure is mine.

DESCRIBING PEOPLE

DESCRIBIR A LAS PERSONAS

To describe a person, we need to memorize two types of verbs" To be"and "To have."

Para describir a una persona, se necesita memorizar dos tipos de verbos "Ser o Estar/Haber o Tener."

Present tense indicative Presente indicativo	Present tense indicative Presente indicativo
To be: Ser o Estar	**To have: Haber o Tener**
I am (I'm) : **Yo soy**/Yo estoy	**I have** (I've): **Yo tengo**
You are (you're): **Tú eres**/Tú estás	**You have** (you've): **Tú tienes**/Ústed tiene
He is (he's): **Él es**/Él está	**He has** (he's): **Él tiene**
She is (she's): **Ella es** / Ella está	**She has** (she's): **Ella tiene**
It is (it's): **Esto es**/Esto está	**It has** (It's): **Esto tiene**
We are (we're): **Somos** / Estámos	**We have** (we've): **Nosotros tenemos**
You are (you're): **Son**/Están	**You have** (you've): **Ústedes tienen**
They are (they're): **Ellos o Ellas son**/Ellos o Ellas están	**They have** (they've): **Ellos o Ellas tienen**

CÓMO DESCRIBIR FÍSICAMENTE A UNA PERSONA

Tall: **Alto (a)**	Attractive: **Atractivo**	Wavy hair: **Cabello ondulado**
Short: **Bajo (a)**	Ugly: **Feo (a)**	Curly hair: **Cabello rizo**
Fat: **Gordo (a)**	**Eyes:** Ojos	Straight hair: **Cabello lacio**
Thin: **Delgado (a)**	Blue eyes: **Ojos azules**	Short hair: **Cabello corto**
Slim: **Delgado (a)**	Gray eyes: **Ojos grises**	Long hair: **Cabello largo**
Skinny: **Flaco (a)**	Green eyes: **Ojos verdes**	Bald: **Calvo (a)**
Young: **Jóven**	Brown eyes: **Ojos cafés**	**Skin**: Piel
Old: **Viejo (a)**	**Hair**: Cabello	Dark skin: **Piel morena**
Cute: **Lindo (a)**	Blond hair: **Cabello rubio**	Black skin: **Piel negra**
Handsome: **Guapo**	Brown hair: **Cabello café**	Tan skin: **Piel bronceada**
Heavy set: **Corpulento**	Black hair: **Cabello negro**	White skin: **Piel blanca**
Pretty/Beautiful: **Bonita**	Red hair: **Pelirojo (a)**	Pale skin: **Piel pálida**
Average: **Estatura media**	Frizzy hair: **Cabello chino**	
Middle aged: **Edad promedio**		

Describe physically yourself, then those people below
Describe físicamente a ti mismo, después a estas personas

1) What do you look like?
1) ¿Cómo te describes?

2) What does he look like?
2) ¿Cómo describes a él?

3) What does she look like?
3) ¿Cómo describes a ella?

EXERCISE/EJERCICIO: **Translate into English**/Traduce en Inglés.

1- Karina es alta, ella tiene los ojos verdes y es delgada.
2- Peter tiene cabello café, él es joven y es muy lindo.
3- Jenny y William son bajos, ellos tienen cabello rizo y piel morena.

VOCABULARY / VOCABULARIO
Expressing feelings/Expresando cómo se siente

Happy/Content: Feliz/Contento	**Sad/Depressed**: Triste/Deprimido (a)
Angry/Mad: Enojado (a)	**Satisfy/Pleased**: Satisfecho (a)
Confused: Confundido (a)	**Desperate**: Desesperado (a)
Upset/Disturb: Molesto (a)	**Excited**: Emocionado (a)
Wonderful: Maravilloso (a)	**Sick**: Enfermo (a)
Anxious: Anxioso (a)	**Great**: Grandioso (a)
Concerned: Preocupado (a)	**Disoriented**: Desorientado (a)
Worried: Preocupado (a)	**Lost**: Perdido (a)

Answer the questions below using: "To be" or "To feel"
Contesta las preguntas usando: El verbo "Ser o Estar" o "Sentir"

1) How do you feel?
1) ¿Cómo te sientes?

2) How does he feel?
2) ¿Cómo se siente él?

3) How does she feel?
3) ¿Cómo se siente ella?

4) How do they feel?
4) ¿Cómo se sienten?

VOCABULARY – A PERSON'S TEMPERAMENT

Smart: Inteligente	**Very comprehensive**: Muy comprehensivo (a)
Very easy to please: Fácil de complacer	**A hard working person**: Muy trabajador (a)
Hard to please: Dificíl de complacer	**Well educated**: Muy educado (a)
A bad temperament: Un mal temperamento	**Very friendly**: Muy amiguero
A good temperament: Un buen temperamento	**Very patient**: Muy paciente
A nice person: Una linda persona	**Impatient**: Impaciente
Very Honest: Muy honesto (a)	**Dishonest**: Deshonesto (a)
Very supportive: Muy apoyador	**Soft**: Tierno (a)
Trust worthy: De confianza	**Sweet**: Dulce, tierno (a)
Very jealous: Muy celoso (a)	**Lazy**: Perezoso (a)
Serious: Serio (a)	**Responsible**: Responsable
Gentle: Gentíl	**A trouble maker**: Peleonero (a)
Very attentive: Muy atento (a)	**Loving**: Cariñoso (a)
A good listener: Muy atento (a)	**Communicative**: Comunicativo (a)
Silly: Tonto (a)	**Aggressive**: Agresivo (a)

Answer the questions below using: "To be" or "To have"
Contesta las preguntas usando: El verbo "Ser o Estar" o "Tener"

Questions and answers/Preguntas y respuestas
Pick one of the answers/Escoge una de las respuestas

What do you think of Paul?	I think he is/<u>I think he has</u>...................
¿Qué piensas de Paul?	**<u>Pienso que es</u> o pienso que él tiene**...........
What do you think of me?	I think you are or <u>I think you have</u>............
¿Qué piensas de mí?	**<u>Pienso que tú eres</u> o pienso que tú tienes**...
What do you think of her?	I think she is or <u>I think she has</u>...................
¿Qué piensas de ella?	**<u>Pienso que ella es</u> o pienso que ella tiene**.....
What do you think of him?	I think he is or <u>I think he has</u>...................
¿Qué piensas de él?	**<u>Pienso que él es</u> o pienso que él tiene**........
What do you think of them?	I think they are or <u>I think they have</u>...........
¿Qué piensas de ellos (as)?	**<u>Pienso que ellos son</u> o pienso que ellos tienen**

COLORS

LOS COLORES

White: **Blanco**	Beige: **Beige**
Black: **Negro**	Cream: **Crema**
Red: **Rojo**	Silver: **Plata**
Blue: **Azúl**	Gold: **Oro**
Orange: **Naranja**	Burgundy: **Vino tinto**
Pink: **Rosa**	Dark blue or navy blue: **Azúl marino**
Purple: **Morado**	Sky blue or light blue: **Azúl celeste**
Gray: **Gris**	Yellow: **Amarillo**
Brown: **Café**	Mustard: **Mostaza**
Green: **Verde**	

Exercise/Ejercicio: **What color is it?** /¿Qué color es?

1-Wthei:_____   6- Edr:_____

2-Lbcak:_____   7-Puperl: _____

3-Lyweol:_____   8- Ubel: _____

4-Enorag:_____   9- Pikn: _____

5-Wnobr:_____   10-Stardmu: _____

Exercise:

1-What color is the house? R) The house is_____

2-What color is the_____? R) The _____is_____

3-What color is the _____? R) The_____is_____

4-What color is the _____? R) The_____is_____

CLOTHES AND ACCESSORIES

ROPAS Y ACCESORIOS

A hat: **Un sombrero**	Pants: **Pantalónes**
A shirt: **Una camisa**	A waist belt: **Un cinturón de vestir**
A black shirt: **Una camisa negra**	A skirt: **Una falda**
A t-shirt: **Una playera**	A short skirt: **Una mini falda**
A white t-shirt: **Una playera blanca**	Earings: **Aretes**
Sun glasses: **Lentes obscuros**	Socks: **Calcetínes**
A neckless: **Un collar**	A handkerchief: **Un pañuelo**
A bracelet: **Una pulsera**	A sweater: **Una sudadera**
A watch: **Un reloj de pulsera**	A suit: **Un traje**
A tie: **Una corbata**	Hosiery: **Una media**
A green jacket: **Un chaleco verde**	Jeans: **Pantalónes de mezclilla**
A dress: **Un vestido**	A cap: **Una gorra**
Shorts: **Un shor**	A green cap: **Una gorra verde**
A scarf: **Una bufanda**	Sandals: **Sandalias**
Gloves: **Guantes**	Boots: **Botas**
A gold chain: **Una cadena de oro**	Running shoes: **Tenís**
A ring: **Un anillo**	Underwear: **Una ropa interior**
A gold ring: **Un anillo de oro**	A bathing suit: **Un traje de baño**
Shoes: **Zapatos**	A swimming suit: **Un traje de baño**

Questions in Present Tense Preguntas en Tiempo Presente	Answers in Present Tense Respuestas en Tiempo Presente
What are you wearing today? **¿Qué traes o (llevas) puesto hoy?**	1-I am wearing today .... **Traigo o (llevo) puesto hoy............................**
What is he wearing today? **¿Qué trae o (lleva) puesto hoy?**	2-He is wearing today .... **Él trae o (lleva) puesto hoy ....**
What is she wearing today? **¿Qué trae o (lleva) puesto hoy?**	3-She is wearing today.................................... **Ella trae o (lleva) puesto hoy ....**
What are they wearing today? **¿Qué traen o (llevan) puesto hoy?**	4-They are wearing today .... **Ellos (as) traen o (llevan) puesto hoy..............**
Questions in Past Tense Preguntas en Tiempo Pasado	**Answers in Past Tense** Respuestas en Tiempo Pasado
What were you wearing yesterday? **Qué traías puesto ayer?**	1-I was wearing yesterday................................ **Yo traía o (llevaba) puesto ayer ....**
What was he wearing yesterday? **¿Qué traía puesto ayer?**	2-He was wearing yesterday............................ **Él traía o (llevaba) puesto ayer ....**
What was she wearing yesterday? **¿Qué traía puesto ayer?**	3-She was wearing yesterday .... **Ella traía o (llevaba) puesto ayer..................**
What were they wearing yesterday? **¿Qué traían puesto ayer?**	4-They were wearing yesterday........................ **Ellos traían o (llevaban) puesto ayer…………...**
Questions in Future Tense Preguntas en Tiempo Futuro	**Answers in Future Tense** Respuestas en Tiempo Futuro
What will you be wearing tomorrow? **¿Qué traerás puesto mañana?**	1-I will be wearing tomorrow .... **Yo traeré o (llevaré) puesto mañana ....**
What will he be wearing tomorrow? **¿Qué traerá o (llevará) puesto mañana?**	2-He will be wearing tomorrow........................ **Él traerá o (llevará) puesto mañana...............**
What will she be wearing tomorrow? **¿Qué traerá o (llevará) puesto mañana?**	3-She will be wearing tomorrow....................... **Ella traerá o (llevará) puesto mañana….........**
What will they be wearing tomorrow? **¿Qué traerán puesto mañana?**	4-They will be wearing tomorrow...................... **Ellos (as) (llevarán) puesto mañana...............**
What are you going to wear tomorrow? **¿Qué vas a traer puesto mañana?**	I am going to wear tomorrow............................ **Voy a traer puesto mañana ....**
What is he going to wear tomorrow? **¿Qué va a traer puesto mañana?**	He is going to wear tomorrow............................ **Él va a traer puesto mañana ....**
What is she going to wear tomorrow? **¿Qué va a traer puesto mañana?**	She is going to wear tomorrow........................... **Ella va a traer puesto mañana ....**
What are they going to wear tomorrow? **¿Qué van a traer puesto mañana?**	They are going to wear tomorrow........................... **Ellos(as) van a traer puesto mañana..................**

SHOPPING DIALOGUE
DE COMPRA DIALOGO

Clerk: Can I help you?/ **¿Puedo ayudarte? o ¿Puedo ayudarle?**

Customer: Yes, I'm looking for a suit/ **Si, estoy buscando un traje.**

Clerk: What size are you? / **¿Qué talla eres? o ¿Qué talla es ústed?**

Customer: I'm medium/ **Soy de talla mediana.**

Clerk: How about this one? / **¿Qué te parece este? o ¿Qué le parece este?**

Customer: That's nice. Can I try it on?/ **Es bonito (a). ¿Puedo probarlo?**

Clerk: Certainly, the dressing room is on your right.
Seguro, el cuarto de vestir está a su derecha.

Customer: Thank you! / **Gracias!**

Clerk: How does it fit? / **¿Cómo te queda? o ¿Cómo le queda?**

Customer: It's too small. Do you have a larger size?
Es demasiado chico (a) ¿Tiene talla más grande?

Clerk: Yes, here you are/ **Si, aqui tiene.**

Customer: Thank you! I will take it/ **Gracias! lo tomaré.**

Clerk: Ok, how would you like to pay? **Ok, ¿Cómo te gustaría pagar?**

Customer: Credit card please, here's my credit card visa
Tarjeta de credito por favor, aquí tiene.

Clerk: Thank you! Could you please sign here?
Gracias! ¿Podrías firmar aquí por favor?

Customer: Sure/ **Seguro**

Clerk: Thanks! for shopping with us, goodbye!
Gracias por su compra, adiós!

Customer: Bye bye! / **Adiós!**

THE MONTHS OF THE YEAR

LOS MESES DEL AÑO

January	**Enero**
February	**Febrero**
March	**Marzo**
April	**Abril**
May	**Mayo**
June	**Junio**
July	**Julio**
August	**Agosto**
September	**Septiembre**
October	**Octubre**
November	**Noviembre**
December	**Diciembre**

Exercise:Translate into Spanish/Traduce en español.

1- My children were born in October.

_____

2- They graduated in July, last year.

_____

3- In April I will be going on vacation.

_____

Ejercicio: Traduce en Inglés/Translate into English.

1- Mi cumpleaño es el 7 de Septiembre.

_____

2- Vamos a organizar una fiesta en Diciembre.

_____

3- Cuatro de Julio es la independencia de Estados Unidos.

_____

Exercise: Match the Months of the Year.

Ejercicio: Ponga en orden los Meses del Año.

January	**Marzo**
February	**Mayo**
March	**Junio**
April	**Julio**
May	Septiembre
June	**Octubre**
July	Noviembre
August	**Diciembre**
September	**Enero**
October	**Febrero**
November	**Abril**
December	**Agosto**

THE DAYS OF THE WEEK
LOS DÍAS DE LA SEMANA

Monday	Lunes
Tuesday (Tusdei)	Martes
Wednesday (wensdei)	Miércoles
Thursday (tersdei)	Jueves
Friday (fuaidei)	Viernes
Saturday (saterdei)	Sábado
Sunday (sondei)	Domingo

1- Today is Monday we need to go to school.

_____

2- Wednesday, is the perfect day for a business meeting.

_____

3- Next Friday, my family and I will travel to Paris.

_____

4- On Saturday there will be a party at Patrick´s house.

_____

Questions

1- What date is today?   **Answer :** Today is _____.
2- What day is today?   **Answer :** Today is _____.
3- What day was yesterday?   **Answer :** Yesterday was_____.
4- What date was yesterday?   **Answer :** Yesterday was_____.

Exercise: Match the vocabulary with the correct answer.

Ejercicio: Ponga en orden el vocabulario con la respuesta correcta.

Week	Fin de semana	In a week	Dentro de una semana
Weekday	Semana	Last night	Hace cuatro días
Weekend	Mañana	Tonight	Mañana por la mañana
Today	Hoy	This evening	Está noche
Tomorrow	Día entre semana	Tomorrow morning	Está noche
Yesterday	Ayer	Four days ago	Anoche
The day after tomorrow	Anteayer	Noon	Media noche
The day before yesterday	Pasado mañana	Midnight	Y cuarto
The day before	Anteayer	And a half	Y media
The day after	El día antes	And a quater	Medio día
Three days later	La semana pasada		
This week	Está semana		
Next week	El lunes pasado		
Last week	Tres días más tarde		
Last Monday	La próxima semana		

What time is it? Let's count the numbers before telling the hour.

¿Qué hora es? Contamos los números antes de decir la hora.

One–Two–Three–Four–Five–Six–Seven–Eight–Nine–Ten–Eleven–Twelve–Thirteen–Fourteen–Fifteen–Sixteen–Seventeen–Eighteen–Nineteen–Twenty–Twenty one–Twenty nine–Thirty–Thirty one–Thirty nine–Fourty–Fourty one–Fourty nine–Fifty–Fifty one–Fifty nine–Sixty–Sixty one–Sixty nine–Seventy–Seventy one–Seventy nine–Eighty–Eighty one–Eighty nine–Ninety–Ninety one–Ninety nine–One hundred–One thousand–One million.

Uno – Dos – Tres – Cuatro – Cinco – Seis – Siete – Ocho – Nueve – Diez – Once – Doce – Trece – Catorce – Quince – Dieciséis – Diecisiete – Dieciocho –Diecinueve –Veinte – Veintiuno – Veintinueve – Treinta – Treinta y uno – Treinta y nueve – Cuarenta – Cuarenta y uno – Cuarenta y nueve – Cincuenta – Cincuenta y uno – Cincuenta y nueve – Sesenta – Sesenta y uno –Sesenta y nueve – Setenta – Setenta y uno – Setenta y nueve – Ochenta – Ochenta y uno – Ochenta y nueve – Noventa – Noventa y uno – Noventa y nueve – Cien – Mil – Un millón.

Questions

1- How much does it cost?/**¿Cuánto cuesta?** - **Answer :** That's/**Cuesta**_____.

2- How much do you charge?/**¿Cuánto cobrás?** - **Answer :** I charge/**Cobro**_____.

3- What's the price?/**¿Cuál es el precio?** - **Answer :** It's/**Son**_____.

4- What's the fee?/**¿Cuál es el precio?** - **Answer :** That's/**Cuesta**_____.

Example:

1530 = Fifteen-thirty
1860 =
1660 =
1977 =
2004 =
1730 =
1997 =
2012 =
1760 =
2015 =
2013 =

Ejercicio: **Utiliza los números para decir que año es.**

Ejemplo:

1530 = Mil quinientos treinta
1860 =
1660 =
1977 =
2004 =
1730 =
1997 =
2012 =
1760 =
2015 =
2013 =

To be born: **Nacer**
I was born/ **Yo nací**_____
You were born/ **Tú naciste**_____
He was born/ **Él nació**_____
She was born/ **Ella nació**_____
It was born/ **Nació** _____
We were born/ **Nosotros nacimos**_____
You were born/ **Ustedes nacieron**_____
They were born/ **Ellos o Ellas nacieron**_____

TELLING TIME ON THE HOUR

DECIR LA HORA

What time is it? / ¿Qué hora es?

It's two o'clock AM/PM
Son las dos en punto

Three ways: tres formas

It's one twenty seven AM/PM
Es la una veintisiete

Two ways: dos formas

It's one fifty AM/PM
Una cincuenta

It's ten to two AM/PM
Diez para las dos

Exercise: Ejercicio

What time is it?	**What time is it?**	**What time is it?**	**What time is it?**
2:00 o'clock	_____ o'clock	_____ o'clock	_____ o'clock
¿Qué hora es?	¿Qué hora es?	¿Qué hora es?	¿Qué hora es?
2:00 en punto	_____ en punto	_____ en punto	_____ en punto

Exercise: How do you say in English? /¿Cómo se dice en Inglés?

Es la una cinco de la mañana: _____

Son las 3 y cuarto de la noche: _____

Son las 4 y media de la mañana: _____

Es un cuarto para la una: _____

ORDINAL NUMBERS
NÚMERO ORDINALES

First (1st)	**Primero**
Second (2nd)	**Segundo**
Third (3rd)	**Tercero**
Fourth (4th)	**Cuarto**
Fifth (5th)	**Quinto**
Sixth (6th)	**Sexto**
Seventh (7th)	**Séptimo**
Eigth (8th)	**Octavo**
Nineth (9th)	**Noveno**
Tenth (10th)	**Décimo**
Eleventh (11th)	**Undécimo**
Twelfth (12th)	**Duodécimo**
Thirteenth (13th)	**Décimotercero**
Fourteenth (14th)	**Décimocuarto**
Fifteenth (15th)	**Décimoquinto**
Sixteenth (16th)	**Décimosexto**
Seventeenth(17th)	**Décimoseptimo**
Eighteenth (18th)	**Décimoctavo**
Nineteenth (19th)	**Décimonoveno**
Twentieth (20th)	**Vigésimo**
Twenty-first (21st)	**Vigésimo primero**
Thirtieth (30th)	**Trigésimo**
Fortieth (40th)	**Cuadragésimo**
Fiftieth (50th)	**Quincuagésimo**
Sixtieth (60th)	**Sexagésimo**
Seventieth (70th)	**Septuagésimo**
Eightieth (80th)	**Octogésimo**
Ninetieth (90th)	**Nonagésimo**
One hundredth (100th)	**Centésimo**

1- Our classroom is on the fifth floor/**1-Nuestra clase está en el quinto piso.**
2- He left his backpack on the third floor/**2-Dejó su mochila en el tercer piso.**
3- Her friends are studying English in sixth grade/**3-Sus amigos están estudiando Inglés al sexto grado.**

Note: Those numbers are used into a sentence for anniversary, day, month, year, floor, level, street and grade.

THE FAMILY

LA FAMILIA

Parents	**Padres**	Grandmother	**Abuela**
Mother	**Madre**	Grandfather	**Abuelo**
Father (fader)	**Padre**	Grandparents	**Abuelos**
Mom	**Máma**	Grandchildren	**Nietos/Nietas**
Dad (ded)	**Pápa**	Granddaughter	**Nieta**
Child (chaild)	**Hijo/Hija**	Grandson	**Nieto**
Baby	**Bebé**	Great-grandmother	**Bisabuela**
Daughter (dauder)	**Hija**	Great-grandfather	**Bisabuelo**
Son	**Hijo**	Wife (waif)	**Esposa**
Adopted daughter	**Hija adoptiva**	Husband	**Esposo**
Adopted son	**Hijo adoptivo**	Cousin (causen)	**Primo/Prima**
Sister	**Hermana**	Brother in law	**Cuñado**
Brother	**Hermano**	Sister in law	**Cuñada**
Twin brother	**Hermano mellizo**	Father in law	**Suegro**
Twin sister	**Hermana melliza**	Mother in law	**Suegra**
Stepmother	**Madrasta**	God mother	**Madrina**
Stepfather	**Padrastro**	God father	**Padrino**
Nephew	**Sobrino**	Niece (nis)	**Sobrina**
Aunt (ent)	**Tía**	Uncle	**Tío**

Practice by asking questions about different family members.

Práctica preguntando a cerca de diferentes miembros de la familia.

Question/Pregunta: How many brothers do you have?/**¿Cuántos hermanos tienes?**
Answer/Respuesta: I have one brother and one sister/**Tengo un hermano e una hermana.**
Question/Pregunta: Are you the youngest or the oldest?/**¿Eres el menor o el mayor?**
Answer/Respuesta: I am the oldest /**Soy el mayor.**

Question/Pregunta: What is your brother`s name? or What´s your brother`s name?
¿Cómo se llama tu hermano? o ¿Cómo se llama su hermano?

Answer/Respuesta: My brother`s name is Peter/**Mi hermano se llama Peter.**

Exercise/Ejercicio

1- My mother's sister is my_____
2- **La hermana de mi máma es mi**_____
3- My daughter's brother is my_____
4- **El hermano de mi hija es mi**_____
5- My father's daughter is my_____
6- **La hija de mi pápa es mi** _____
7- My mom and dad are my_____
8- **Mi máma y mi pápa son mis**_____
9- My sister's son is my_____
10-**El hijo de mi hermana es mi** _____

COUNTRIES AND NATIONALITIES
PAÍSES Y NACIONALIDADES

Exercise: Guess the language of the country and its nationality.

Ejercicio: Adivine el idioma de cada país y su nacionalidad.

Country/País	Nationality/Nacionalidad	Language/Idioma
The United States Estados Unidos		
The United Kingdom Inglatera		
Russia/Rusia		
Germany/Alemania		
Mexico/México		
Canada/Cánada		
France/Francia		
Spain/España		
Japan/Japón		
Australia		
China		
Poland/Polonia		
Denmark/Dinamarca		
Turkey/Turquía		
Brazil		
Bolivia		

Question/Pregunta: Where are you from?/ What's your native language?
¿De dónde eres? o ¿De dónde es ústed?/ ¿Cúal es su idioma natal?
Answer/Respuesta: I am from the United States/ **(Yo) soy de los Estados Unidos.**
Answer/Respuesta: I speak English/ **(Yo) hablo Inglés.**

OCCUPATIONS/PROFESSIONS

OCUPACIONES/PROFESIONES

Mechanic **Mecanico (a)**	Seamstress **Costurera**	Fireman **Bombero**	Pilot (pailot) **Piloto**
Butcher (bocher) **Carnicero (a)**	Barber **Barbero**	Soldier **Soldado**	Clown **Payaso (a)**
Gardener **Jardinero (a)**	Plumber (plomer) **Plomero (a)**	Baker (beker) **Panadero (a)**	Farmer **Granjero (a)**
Lawyer (loyer) **Abogado (a)**	Painter **Pintor (a)**	Carpenter **Carpintero (a)**	Tailor (teiler) **Costurero (a)**
Actor/Actress Actor/**Actríz**	Artist **Artista**	Doctor **Doctor**	Dentist **Dentista**
Violinist **Violinista**	Secretary **Secretaria**	Singer **Cantante**	Scientist (sayentis) **Científíco (a)**
Police officer **Policía**	Chemist (kimist) **Quimico (a)**	Nurse (ners) **Enfermero (a)**	Inventor **Inventor (a)**
Brick layer **Albañil**	Hair dresser **Estilista**	Teacher **Maestro (a)**	Surgeon **Cirujano (a)**

Practice/**Práctica**

Question: What do you do for a living?
Pregunta: ¿A qué te (se) dedica(s)?
Question: What does he do for a living?
Pregunta: ¿A qué se dedica?
Question: What does she do for a living?
Pregunta: ¿A qué se dedica?
Question: What do they do for a living?
Preguta: ¿A qué se dedican?

I am a teacher or I work as a teacher.
Soy maestro (a) o trabajo como maestro
He is a doctor or he works as a doctor.
És doctor o trabaja como doctor.
She is a nurse or she works as a nurse.
És enfermera o trabaja como enfermera.
They are pilots or they work as pilots.
Ellos son pilotos o trabajan como pilotos.

Exercise: What do they do? Ejercicio: ¿A qué se dedican?

He is a _____

He works as a _____

He is a _____

Dialogue: At the airport/Dialogo: En el aeropuerto

Traveler: Good morning
Viajero (a): Buenos días.

Flight attendant: Good morning, may I have your passport and your ticket please?
Aeromozo (a): Buenos días, ¿puedo tomar su pasaporte y su boleto por favor?

Traveler: Sure, here you are.
Viajero (a): Seguro, aqui tiene.

Flight attendant: Everything is in order.
Aeromozo (a): Todo esta en órden.

Traveler: Can I keep my carry-on baggage?
Viajero (a): ¿Puedo guardar mi equipaje de mano?

Flight attendant: Sure, here is your boarding pass, your seat number is 20B.
Aeromozo (a): Seguro, aquí tiene su pase de abordar, su número de asiento es 20B.

Traveler: Is the flight delayed?
Viajero (a): ¿El vuelo se retraso?

Flight attendant: No, sir, you will board the airplane at gate 9. Have a nice trip!
Aeromozo (a): No, señor, ústed abordará el avión a la puerta 9. ¡Que tenga un lindo viaje!

Traveller: Thank you!
Viajero (a): Gracias!

Flight attendant: You are welcome.
Aeromozo (a): De nada.

AIRLINE RESERVATIONS

RESERVAR UN BOLETO DE AVION

Reservations clerk - American airline, good morning. May I help you?

Recepcionista -American airline, buenos días. ¿Puedo ayudarle?

Keny - Yes, do you have a flight to Mexico next Tuesday afternoon?

Keny - Si, tiene vuelos para México próximo Martes en la tarde?

Reservations clerk - Economy, business class or first class?

Recepcionista - Económico, clase de negocio o primera clase?

Keny -Economy, please/**Keny -** Económico, por favor.

Reservations clerk -Please hold on, yes, there´s a flight at 12:45 and one at 4:00 pm.

Recepcionista- Favor de esperar......si, hay un vuelo a las 12:45 y uno a las 4:00pm.

Keny - I prefer the one at 12:45 pm, how much does it cost?

Keny- Prefiero el de las 12:45 pm, ¿cúanto cuesta?

Reservations clerk -The cost will be $400 dollars. Would you like me to reserve?

Recepcionista- El costo séra $400 dólares. ¿Le gustaría que reserve?

Keny - Yes, please/**Keny -** Si, por favor.

Reservations clerk -Can I have your name and email address please?

Recepcionista - ¿Puedo tomar su nombre y su correo electrónico por favor?

Keny -My name is Keny Smith, my email address is: Kenny@gmail.com

Keny - Mi nombre es Keny Smith, mi correo electrónico es <u>Kenny@gmail.com</u>

Reservations clerk - Ok, Mr. Kenny, please hold on a minute…. now you have been booked. The flight will leave at 12:45 pm and your arrival to Mexico will be at 4:00 pm, Local time, an email has been sent to you.

Recepcionista - Ok, señor Kenny, favor de esperar un minuto…se ha hecho su reservación. El vuelo partirá a las 12:45 pm y la llegada a México será a las 4:00 pm, tiempo local, un correo le fue enviado.

Keny - Thank you! /**Keny -** Gracias!

Reservations clerk - You are more than welcome Sir. Have a wonderful trip.

Recepcionista - De nada señor. Que tenga un excelente viaje.

MAKE A HOTEL RESERVATION

HACER UNA RESERVACIÓN DE HOTEL

Receptionist: Hello, Sunset Hotel, how may I help you?
Recepcionista: Hola, sunset Hotel, ¿cómo le puedo ayudar?

Watson: Hi, I`d like to make a reservation.
Watson: Hola, me gustaría hacer una reservación.

Receptionist: Just a moment, for what date?
Recepcionista: Un momento, ¿con qué fecha?

Watson: April 15th/Watson: 15 de Abril.

Receptionist: How many nights will you be staying?
Recepcionista: ¿Por cúantas noches?

Watson: 2 nights, what's the room rate?
Watson: 2 noches, ¿qué costo tiene el cuarto?

Receptionist: 60 dollars a night plus tax. Would you like me to reserve a room for you?
Recepcionista: 60 dólares más impuesto por noche. ¿Le gustaría que le haga la reservación?

Watson: Yes, please/Watson: Si, por favor.

Receptionist: Your name, please?
Recepcionista: ¿Su nombre, por favor?

Watson: **Watson Joseph**

Receptionist: Mr. Watson, how will you be paying?
Recepcionista: Sr. Watson ¿cómo pagará ústed?

Watson: Credit card visa/Watson: Tarjeta de credito.

Receptionist: Card number please.
Recepcionista: Número de tarjeta por favor.

Watson: 345687906736654.

Receptionist: Expiration date?
Recepcionista: ¿Fecha de caducidad?

Watson: October 4ᵗʰ,2014 / Cuarto de octubre 2014.

Receptionist: Ok, You are all set, your booking confirmation number is 3478. We´ll see you on the 15ᵗʰ, thank you for booking with us.
Recepcionista: Ok, listo, su número de confirmación es 3478. Le veremos el 15, gracias por reservar con nosotros.

AT THE RESTAURANT
EN EL RESTAURANTE

Waiter/Waitress - Good morning, Sir!
Mesero (a) - Buenos días, Señor!

Customer - Good morning! Can I have the menu, please?
Cliente - Buenos días ¿Puedo ver el menú, por favor?

Waiter/Waitress - Sure! here is the menu.......would you like to order?
Mesero (a) - Seguro! aqui está el menú........le gustaría ordenar?

Customer - Yes, please! What's the main menu?
Cliente - Si, por favor ¿Cúal es el menú principal?

Waiter/Waitress - Our main menu for today is molcajete!
Mesero (a) - Nuestro menu principal por hoy es molcajete!

Customer -What are the ingredients?
Cliente - ¿Cúales son los ingredientes?

Waiter/Waitress - Shrimp, beef and cherry tomatoes, altogether with cheese.
Mesero (a) - Camarón, carne de res y tomates, mezclado con queso.

Customer - Sounds good! I´ll take it!
Cliente - Suena bien! Lo tomaré.

Waiter/Waitress - And to drink?
Mesero (a) - ¿Y para beber?

Customer - A glass of red wine, please!
Cliente - Un vaso de vino tinto, por favor!

Waiter/Waitress - Any dessert?
Mesero (a) - Algo de postre?

Customer – Nothing for dessert just an orange juice to finish my meal!
Cliente – Nada de postre, solo jugo de naranja para terminar mi comida!

Waiter/Waitress - Just a moment please, I´ll get back to you soon!
Mesero (a) - Un momento por favor, regreso pronto!

Customer - Thank you!/Cliente - Gracias!

Exercise: Write the name of fruits and vegetables in Spanish/English.

Ejercicio: Escribe los nombres de frutas y verduras en Español/Inglés.

Fruits/Frutas	Find the Meaning in Spanish Encuentra el significado en Español	Vegetables Verduras	Encuentra el significado en Inglés Find the Meaning in English
Banana		Cebolla	
Water melon		Maíz	
Pumpkin		Zanahoria	
Orange		Pepino	
Tomato		Apio	
Strawberry		Lechuga	
Grape		Brócoli	
Mango		Frijol	
Avocado		Frijol verde	
Cherry		Repollo	
Apple (apol)		Espinaca	
Pear		Ajo	
Papaya		Repollo rojo	
Peach (pich)		Papas	
Lemon		Champiñón	
Lime (laim)			
Pineapple			

Exercise: Pick some fruit names and vegetables, then explain how they benefit us.

Ejercicio: Elige algunos nombres de frutas y verduras, después explica cómo nos beneficia.

1-

2-

3-

4-

5-

_____

Exercise: Complete the sentences by guessing the words.

A- Kara drank alot of Ch_____yesterday.

B- My parents made a few C_____last Saturday.

C- We don´t have many Ap_____in the fridge.

D- My aunt doesn´t put much On_____on the pizza.

E- Julian bought a few Or_____in the supermarket 2 days ago.

Ejercicio: Completa las frases adivinando las palabras.

A- Johana cocinó mucho Ch_____anoche.

B- No hay A_____en la botella.

C- Podemos preparar algo de Pe_____y despúes comer algo.

D- A Joseph le encanta Pa_____y Es_____.

E- Karolina no le gusta comer Br_____en la mañana.

ASKING AND GIVING DIRECTIONS
UBICACIONES

Dialogue -Directions I

Dialogo –Dirección I

Excuse me, is there a bank near here?
Disculpa, ¿hay un banco cerca de aqui?

Yes, There's a bank on the corner.
Si, hay un banco en la esquina.

Thank you!
Gracias!

You're welcome.
De nada.

Dialogue - Directions II

Dialogo –Dirección II

Excuse me, is there a mall near here?
Disculpa, ¿hay un centro comercial cerca de aqui?

Yes, there's one near here.
Si, hay uno cerca de aqui.

How do I get there?
¿Cómo llegar allá?

At the traffic light, make a left and go straight on. It's on the left.
Al semáforo, a la izquierda, ve todo derecho. Está a la izquierda

Is it far?/ Not really.
¿Está lejos?/Realmente no.

Thank you!/Gracias!
Please don't mention it.
Por favor, ni lo digas.

Exercise: Ask for and give directions /Ejercicio: Preguntar y dar ubicaciones.

1- _____

2- _____

3- _____

4- _____

5- _____

6- _____

VOCABULARY

VOCABULARIO

Where is? -
¿Dónde está...?

Where are?
¿Dónde están...?

Where are you?
¿Dónde está ústed?

Turn on to
Gira a

How do I get to...?
¿Cómo llego a...?

How far is the...?
¿Qué tan lejos está el/la?

The mall
El Centro commercial

The supermarket
El supermercado

The corner
La esquina

Underneath of
Debajo de

Over here
Por aqui/Por acá

Around the corner
A la vuelta

Straight ahead
Todo derecho

At the corner of
A la esquina de

Turn right
Gira a la derecha

A mile away
Una milla

17 minutes away
17 minutos

To the North
Al Norte

To the East
Al Este

The beach
La playa

The book store
La librería

The building
El edificio

The University
La Universidad

The place
El lugar

The church
La iglesia

The school
La escuela

The library
La biblioteca

The traffic light
El semáforo

On top of
Sobre

Against
En contra de

Over there
Por allí/Por allá

In front of
En frente de

Far from
Lejos de

Across
Al otro lado de

5 blocks away
5 cuadras

Towards
Hacía

10 Kilometers away
10 kilometros

What's your favorite holiday and season of the year? Explain why?

¿Cúal es su día festivo favorito y estación del año? Explica porqué.

The Seasons of the year Estaciones del año		U.S. Holidays Días festivos de Estados Unidos	
Spring	Primavera	**Christmas**	Navidad
Summer	Verano	**Thanksgiving**	Día de acciones de gracia
Autumn/Fall	Otoño	**Fourth of July**	Cuatro de Julio
		Labor Day	Día del trabajador
Winter	Invierno	**Veterans' Day**	Día de veteranos
		New Year's Eve	Noche buena
		New Year's Day	Día de año nuevo
		Easter	Pascua
		Valentine's Day	Día de San Valentín

¿CÓMO ES EL CLIMA HOY?

Exercise/Ejercicio:

Match the vocabulary

Ponga en orden el vocabulario.

7- It's sunny	Está nublado
8- It's cloudy	Está soleado
9- It's rainy	Está nevando
10- It's snowy	Está lloviendo
11- It's partly cloudy	Está tormentoso
12- It's stormy	Es parte nublado
13- It's lightning	Hace viento
14- It's windy	Hay truenos
15- It's hailing	Hay niebla
16- It's foggy	Está granizando
17- It's sleeting	Está helado
18- It's freezing	Hay agua nieve
19- It's hot	Hace frío
20- It's cold	Hace calor
21- It's warm	Está cálido

Practice/ Práctica

Select the correct word/Selecciona la palabra correcta.

1- Yesterday was a beautiful day to go to the beach. It was_____(icy, sunny) and warm.
2- It will be cloudy today with a chance of_____(pouring rain, freezing) all day.
3- Drive carefully tonight because it will be_____(partly cloudy, warm, rainy) out there.

Practice/ Práctica

Select the correct word/Selecciona la palabra correcta.

1- No hay nube en el cielo. Es totalmente_____(nublado, claro, calor).
2- Va a ser mucho calor hoy. Augmentará hasta 110_____(grado, llovioso) Celsius.
3- Podría llover hoy habrá_____(inundaciónes, granizo, viento) en la calle.

DIALOGUE – FORMAL: A PHONE CALL TO A LAW FIRM

DIALOGO – FORMAL: UNA LLAMADA A UN DESPACHO JURÍDICO

-Good afternoon, GIS firm, how may I help you?
-Buenas tardes, despacho GIS, ¿En qué le puedo ayudar?

-Good afternoon, I'd like to speak to Mr. Joseph please.
-Buenas tardes, me gustaría hablar con el Señor Joseph por favor.

-I'm afraid Mr. Joseph is not available at the moment.
-Temo que el Señor Joseph no está disponible por el momento.

-When do you expect him to come back?
-¿Cúando espere que regrese?

-If he is not delayed, in approximately half an hour.
-Si no se tarda, aproximadamente media hora.

-Could you please ask him to call me back?
-¿Podría por favor pedirle que me llame de vuelta?

-Sure, who is calling please?
-Seguro, ¿Quién llama por favor?

-My name is Jeanette Baker, I consulted with Mr. Joseph before.
-Mi nombre es Jeanette Baker, me comunique con el Señor Joseph anteriormente.

-Does he have your number?
- ¿Tiene su número?

-Yes, I believe he does, however, maybe I'd give it to you just in case.
-Si, creo, de todo modo, se le entregaré solo en caso.

-Yes, that would be best, hold on please while I find a pen.
-Si, sería mejor, espera por favor mientras hallo una pluma.

-Alright, go ahead please.
-De acuerdo, adelante por favor.

-**My number is 619 678 8510**
-Mi número es 619 678 8510

-**Let me read that back to you: 619 678 8510**
-Dejame repetirselo: 619 678 8510

-**That's correct/** Correcto.

-**Sorry. I didn't quite catch your name, could you spell it for me please?**
-Perdone, no capte por completo su nombre, ¿podría deletreármelo por favor?

-Of course my first name is Jeanette: **J-E-A-N-E-T-T-E and my last name: B-A-K-E-R**
-Seguro mi nombre es Jeanette: J-E-A-N-E-T-T-E y mi appellido es: B-A-K-E-R

-**O.k I made a note of that, I'll ask Mr. Joseph to call you back as soon as he returns.**
-O.K tome nota, pediré al Señor Joseph que le llame cuando regrese.

-**Thank you very much, good bye!**
-Muchas gracias, adiós!

PARTS OF THE BODY

PARTES DEL CUERPO

Head	**Cabeza**	Toe	**Dedo del pie**
Neck	**Cuello**	Spine	Columna vértebral
Throat	**Garganta**	Rib	**Costilla**
Nape of the neck	**Nuca**	Skin	**Piel**
Shoulder	**Hombro**	Lungs	**Pulmones**
Chest	**Pecho**	Stomach	**Estòmago**
Abdomen	**Abdomen**	Liver	**Higado**
Back	**Espalda**	Kidneys	**Riñones**
Arm	**Brazo**	Bladder	**Vejíga**
Elbow	**Codo**		
Hand	**Mano**		
Wrist	**Muñeca**		

Find the meaning

Encuentra el significado

Fist	**Puño**	Lips	
Finger	**Dedo**	Chin	
Little finger	**Meñique**	Front	
Index finger	**Indice**	Beard	
Thumb	**Pulgar**	Eyelash	
Fingernail	**Uña**	Nose	
Waist	**Cintura**	Boob	
Hip	**Cadera**	Palm	
Bottom	**Gluteos**	Bicep	
Leg	**Pierna**	Tricep	
Thigh	**Muslo**	Moustache	
Knee	**Rodilla**	Hair	
Calf	**Pantorilla**	Tongue	
Ankle	**Tobillo**	Cheek	
Foot	**Pie**		
Heel	**Talòn**		

THREE STEPS TO LEARN EASIER ENGLISH OR SPANISH

TRES PASOS PARA APRENDER MÁS FÁCIL INGLÉS O ESPAÑOL

THERE ARE 3 THINGS WE MUST LEARN TO SPEAK
ANY LANGUAGE, ESPECIALLY ENGLISH OR SPANISH
HAY 3 COSAS DEBEMOS SABER PARA APRENDER HABLAR
CUALQUIER IDIOMA, ESPECIALMENTE INGLÉS O ESPAÑOL

1- **Know how to conjugate any verb in present tense indicative, past tense, future and conditional tense.**

1- Saber cómo conjugar cualquier verbo en tiempo presente, pasado, futuro y condicional.

2- **Learn the prepositions and articles to complete your phrases or sentences in English or Spanish.**

2- Aprender las preposiciones y los artículos para completar sus frases en Inglés o Español.

3- **Study and memorize the vocabularies.**

3- Estudiar y memorizar los vocabularios.

SOME PREPOSITIONS AND ARTICLES TO COMPLETE YOUR PHRASES
ALGUNAS PREPOSICIONES Y ARTÍCCULOS PARA COMPLETAR SUS FRASES

In the = en el, en la, en las, en los - **In** = en - **Behind** = detrás de/atrás de - **With the** = con el, con la, con las, con los - **At the** = en el, en la, en las, en los - **Before** = antes - **After** = despúes - **So/Then** = entonces, después - **To** = a, de, para - **With** = con - **For** = para, por - **Of the** = del, de la, de los, de las - **From the** = del, de la, de los, de las - **To the** = al, a la, a las, a los - **On** = sobre - **About** = a cerca de - **A** = un, una - **An** = un, una - **The** = el, la, las, los.

HOW TO USE THE ARTICLES: The - A - An
CÓMO USAR LOS ARTICULOS: El, la, los, las – un, una

In English, we use **"The"** (means in Spanish **"el, la, los, las"**) as a definite article with a name that begins with a vowel or a consonant, **this rule is the same in Spanish**. We use **"A"** as an indefinite article before a name that begins with a consonant and **"An"** as an indefinite article before a name that begins with a vowel **(a, e, i, o, u), this rule does not apply in Spanish**, we can only use **"A"/"An"** (means in Spanish **"Un/Una"**) for masculine or feminine gender, no matter if it's a vowel or a consonant.

En Inglés utilizamos **"The"** (significa en Español "el, la, los, las") como artículo definido con un nombre que comienza con una vocal o consonante, esa regla es igual en Español. Utilizamos **"A"** como un artículo indefinido antes de un nombre que comienza con un consonante y **" An"** como artículo indefinido antes de un nombre que comienza con una vocal, está regla no se aplica.

En Español, empleamos "A"/"An" (significa en Español "Un/Una") para género masculino o femenino, sin importar que sea vocal o consonante.

Example/Ejemplo:

1- **The pens**/Las plumas -**The chair**/La silla -**The apple**/La manzana - **The eagles**/Las aguilas.
2- **A dog**/Un perro - **A cat**/Un gato - **An apple**/Una manzana -A**n orange**/Una naranja -**An eagle**/Un águila - **An eraser**/Un borrador - **An umbrella**/Un paragua.

HOW TO CONJUGATE VERBS IN PRESENT TENSE
CÓMO CONJUGAR LOS VERBOS EN TIEMPO PRESENTE.

1- It is not complicated to conjugate verbs in English. We only need to start with a subject or a personal pronoun plus the base form of the verb. Then in the **3rd person** singular pronouns (**he /she/ it**) we must add a "**S**" to the ending of the verb. An exception to this rule is the verb "**to have**" which changes to "**has**" in the **3rd person**.

2- All the verbs in present tenses which end in **o, ss, ch, sh,** and **x** add an - **Es** to the ending of the verb.

3- All the verbs in the present tenses that end in **Y** change. You must change **Y** to an **I** then **add - ES** to the ending of the verb. An exception to this rule is the verb "**to play**" "**to say**" "**to pray**" "**to pay**" "**to buy**" etc, which changes to "**plays**" "**says**" "**prays**" "**pays**" "**buys**" in the **3rd person. It is not allowed to add "S" after (can, must, should, may, might etc).**

In Spanish, none of these rules are used to conjugate the verbs in the present tense, but all the verbs which end in "**ar**" have their ending in the present tense in "**o, as, a, amos, an, an**". Those with "**er**" end in the present tense in "**o, es, e, emos, en, en**". Finally those wich end in "**ir**" end in the present tense in "**o, es, e, imos, en, en**" (i.e: "**to sing**" cantar, "**to drink**" beber "**to compete**" competir). Note that in Spanish there are few exceptions with some irregular verbs, example: **I go** (yo voy).

Al igual que el idioma Español, hay un montón de verbos de acción en el idioma de Inglés que pueden ayudarnos a expresar nuestros pensamientos. Hay una sola manera de saber cómo conjugarlos en el tiempo presente.

1- No es complicado conjugar verbos en Inglés. Sólo tiene que comenzar con un pronombre personal, más la forma base del verbo. Luego, en la tercera persona en singular (**he / she / it**) hay que añadir una "**S** " al final del verbo. Una excepción a esta regla es el verbo "**to have**" (tener) que cambia a "**has**" (tiene) en la tercera persona.

2- Todos los verbos en los tiempos presente que terminan en **o, ss, ch, sh, x,** hay que añadir "**Es**" al final del verbo.

3- Todos los verbos en los tiempos presente que terminan en **Y** cambia. Se debe cambiar la "**Y**" en "**I**" y luego añadir "**Es**" al final del verbo. Una excepción a esta regla es el verbo **"to play"** jugar, **"to say"** decir, **"to pray"** rezar, **"to pay"** pagar, **"to buy"** comprar, etc, que cambia a **"plays","** says **"," prays ", " pays","buys"** en la tercera persona. No está permitido agregar "**S**" despúes de **(can, must, should, may, might).**

En Español, ninguna de esas reglas se aplica para conjugar los verbos en el tiempo presente, pero todos los verbos que terminan en **"ar"** tienen su final en el tiempo presente en **"o, as, a, amos, an, an".** Aquellos que se terminan en **"er"** en el tiempo presente se terminan en **"o, es, e, emos, en, en."** Finalmente, los verbos en **"ir"** en el tiempo presente tienen una terminación en **"o, es, e, imos, en, en"** (Ejemplo: **"cantar", "beber", "competir"**). Nota en Español hay pocas excepciones con algunos verbos irregulares, Ejemplo: **I go** (yo voy).

Personal pronouns/Pronombres personales

I (ay) = Yo
You (iu) = Tú o ústed
He (hi) = Él
She (shi) = Ella
It (it) = Esto
We (wi) = Nosotros
You (iu) = Ústedes
They (dei) = Ellos o ellas

Present tense/Tiempo presente

To speak = hablar
I (ay) speak = Yo hablo
You speak = Tú hablas/ústed habla
He (hi) speaks = Él habla
She (shi) speaks = Ella habla
It (it) speaks = Esto habla
We (wi) speak = Nosotros hablamos
You (iu) speak = Ústedes hablan
They (dei) speak = Ellos/Ellas hablan

Present tense/Tiempo presente

To have = haber, tener
I (ay) have = Yo tengo
You (iu) have = Tú tienes/ústed tiene
He (hi) has = Él tiene
She (shi) has = Ella tiene
It (it) has = Esto tiene
We (wi) have = Nosotros tenemos
You (iu) have = Ústedes tienen
They (dei) have = Ellos/Ellas tienen

To go (tu go) = Ir
I go (ay go) = **Yo voy**
You go (iu go) = **Tu vas/ústed va**
He goes (hi goss) = **Él va**
She goes (shi goss) = **Ella va**
It goes (it goss) = **Esto va**
We go (wi go) = **Nosotros vamos**
You go (iu go) = **Ústedes van**
They go = **Ellos /Ellas van**

To kiss (tu kiss) = Besar
I kiss = **Yo beso**
You kiss = **Tu besas/ ústed besa**
He kisses (hi kisiss) = **Él besa**
She kisses (shi kisiss) = **Ella besa**
It kisses (it kisiss) = **Esto besa**
We kiss = **Nosotros besamos**
You kiss = **Ústedes besan**
They kiss = **Ellos/Ellas besan**

To search (tu serch) = Buscar	To push (tu push) = Empujar
I search (ay serch) **Yo busco**	I push (ay push) **Yo empujo**
You search (iu serch) **Tu buscas/ústed busca**	You push (iu push) **Tu empujas/ústed empuja**
He searches (hi serchiss) **Él busca**	He pushes (hi pushiss) **Él empuja**
She searches (shi serchiss) **Élla busca**	She pushes (shi pushiss) **Ella empuja**
It searches (it serchiss) **(Esto) busca**	It pushes (it pushiss) **(Esto) empuja**
We search (wi serch) **Nosotros buscamos**	We push (wi push) **Nosotros empujamos**
You search (iu serch) **Ústedes buscan**	You push (iu push) **Ústedes empujan**
They search (dei serch) **Ellos/ellas buscan**	They push (dei push) **Ellos/ellas empujan**

To wax (tu wacs) = Encerar
I wax (ay wacs) = **yo encero**
You wax = **tu enceras**
He waxes (hi wacsiss) = **él encera**
She waxes = **ella encera**
It waxes (it wacsiss) = **(esto) encera**
We wax = **nosotros enceramos**
You wax = **ústedes enceran**
They wax = **ellos/ellas enceran**

To fax (tu facs) = Faxear
I fax (ay facs) = **yo faxeo**
You fax = **tu faxeas/ústed faxea**
He faxes (hi facsiss) = **él faxea**
She faxes = **ella faxea**
It faxes (it facsiss) = **(esto) faxea**
We fax = **nosotros faxeamos**
You fax = **ústedes faxean**
They fax = **ellos/ellas faxean**

To try (tu chruay) = Tratar (intentar/probar) To play (plei) = Jugar

I try (ay chruay)
Yo trato

I play (ay plei)
Yo juego

You try (iu chruay)
Tu tratas/ústed trata

You play (iu plei)
Tu juegas/ústed juega

He tries (hi chruays)
Él trata

He plays (hi pleiss)
Él juega

She tries (shi chruays)
Ella trata

She plays (shi pleiss)
Ella juega

It tries (it chruays)
Esto trata

It plays (it pleiss)
Esto juega

We try (wi chruay)
Nosotros tratamos

We play (wi plei)
Nosotros jugamos

You try (iu chruay)
Ústedes tratan

You play (iu plei)
Ústedes juegan

They try (dei chruay)
Ellos/Ellas tratan

They play (dei plei)
Ellos/Ellas juegan

Some helping vocabularies to complete your sentence in the present tense:
Today, this morning, this afternoon, **this evening, tonight**, now, right now.

Algunos vocabularios para completar sus frases en el tiempo presente:
Hoy, está mañana, está tarde, **está noche, está noche,** ahora, ahora mismo.

NEGATIVE FORMS
FORMAS NEGATIVAS

To transform a verb into a negative sentence in the present tense we need to add the negative form do not (don't) or does not (doesn't) plus the base form of the verb. In Spanish only add "No" after the personal pronoun before the verb. Example: "Yo no quiero" I do not (I don't) want.

Para transformar un verbo en forma negativa en el tiempo presente tenemos que añadir la forma negativa do not (don't) or does not (doesn't) más la forma base del verbo. En Español se agrega solamente **"No"** despúes del pronombre personal antes del verbo. Ejemplo: **"Yo no quiero"** I do not (don't) want.

Exercise: Complete the sentence in the right–hand column **using different verbs**.

Ejercicio: Complete la frase de la columna derecha usando diferentes verbos.

I do not (**don't**) + verb Yo no + verbo	I **do not speak** Chinese with my students. **(Yo) no hablo** Chino con mis estudiantes.
You do not (**don't**) + verb Tu no + verbo	
He does not (**doesn't**) + verb Él no + verbo	
She does not (**doesn't**) + verb Ella no + verbo **It** does not (**doesn't**) + verb	
Esto no + verbo **We** do not (**don't**) + verb	
Nosotros no + verbo **You** do not (**don't**) + verbo	
Ústedes no + verbo **They** do not (**don't**) + verb	
Ellos o Ellas + verbo	

VERBS + INFINITIVE
VERBOS + INFINITIVO

When a verb is followed by another verb, the second verb is the infinitive.
Example: You decide to ask/They offer to sell/We manage to convince.

Cuando un verbo se sigue con otro, el segúndo es el infinitivo.
Ejemplo: Yo decido preguntar/Ellos ofrecen vender/Manejamos convencer.

- **Translate into Spanish the following sentences:**
- Traduce en Español las frases siguientes:

- He decides <u>to ask</u> if they want <u>to go</u> to Acapulco for this summer.
- They agree <u>to buy</u> the house during Christmas.

Exception: There are certain verbs that we need to memorize which we should never add (To) followed by another verb in English (Must, Can etc). Examples: We must drink water/I can write and read/You may drive for me/ You might get what you need at the store.

Excepción: Hay ciertos verbos que tenemos que memorizar que nunca debemos añadir (To) cuando se sigue por otro verbo en Inglés (Must, Can etc). Ejemplos: **We <u>must</u> drink water** (Debemos beber agua), **I <u>can</u> write and read** (Puedo escribir y leer), **You <u>may</u> drive for me** (Puedes conducir por mí), **You <u>might get</u> what you need at the store** (Es posible que consigues lo que necesitas en la tienda).

Note: Even we use the negative form into a sentence, if the first verb is followed by another verb, we still need to add the second verb in infinitive.

Nota: Incluso al utilizar la forma negativa en una frase, si el primer verbo va seguido de otro verbo, aún tenemos que añadir el segundo verbo en infinitivo.

Negative Form (More common)
Example1- They do not (**don't**) decide to ask for a contract.
Ejemplo1- Ellos no deciden pedir un contrato.

Negative Form (Not common)
Example 2-They decide not to ask for a contract.
Ejemplo2- Ellos no deciden pedir un contrato.

EXERCISE: MAKE 4 SENTENCES WITH THE FOLLOWING VERBS IN AFFIRMATIVE FORM:

EJERCICIO: HÁZ 4 FRASES CON LOS SIGUIENTES VERBOS EN FORMA AFIRMATIVA:

Need to know/Want to see/Try to convince/Accept to buy.

Necesitar saber o (conocer)/Querer ver/Intentar convencer/Aceptar de comprar.

1- _____

2- _____

3- _____

4- _____

EXERCISE: MAKE 4 SENTENCES WITH THE FOLLOWING VERBS IN NEGATIVE FORM:

EJERCICIO: HÁZ 4 FRASES CON LOS SIGUIENTES VERBOS EN FORMA NEGATIVA:

Need to know/Want to see/Try to convince/Accept to buy.

Necesitar saber o (conocer)/Querer ver/Intentar convencer/Aceptar de comprar.

1- _____

2- _____

3- _____

4- _____

REGULAR VERBS AND IRREGULAR VERBS (PAST)

VERBOS REGULARES E IRREGULARES (TIEMPO PASADO)

In the English language, there are two other types of verbs, regular and irregular. All the action verbs that end in **ED** in the past are called regular verbs. In all other cases, the verbs do not end in **ED** in the past, are called irregular verbs. These verbs end in many different endings. There is no special rule to change these irregular verbs. Only by practice, and memorization can these irregular verbs be learned.

In Spanish, none of these rules are used to conjugate the verbs in past tense. All the verbs which end in **"ar"** have their ending in past tense in **"ba, bas, ba, bamos, ban, ban"**. Those with **"er"** end in past tense in **"ía, ías, ía, íamos, ían, ían."** Finally those wich end in **"ir"** end in past tense in **"ía, ías, ía, íamos, ían, ían"**(i.e: **"to sing"** cantar, **"to drink"** beber,**"to compete"** competir). There are few exceptions to this rule in the case of some irregular verbs in Spanish, example: **"to be"** (ser o estar) - **I was** (yo era o yo estuve).

En el idioma Inglés, hay dos tipos de verbos, regulares e irregulares. Todos los verbos de acción que terminan en **ED** en el pasado se llaman verbos regulares. En otros casos, los verbos no terminan en **ED** en el pasado, se llaman verbos irregulares. Estos verbos terminan diferentes. No hay una regla especial para estos verbos irregulares. Solamente mediante la práctica y la memorización se pueden aprender estos verbos irregulares.

En Español, ninguna de esas reglas se aplica para conjugar los verbos en tiempo pasado (pretérito imperfecto). Todos los verbos que terminan en **"ar"** tienen su final en tiempo pasado en **"ba, bas, ba, bamos, ban, ban."**Aquellos que se terminan en **"er"** en tiempo pasado se terminan en **"ía, ías, ía, íamos, ían, ían."** Finalmente los que tienen una terminación en **"ir"** en tiempo pasado se terminan en **"ía, ías, ía, íamos, ían, ían"** (ejemplo: to sing**"cantar,"** to drink **"beber,"** to compete**"competir"**). Hay pocas excepciones para está regla en el caso de algunos verbos irregulares en Español, ejemplo: **"to be"**(ser o estar) - **I was** (yo era o yo estuve).

REGULAR VERBS
VERBOS REGULARES

Present tense/Tiempo presente - **Past tense**/Tiempo pasado

To abandon (abandon) **abandonar**	Abandoned (abandond) **abandonaba**
To adapt (adapt) **adaptar**	Adapted (adaptid) **adaptaba**
To add **sumar, agregar**	Added (addid) **sumaba, agregaba**
To admire (admaier) **admirar**	Admired (admaierd) **admiraba**
To admit (admit) **confesar**	Admitted (admitid) **confesaba**
To announce (anons) **anunciar**	Anounced (anonst) **anunciaba**
To answer (enser) **contestar**	Answered (enserd) **contestaba**
To appear (apir) **aparecer**	Appeared (apird) **aparecía**
To ask (asc) **preguntar**	Asked (askt) **preguntaba**
To ask for (asc for) **pedir**	Asked for (askt for) **pedía**
To attack (atac) **atacar**	Attacked (atact) **atacaba**
To attend (atend) **asistir**	Attended (atendid) **asistía**
To award (aword) **otorgar**	Awarded (awordid) **otorgaba**
To achieve (achiv) **lograr**	Achieved (achivt) **lograba**
To bake (beik) **hornear**	Baked (beikt) **horneaba**
To believe (biliv) **creer**	Believed (bilivd) **creía**
To brush (brash) **cepillar**	Brushed (brasht) **cepillaba**
To burn (bern) **quemar**	Burned (bernd) **quemaba**
To call (coll) **llamar**	Called (cold) **llamaba**
To change (cheinch) **cambiar**	Changed (cheincht) **cambiaba**
To clean (klin) **limpiar**	Cleaned (klind) **limpiaba**
To climb (claimb) **escalar**	Climbed (claimbd) **escalaba**
To close (clos) **cerrar**	Closed (closd) **cerraba**
To cook (cuc) **cocinar**	Cooked (cuct) **cocinaba**

Note: Some regular verbs in English are considered irregular in Spanish, only by practice and memorization can these irregular verbs be learned.

Nota: Algunos verbos regulares en Inglés son considerados irregulares en Español, Solamente mediante la práctica y la memorización se pueden aprender estos verbos irregulares.

IRREGULAR VERBS

VERBOS IRREGULARES

Present tense/Tiempo presente - **Past tense**/Tiempo pasado

To read (rid) **leer**	Read (red) **leía**
To ride (raid) **pasear**	Rode (rod) **paseaba**
To ring (ring) **sonar**	Rang (reng) **sonaba**
To run (ran) **correr**	Ran (ren) **corría**
To rise (raiss) **subir**	Rose (rouss) **subía**
To say (sei) **decir**	Said (seid) **decía**
To see (si) **ver**	Saw (so) **veía**
To sing (sing) **cantar**	Sang (seng) cantaba
To sell (seil) **vender**	Sold (sold) vendía
To send (send) **enviar**	Sent (sent) **enviaba**
To sit (sit) **sentar**	Sat (sat) **sentaba**
To shut (shut) **cerrar**	Shut (shat) **cerraba**
To sleep (slip) **domir**	Slept (slerpt) **dormía**
To speak (spik) **hablar**	Spoke (spork) **hablaba**
To stand (stend) **pararse**	Stood (stud) **paraba**
To strike (straik) **golpear**	Struck (stroc) **golpeaba**
To slide (slaid) **resbalar**	Slid (slid) **resbalaba**
To spend (spend) **gastar**	Spent (spent) **gastaba**
To sweep (suip) **barrer**	Swept (swept) **barría**
To swim (suim) **nadar**	Swam (suem) **nadaba**
To steal (stil) **robar**	Stole (storl) **robaba**
To swear (suer) **jurar**	Swore (sour) **juraba**
To spring (spring) **brincar**	Sprang (sprang) **brincaba**
To spread (spred) **extender**	Spread (spred) **extendía**
To take (teic) **tomar**	Took (tuk) **tomaba**
To teach (tich) **enseñar**	Taught (tort) **enseñaba**
To tear (ter) **rascar**	Tore (tor) **rascaba**
To think (tenk) **pensar**	Thought (fort) **pensaba**
To tell (tel) **decir**	Told (told) **decía**

Example:

1- They <u>thought</u> that last year was going to be a great baseball season.
2- That team never <u>scored</u> below 90 and that was a surprise to see them lose the game.
3- Last year we <u>recalled</u> our mother's sweet roll recipe for Christmas.
4- He <u>was</u> very upset right after seeing his favorite team loses the championship.

Ejemplo:

1- Ellos <u>pensaban</u> que el año pasado iba a ser una gran temporada de béisbol.
2- Ese equipo nunca <u>anotaba</u> debajo de 90 y fue una sorpresa verlos perder el juego.
3- El año pasado <u>recordábamos</u> la receta de nuestra madre para hacer galleta para navidad.
4- Él <u>estaba</u> muy molesto después de ver a su equipo favorito perder el campeonato.

Some helping vocabularies to complete your sentences in past tense:

Last year, last month, yesterday, last night, last week, two weeks ago, two minutes ago, two years ago, one day ago, on July 13th, 2012.

Algunos vocabularios para completar sus frases en tiempo pasado:

El año pasado, el mes pasado, ayer, anoche, la semana pasada, hace dos semanas, hace dos minutos, hace dos años, hace un día, el 13 de julio, 2012.

Exercise: Transform the verbs in brackets in past tense and translate into Spanish

1- We (accept) to visit Ibiza this coming year 2016.
2- We (need) to be productive in order to make our society a better place.
3- They (have) many nice things to see in Paris.

NEGATIVE FORMS
FORMAS NEGATIVAS

To transform a verb into a negative sentence in past tense we need to add the negative form did not (didn't) plus the base form of the verb. In Spanish only add "No" after the personal pronoun before the verb. Example: ("Yo no dormía" I did not sleep).

Para transformar un verbo en forma negativa en tiempo pasado tenemos que añadir la forma negativa did not (didn't) más la forma base del verbo. En Español se agrega solamente **"No"** despúes del pronombre personal antes del verbo. Ejemplo: (**"Yo no dormía"** I did not sleep).

Exercise: Complete the sentence in the right-hand column using different verbs from the previous regular or irregular verbs list.

Ejercicio: Complete la frase con diferentes verbos previamente visto en la lista de los verbos regulares e irregulares usando la columna derecha.

I did not (**didn't**) + verb Yo no + verbo	**I did not have a chance to visit my grandma last year** Yo no tenía oportunidad visitar a mi abuela el año pasado
You did not (**didn't**) + verb Tu no + verbo	
He did not (**didn't**) + verb Él no + verbo	
She did not (**didn't**) + verb Ella no + verbo	
It did not (**didn't**) + verb Esto no + verbo	
We did not (**didn't**) + verb Nosotros no + verbo	
You did not (**didn't**) + verb Ústedes no + verbo	
They did not (**didn't**) + verb Ellos o Ellas no + verbo	

Future tense

As in Spanish, there are plenty of action verbs in English, which can help us to express our thoughts. There is only one way to conjugate them in future tense and conditional tense.

1- To conjugate the verbs in future tense is not complicated. We only need to start with a subject or a personal pronoun, plus **"will"** and the base form of the verb.

In Spanish, none of these rules are needed to conjugate the verbs in future tense, but all the verbs which end in **"ar"** have their ending in future tense in **"aré, rás, rá, remos, rán, rán"**. Those with **"er"** end in future tense in **"ré, rás, rá, remos, rán, rán."** Finally, those wich end in **"ir"** end in future tense in **"ré, rás, rá, remos, rán, rán."** (i.e: **"to sing"** cantar, **"to drink"** beber, **"to compete,"** competir).

Tiempo futuro

Al igual que el idioma Español, hay un montón de verbos de acción en Inglés que pueden ayudarnos a expresar nuestros pensamientos. Hay una sóla manera de saber cómo conjugarlos en tiempos futuro y condicional.

1- No es complicado conjugar verbos en tiempo futuro. Solamente tiene que comenzar con un pronombre personal, más "**will**" y la forma base del verbo.

En Español, ninguna de esas reglas se ocupa para conjugar los verbos en tiempo futuro, pero todos los verbos que terminan en **"ar"** tienen su final en tiempo futuro con terminación **"ré, rás, rá, remos, rán, rán."** Aquellos que se terminan en **"er"** en tiempo futuro terminan en **"ré, rás, rá, remos, rán, rán."** Finalmente, los que tienen una terminación en **"ir"** en tiempo futuro terminan en **"ré, rás, rá, remos, rán, rán"** (ejemplo: **"to sing"**, cantar, **"to drink,"** beber, **"to compete,"** competir).

I will drink	**Yo** beberé
You will drink	**Tu** beberás
He will drink	**Él** beberá
She will drink	**Ella** beberá
It will drink	**Esto** beberá
We will drink	**Nosotros** beberemos
You will drink	**Ústedes** beberán
They will drink	**Ellos o Ellas** beberán

Example/Ejemplo

Negative forms/Formas negativas

To transform a verb into a negative sentence in future tense we need to add the negative form will not (won't) plus the base form of the verb. In Spanish only add "No" after the personal pronoun before the verb. (Example: "yo no iré" I will not go).

Para transformar un verbo en forma negativa en tiempo futuro tenemos que añadir la forma negativa will not (won't) más la forma base del verbo. En Español se agrega solamente **"No"** despúes del pronombre personal antes del verbo (Ejemplo:**"yo no iré"** I will not go).

Exercise: Complete the sentence in the right-hand column using different verbs from the previous regular or irregular verbs list.

Ejercicio: Complete la frase con diferentes verbos previamente visto en la lista de los verbos regulares e irregulares usando la columna derecha.

Future tense/Tiempo futuro	Answer part/Respuesta
I will not(**won't**)+verb Yo no+verbo	I will not go to the beach this summer. Yo no iré a la playa este verano.
You will not(**won't**)+verb Tu no+verbo	
He will not(**won't**)+verb Él no+verbo	
She will not(**won't**)+verb Ella no+verbo	
It will not(**won't**)+verb Esto no + verbo	
We will not(**won't**)+verb Nosotros no+verbo	
You will not(**won't**)+verb Ústedes no+verbo	
They will not(**won't**)+verb Ellos o Ellas no+verbo	

Conditional tense

2- To conjugate the verbs in conditional tense is not complicated. We only need to start with a subject or a personal pronoun, plus **"would"** and the base form of the verb. **In Spanish, none of these rules are needed to conjugate the verbs in condicional tense**, but all the verbs which end in **"ar"** have their ending in condicional tense in **"ría, rías, ría, ríamos, rían, rían."** Those with **"er"** end in conditional tense in **"ría, rías, ría, ríamos, rían, rían."** Finally, those wich end with **"ir"** end in conditional tense in **"ría, rías, ría, ríamos, rían, rían."** (i.e: **"to sing"** cantar, **"to drink"** beber, **"to compete"** competir).

Tiempo condicional

2- No es complicado conjugar los verbos en condicional. Solamente tiene que comenzar con un pronombre personal, más **"would"** y la forma base del verbo. **En Español, ninguna de esas reglas se ocupa para conjugar los verbos en tiempo condicional,** pero todos los verbos que terminan en **"ar"** terminan en tiempo condicional con **"ría, rías, ría, ríamos, rían, rían."** Aquellos que se terminan en **"er"** en tiempo condicional se terminan en **"ría, rías, ría, ríamos, rían, rían."** Finalmente los que tienen terminación en **"ir"** en tiempo condicional se terminan en **"ría, rías, ría, ríamos, rían, rían."** (Ejemplo: **"to sing"** cantar, **"to drink"** beber, **"to compete"** competir).

Example/Ejemplo

Conditional tense	Tiempo condicional
I would dance	**Yo** bailaría
You would dance	**Tu** bailarías
He would dance	**Él** bailaría
She would dance	**Ella** bailaría
It would dance	**(Esto)** bailaría
We would dance	**Nosotros** bailaríamos
You would dance	**Ústedes** bailarían
They would dance	**Ellos o Ellas** bailarían

NEGATIVE FORMS

FORMAS NEGATIVAS

To transform a verb into a negative sentence in conditional tense we need to add the negative form would not (wouldn't) plus the base form of the verb. In Spanish only add "No" after the personal pronoun before the verb. (Example: "yo no iría" I would not go).

Para transformar un verbo en forma negativa en tiempo condicional tenemos que añadir la forma negativa would not (wouldn't) más la forma base del verbo. En Español se agrega solamente "**No**" despúes del pronombre personal antes del verbo, ejemplo: "**yo no iría**" I would not go.

Exercise: Complete the sentence in the right-hand column using different verbs from the previous regular or irregular verbs list.

Ejercicio: Complete la frase con diferentes verbos previamente visto en la lista de los verbos regulares e irregulares usando la columna derecha.

Conditional Tense Tiempo Condicional	Answer part/Respuesta
I would not (**wouldn't**) + verb Yo no + verbo	**I would not go to the party if I wasn't invited.** Yo no iría a la fiesta si no fuera invitado.
You would not (**wouldn't**) + verb Tu no + verbo	
He would not (**wouldn't**) + verb Él no + verbo	
She would not (**wouldn't**) + verb Ella no + verbo	
It would not (**wouldn't**) + verb Esto no + verbo	
We would not (**wouldn't**) + verb Nosotros no + verbo	
You would not (**wouldn't**) + verb Ústedes no + verbo	
They would not (**wouldn't**) + verb Ellos o Ellas no + verbo	

LESSON II

LECCIÓN II

PREPOSITION OF PLACE/PREPOSICIÓN DE LUGAR

There are plenty of prepositions in English, so we will only choose the most significant ones.
Hay muchas preposiciones en Inglés, elegimos solamente los más significantes.

List of the prepositions/Lista de preposiciones:

Outside, inside, behind, in front of, above, over, near, around, opposite, **among, between**, under, below, on top of, next to, beside, by.

Afuera o fuera de, dentro de o adentro de, atrás o detrás de, en frente de, arriba, sobre, cerca de, alrededor de, opuesto de, **en medio de o entre**, abajo de o debajo de, más abajo de, encima de, cerca de, al lado de, por.

Outside = Fuera de o afuera de

Example/Ejemplo:
I wanted to live outside Mexico
Quise vivir fuera de México.

Inside/In = Dentro de o adentro

Example/Ejemplo:
The balls are <u>inside</u> **the box or the balls are** <u>in</u> **the box.**
Las pelotas están adentro de la caja.

Behind = Atrás de o detrás de

Example/Ejemplo:
The parking is behind the hospital.
El estacionamiento está detrás del hospital.

In front of = En frente de

Example/Ejemplo:
I live in front of their houses.
(Yo) vivo frente de sus casas.

Above/Over = Encima de, arriba

Example/Ejemplo:
The bird was <u>above</u> the house or the bird was <u>over</u> the house.
El pájaro estaba encima de la casa.

Below/Under = Más bajo de o abajo de (we use 'below' not 'under' when it means 'lower than').

Example/Ejemplo:
1- Two cats are under the old brick bridge.
   Dos gatos están abajo del viejo puente de ladrillo.

2- We could see the town below us.
   Podríamos ver la ciudad más debajo de nosotros.

Among/Between = Entre (we use between when we can specify something or someone between different things and among is when there is one specific thing in middle of many similar.) Between "entre" se usa, cuando se especifica algo o alguien entre diferentes cosas y among "entre" en medio de cosas similares.

Example/Ejemplo:
1- We could see the deer between the trees.
   Podríamos ver los venados <u>entre</u> los árboles.

2- There was a white cow among the others.
   Hubo una vaca blanca <u>entre</u> las otras.

By/Next to/Near/Beside = Por, cerca de, al lado de.

Example/Ejemplo:

They live by our house or they live near our house or they live beside our house or they live next to our house.

Ellos viven cerca de nuestra casa.

LESSON III

LECCIÓN III

Plural form of nouns/Forma plural de los sustantivos

For the nouns that pass from singular to plural in English it is necessary to add a "S". In Spanish we must add a "S" or "ES" after the nouns no matter how they end.

Para los sustantivos que pasan de singular a plural en Inglés es necesario agregar una **"S"**. En Español debemos de agregar una **"S"** o **"ES"** después de los sustantivos sin importar cómo terminan.

Ex: Desk- Desks - Chair- Chairs - Computer - Computers - Picture - Pictures.
Ej: Escritorio - Escritorios - Silla - Sillas - Computadora - Computadoras - Foto - Fotos.

The nouns that end in "Y" in English with a consonant before when passing from singular to plural changed "Y" in "IES".

Los sustantivos que terminan en **"Y"** en Inglés con un consonante adelante cuando pasan de singular al plural cambia la **"Y"** en **"IES"**.

Ex: Country – Countries – Lady – Ladies – Family – Families.
Ejemplo: País – Países – Dama – Damas – Familia – Familias.

Exception: If the nouns end with "Y" following a vowel when passing from singular to plural is necessary to add only a "S".

Excepción: Si los sustantivos se terminan en **"Y"** siguiendo de una vocal cuando pasa de singular al plural es necesario agregar una **"S"** nada más.

Ex: Boy-Boys-Toy-Toys-Clay-Clays.
Ej: Niño - Niños - Juguete - Juguetes - Arcilla – Arcilla (excepción).

The nouns in English which end in S, CH, X, Z, O add an "ES" to form its plural form.

Los sustantivos que termina en **S, CH, X, Z, O** agregue una **"ES"** para formar su plural.

Ex: Potato-Potatoes-Glass-Glasses-Church-Churches-Box-Boxes.
Ej: Papa - Papas - Vaso- Vasos - Iglesia - Iglesias- Caja - Cajas.

All the nouns in English that end in "FE" change. You must change them in "VES".

Todos los sustantivos en Inglés que terminan en **"FE"** cambia. Debe de cambiarlos en **"VES"**.

Ex: Leaf-Leaves-Shelf-Shelves-Life-Lives-Knife-Knives.
Ej: Hoja - Hojas - Estante -Estantes -Vida -Vidas - Cuchillo - Cuchillos.

We have a few common words in English which have irregular plural forms.

Tenemos unas palabras comúnes en Inglés que tienen formas irregulares.

Ex: Gulf - Gulfs - Roof - Roofs - Proof - Proofs - Safe - Safes - Scarf - Scarfs.
Ej: Golfo - Golfos - Techo - Techos - Prueba - Pruebas - Caja fuerte - Cajas fuertes (excepción) - Bufanda - Bufandas.

Exist some nouns in English when they're passing to the plural they change differently.

Existen algunos sustantivos en Inglés cuando pasan al plural cambian diferentemente.

Ex: Man - Men - Woman - Women - Child - Children - Foot - Feet - Ox - Oxen - Tooth - Teeth - Mouse - Mice.
Ej: Hombre - Hombres - Mujer - Mujeres - Niño - Niños - Pie - Pies - Buey - Bueyes - Diente - Dientes - Ratón - Ratónes.

Exist some nouns in English when they're passing to plural they don't change.

Existen algunos sustantivos en Inglés cuando pasan al plural no cambian.

Ex: Sheep - Sheep - Deer - Deer - Hose - Hose - Fish - Fish
Ej: Oveja - Ovejas - Venado - Venados - Media - Medias - Pescado - Pescados.

Exercise/Ejercicio

Create your sentences with outside, inside, behind, in front of, above, near.

Crea sus frases con: fuera de o afuera de, dentro de, detrás de, frente de, arriba de, cerca de

1- _____

2- _____

3- _____

4- _____

5- _____

6- _____

LESSON IV

LECCION IV

There is/There are: Hay

We use "There is" and "There are" for present tense singular and plural to show the existence of something, for negative: There is no/There are no, for questions: Is there?/Are there?

Utilizamos **"There is" y "There are"** (hay) en tiempo presente singular y plural para demostrar la existencia de algo, en negativo: **There is no/There are no** (no hay), para preguntas: **Is there?/Are there?** (¿hay?).

Example: There is a person coming to my house tonight.
Ejemplo: **Hay una persona que va venir a mi casa está noche.**

Example: There are three dogs upstairs in my house.
Ejemplo: **Hay tres perros arriba en mi casa.**

There was: Hubo/Había/There were: Hubo/Habían

We use "There was" and "There were" for past tense singular and plural to show that something existed in the past.

For negative: There was no/There were no.
For questions: Was there?/Were there?

Utilizamos **"There was" y "There were"** (hubo) en tiempo pasado singular y plural para demostrar la existencia de algo, en negativo: **There was no/There were no"** (no hubo), para preguntas: **Was there?/Were there?** (¿hubo?).

Example: There was a ship that entered the bay.
Ejemplo: **Hubo un barco que entraba a la bahía.**

Example: There were many ants that crossed the street.
Ejemplo: **Hubo muchas hormigas que cruzaban la calle.**

There will be: Habrá/Habrán/There would be: Habría/Habrían

We use "There will be" to explain things that will happen in the future. We use "There would be" for conditional tense.

For negative: There will be no (singular, plural)
For question: Will there be? (singular, plural).
For negative: There would be no (singular, plural).
For questions: Would there be?

Utilizamos **"There will be"** (habrá/habrán) **para demostrar la existencia de algo en tiempo futuro y "There would be"** (habría, habrían) en tiempo condicional (singular y plural) para demostrar la existencia de algo, en negativo: **There will be no** (no habrá/no habrán),"**There would be no** (no habría/no habrían).

Para preguntas: **Will there be?** (¿habrá?/¿habrán?),

Would there be? (¿habría/habrían?).

Example: There will be a T.V in my house.
Ejemplo: **Habrá una televisión en mi casa.**

Example: If I did not pay my landlord, there would be trouble.
Ejemplo: **Si no pagaba mi renta, habría problema.**

Exercise/Ejercicio
Fill in the blanks with: There is/There are/There was/There were/There will be/There would be.
Llene los espacios en blanco con: Hay/Hubo o Había/Habrá/Habrán/Habría/Habrían.

1- **Tonight_____people coming to my house for a party.**
2- Esta noche_____gente que va venir a mi casa para una fiesta.
3- **Last week_____two people died in a car accident.**
4- La semana pasada_____dos personas que murieron en un accidente de auto.
5-_____**a new student at school this summer.**
6-_____un nuevo estudiante en la escuela este verano.
7- **This morning_____a lot of snow in my back yard.**
8- Está mañana_____mucha nieve detrás de mi patio.

LESSON V

LECCIÓN V

INTERROGATIVE FORM
FORMA INTEROGATIVA

Sometimes students are confused when asking questions in English or Spanish. The easiest way to make simple questions in English is using the auxiliary **Do** or **does** for present tense. **Did** for past tense. **Will** for future tense and **Would** for conditional tense, plus the personal pronouns and the base form of the verbs. There is an exception to this rule, the verb **"To be"**.

In Spanish, this rule does not apply. To make any questions in Spanish we need to pick the conjugated verb after the personal pronoun and make the question with intonation (Example: **"You work"** tu trabajas. **"Do you work?"** ¿Trabajas? The same thing is used for negative questions (Example: **"You work"** tu trabajas. **"Don't you work?"** ¿No trabajas?

A veces los estudiantes se confunden cuando hacen preguntas en Inglés o Español. La manera más fácil de hacer preguntas sencillas en Inglés es usar el auxiliar "**Do or Does**" en tiempo presente. **"Did"** en tiempo pasado. **"Will"** en tiempo futuro y **"Would"** en tiempo condicional, más los pronombres personales y la forma base de los verbos. Hay una excepción a esta regla, el verbo **"To be" (ser o estar).**

En Español, está regla no se aplica. Para hacer cualquier pregunta necesitamos elegir el verbo conjugado que viene despúes del pronombre personal (Ejemplo: **"You work"** tú trabajas. **"Do you work?"** ¿Trabajas? Misma cosa para preguntas en forma negativas pero con intonaciones (Ejemplo: **"You work"** tú trabajas. **"Don't you work?"** ¿No trabajas?

How to make simple questions in present tense "To have" and "To want": Tener y Querrer
Cómo hacer preguntas sencillas en tiempo presente "**To have**" and "**To want**": Tener y Querrer

Formula: **Do or does + Pronoun + Verb** - Negative: **Don`t or doesn`t + Pronoun + Verb**

Do I have? ¿**Tengo?**	Do I want? ¿**Quiero?**
Do You have? ¿**Tienes?**	Do You want? ¿**Quieres?**
Does He have? ¿**Tiene?**	Does He want? ¿**Quiere?**
Does She have? ¿**Tiene?**	Does She want? ¿**Quiere?**
Does It have? ¿**Tiene?**	Does It want? ¿**Quiere?**
Do We have? ¿**Tenemos?**	Do We want? ¿**Queremos?**
Do You have? ¿**Tienen?**	Do You want? ¿**Quieren?**
Do They have? ¿**Tienen?**	Do They want? ¿**Quieren?**

Negative Questions/Preguntas en Negativas

Don't I have? ¿No tengo?
Don't You have? ¿No tienes?
Doesn't He have? ¿No tiene?
Doesn't She have? ¿No tiene?
Doesn't It have? ¿No tiene?
Don't We have? ¿No tenemos?
Don't You have? ¿No tienen?
Don't They have? ¿No tienen?

Don't I want? ¿No quiero?
Don't You want? ¿No quieres?
Doesn't He want? ¿No quiere?
Doesn't She want? ¿No quiere?
Doesn't It want? ¿No quiere?
Don't We want? ¿No queremos?
Don't You want? ¿No quieren?
Don't They want? ¿No quieren?

Example/Ejemplo

1- **Do we have tickets to go to Hawaii?** ¿Tenemos boletos para ir a Hawaii?

2- **Does she want to visit Paris next summer?** ¿Quiere visitar París el próximo verano?

3- **Do they have a meeting tomorrow morning?** ¿Tienen una reunión mañana en la mañana?

Short answer/Respuesta corta	Long answer/Respuesta larga
1R-Yes, we do. 1R-Si, tenemos.	**1R-Yes, we have tickets to go to Hawaii.** 1R-Si, tenemos boletos para ir a Hawaii.
No, we don't. No, no tenemos	**No, we don't have tickets to go to Hawaii.** No, no tenemos boletos para ir a Hawaii.
2R-Yes, she does. 2R-Si, ella quiere.	**2R-Yes, she wants to visit Paris next summer.** 2R-Si, ella quiere visitar París próximo verano.
No, she doesn't. No, ella no quiere.	**No, she doesn't want to visit Paris next summer.** No, ella no quiere visitar París próximo verano
3R-Yes, they do. Si, ellos tienen.	**3R-Yes, they have a meeting tomorrow morning.** Si, ellos tienen una reunión mañana por la mañana
No, they don't. No, ellos no tienen.	**No, they don't have a meeting tomorrow morning.** No, ellos no tienen una reunión mañana por la mañana.

Create your questions in present tense in affirmative and negative form.
Crea sus preguntas en tiempo presente en forma afirmativa y negativa.

1- _____

2- _____

3- _____

4- _____

How to make simple questions in past tense "To need" and "To work": Necesitar y Trabajar
Cómo hacer preguntas simples en tiempo pasado **"To need"** and **"To work":** Necesitar y Trabajar

Formula: **Did+Pronoun+Verb** - Negative: **Didn`t+Pronoun+Verb**

Did I need? **¿Necesitaba?**   Did I work? **¿Trabajaba?**
Did You need? **¿Necesitabas?**   Did You work? **¿Trabajabas?**
Did He need? **¿Necesitaba?**   Did He work? **¿Trabajaba?**
Did She need? **¿Necesitaba?**   Did She work? **¿Trabajaba?**
Did It need? **¿Necesitaba?**   Did It work? **¿Trabajaba?**
Did We need? **¿Necesitabamos?**   Did We work? **¿Trabajabamos?**
Did You need? **¿Necesitaban?**   Did You work? **¿Trabajaban?**
Did They need? **¿Necesitaban?**   Did They work? **¿Trabajaban?**

Negative questions/Preguntas en formas negativas

Didn't I need? **¿No necesitaba?**   Didn't I work? **¿No trabajaba?**
Didn't You need? **¿No necesitabas?**   Didn't You work? **¿No trabajabas?**
Didn't He need? **¿No necesitaba?**   Didn't He work? **¿No trabajaba?**
Didn't She need? **¿No necesitaba?**   Didn't She work? **¿No trabajaba?**
Didn't It need? **¿No necesitaba?**   Didn't It work? **¿No trabajaba?**
Didn't We need **¿No necesitabamos?**   Didn't We work? **¿No trabajabamos?**
Didn't You need? **¿No necesitaban?**   Didn't You work? **¿No trabajaban?**
Didn't They need? **¿No necesitaban?**   Didn't They work? **¿No trabajaban?**

Example/Ejemplo
1- **Did Sarah study Spanish?/**¿Estudiaba Sarah Español?
2- **Did Jeffrey miss the bus to work?/**¿Faltaba Jeffrey al autobús para ir a trabajar?
3- **Did Stacey sing at the bar?/**¿Cantaba Stacey en el bar?

Short answer/Respuesta corta	Long answer/Respuesta larga
1R-Yes, she did. 1R-Si, ella estudiaba.	**1R-Yes, she studied Spanish.** 1RSi, ella estudiaba Español.
No, she didn't. No, ella no estudiaba.	**No, she didn't study Spanish.** No, ella no estudiaba Español.
2R-Yes, he did. 2R-Si, él faltaba.	**2R-Yes, he missed the bus to work.** 2R- Si, él faltaba el autobús para ir a trabajar.
No, he didn't. No, él no faltaba.	**No, he didn't miss the bus to work.** No, él no faltaba el autobús para ir a trabajar.
3R-Yes, she did. Si, ella cantaba.	**3R-Yes, she sang at the bar.** 3R-Si, ella cantaba en el bar.
No, she didn't. No, ella no cantaba.	**No, she didn't sing at the bar.** No, ella no cantaba en el bar.

Exercise/Ejercicio
Create your questions in past tense in affirmative and negative form.
Crea sus preguntas en tiempo pasado en forma afirmativa y negativa.

1- _____

2- _____

3- _____

4-_____

How to make simple questions in future tense "To dance" and "To study": Bailar y Estudiar

Cómo hacer preguntas simples en tiempo futuro **"To dance"** and **"To study":** Bailar y Estudiar

Formula: Will + Pronoun + Verb - Negative: Won`t + Pronoun + Verb

Will I dance? **¿Bailaré?**   Will I study? **¿Estudiaré?**
Will You dance? **¿Bailarás?**   Will You study? **¿Estudiarás?**

Will He dance? **¿Bailará?**	Will He study? **¿Estudiará?**
Will She dance? **¿Bailará?**	Will She study? **¿Estudiará?**
Will It dance? **¿Bailará?**	Will It study? **¿Estudiará?**
Will We dance? **¿Bailaremos?**	Will We study? **¿Estudiaremos?**
Will You dance? **¿Bailarán?**	Will You study? **¿Estudiarán?**
Will They dance? **¿Bailarán?**	Will They study? **¿Estudiarán?**

Negative questions/Preguntas en formas negativas

Won't I dance? **¿No bailaré?**	Won't I study? **¿No estudiaré?**
Won't You dance? **¿No bailarás?**	Won't You study? **¿No estudiarás?**
Won't He dance? **¿No bailará?**	Won't He study? **¿No estudiará?**
Won't She dance? **¿No bailará?**	Won't She study **¿No estudiará?**
Won't It dance? **¿No bailará?**	Won't It study? **¿No estudiará?**
Won't We dance? **¿No bailaremos?**	Won't We study? **¿No estudiaremos?**
Won't You dance? **¿No bailarán?**	Won't You study? **¿No estudiarán?**
Won't They dance? **¿No bailarán?**	Won't They study? **¿No estudiarán?**

Example/Ejemplo
1- **Will she take the book back to the store?**/¿Ella devolverá el libro a la tienda?
2- **Will they visit their parents in Mexico?**/¿Visitarán a sus padres en México?
3- **Will Tim go to the dentist tomorrow?**/¿Irá Tim al dentista mañana?

Short answer/Respuesta corta	Long answer/Respuesta larga
1R-Yes, she will.	**1R-Yes, she will take the book back to the store.**
1R-Si, ella lo devolverá.	1R-Si, ella devolverá el libro a la tienda.
No, she won't.	**No, she won't take the book back to the store.**
No, ella no lo devolverá.	No, ella no devolverá el libro a la tienda.
2R-Yes, they will.	**2R-Yes, they will visit their parents in Mexico.**
2R-Si, ellos visitarán	2R-Si, ellos visitarán sus padres en México.
No, they won't.	**No, they won't visit their parents in Mexico.**
No, ellos no visitarán	No, ellos no visitarán sus padres en México.
3R-Yes, he will	**3R-Yes, he will go to the dentist tomorrow.**
3R-Si, él irá.	3R-Si, él irá al dentista mañana.
No, he won't.	**No, he won't go to the dentist tomorrow.**
No, él no irá.	No, él no irá al dentista mañana.

Create your questions in future tense in affirmative and negative form.
Crea sus preguntas en tiempo futuro en forma afirmativa y negativa.

1- _____

2- _____

3- _____

4- _____

How to make simple questions in conditional tense "To confess" and "To forgive"
Cómo hacer preguntas simples en tiempo condicional "Confesar" y "Perdonar"

Formula: **Would + Pronoun + Verb** - Negative: **Wouldn`t + Pronoun + Verb**

Would I confess? **¿Confesaría?**   Would I forgivve? **¿Perdonaría?**
Would You confess? **¿Confesarías?**   Would You forgive? **¿Perdonarías?**
Would He confess? **¿Confesaría?**   Would He forgive? **¿Perdonaría?**
Would She confess? **¿Confesaría?**   Would She forgive? **¿Perdonaría?**
Would It confess? **¿Confesaría?**   Would It forgive? **¿Perdonaría?**
Would We confess? **¿Confesaríamos?**   Would We forgive? **¿Perdonaríamos?**
Would You confess? **¿Confesarian?**   Would You forgive? **¿Perdonarian?**
Would They confess? **¿Confesarían?**   Would They forgive? **¿Perdonarían?**

Negative questions/Preguntas en formas negativas

Wouldn't I confess? **¿No confesaría?**   Wouldn't I forgive? **¿No perdonaría?**
Wouldn't You confess? **¿No confesarías?**   Wouldn't You forgive? **¿No perdonarías?**
Wouldn't He confess? **¿No confesaría?**   Wouldn't He forgive? **¿No perdonaría?**
Wouldn't She confess? **¿No confesaría?**   Wouldn't She forgive? **¿No perdonaría?**
Wouldn't It confess? **¿No confesaría?**   Wouldn't It forgive? **¿No perdonaría?**
Wouldn't We confess? **¿No confesaríamos?**   Wouldn't We forgive? **¿No perdonaríamos?**
Wouldn't You confess? **¿No confesarian?**   Wouldn't You forgive? **¿No perdonarian?**
Wouldn't They confess? **¿No confesarían?**   Wouldn't They forgive? **¿No perdonarían?**

Example/Ejemplo:

1- **Would you tell the truth if I did?**/ ¿Dirías la verdad si yo lo hiciera?

2- **Would they arrive on time if it was raining?**/ ¿Llegarían a tiempo si estuviera lloviendo?

3- **Would we pass the test tomorrow if we study?**/Pasaríamos la prueba mañana si estudiaríamos?

Short answer/Respuesta corta   **Long answer**/Respuesta larga

1R-Yes, I would. 1R-Si, lo diría.	**1R-Yes, I would tell the truth if you did.** 1R-Si, diría la verdad si lo hicieras.
No, I wouldn't. No, no lo diría.	**No, I wouldn't tell the truth** No, no diría la verdad.
2R-Yes, they would. 2R-Si, llegarían.	**2R-Yes, they would arrive on time if it was raining.** 2R- Si, llegarían a tiempo si estuviera lloviendo.
No, they wouldn't. No, no llegarían.	**No, they wouldn't arrive on time if it was raining.** No, no llegarían a tiempo si estuviera lloviendo.
3R-Yes, we would. 3R-Si, lo pasaríamos.	**3R-Yes, we would pass the test tomorrow if we study.** 3R-Si, pasaríamos la prueba mañana si estudiamos.
No, we wouldn't. No, no lo pasaríamos.	**No, we wouldn't pass the test if we did not study.** No, no pasaríamos la prueba si no estudiabamos.

Contraction with "To be" (tu bi): Ser o Estar

I am (I'm)= **Yo soy/Yo estoy**

You are (you're)= **Tu eres/Tu estás**

He is (he's)= **Él es/Él está**

She is (she's)= **Ella es/Ella está**

It is (it's)= **Esto es/Esto está**

We are (we're)= **Nosotros somos/Nosotros estamos**

You are (you're)= **Ústedes son/Ústedes están**

They are (they're)= **Ellos/Ellas son o Ellos/Ellas están**

To make simple questions with "to be", we must use the present continuous reversing "to be" by adding(1)"ing" after the following verb, example:(Is she working?). We can use as well: (2) adjectives, (3) family members, (4) places and (5) occupations together with "to be" to make questions.

In Spanish, this rule does not apply. To make any questions in Spanish in the present tense with **"to be"** we need to take the base form of the conjugated verb **"to be"** (ser/estar) in affirmative form, then add **"ing"** (ando/endo) after the verb that follows **"to be"** (ser/estar) and pronounce it

With intonation (example: **"She is singing"** ¿Está cantando?), there are few exceptions to this rule. We must use the same technique for the past, future and the conditional tense.

Para hacer preguntas sencillas con **"to be"** (ser/estar), debemos usar el presente continuo volteando **"to be"** (ser o estar), adiciónando (1) **"ing"** (ando/endo) después del verbo que lo sigue, ejemplo: **(Is she working?** ¿Está trabajando?). Podemos usar tambíen: (2) **adjetivos**, (3) **miembros de familia**, (4) **lugares** (5) **ocupaciones** junto con **"to be"** (ser/estar) para hacer preguntas.

En Español, esta regla no se aplica. Para hacer preguntas en Español en tiempo presente con **"to be"** (ser/estar) necesitamos tomar la base del verbo conjugado **"to be"** (ser/estar) en forma afirmativa, agregando **"ing"** (ando/endo) al verbo que lo sigue y pronunciarlo con intonación, ejemplo: (**"She is singing"** ¿Está cantando?), hay pocas excepciones para está regla. Debemos hacer lo mismo para el tiempo pasado, futuro y condicional.

How to make simple questions in present tense with "To be" (ser/estar) plus another verb.
Cómo hacer preguntas simples en tiempo presente con **"To be"** (ser/estar) más otro verbo.

Formula: To be + Pronoun + Verb with "ing"

Present tense continuous	Present tense continuous
Am I sleeping? **¿Estoy durmiendo?**	Am I studying? **¿Estoy estudiando?**
Are You sleeping? **¿Estás durmiendo?**	Are You studying? **¿Estás estudiando?**
Is He sleeping? **¿Está durmiendo?**	Is He studying? **¿Está estudiando?**
Is She sleeping? **¿Está durmiendo?**	Is She studying? **¿Está estudiando?**
Is It sleeping? **¿Está durmiendo?**	Is It studying? **¿Está estudiando?**
Are We sleeping? **¿Estámos durmiendo?**	Are We studying? **¿Estámos estudiando?**
Are You sleeping? **¿Están durmiendo?**	Are You studying? **¿Están estudiando?**
Are They sleeping? **¿Están durmiendo?**	Are They studying? **¿Están estudiando?**

Example/Ejemplo
1- Are you **studying at** school? (Verb)/¿Estás estudiando en la escuela?
2- Are you **married**? (Adjective)/¿Eres casado?
3- Is your **sister** happy now? (Family member)/¿Está tu hermana feliz ahora?
4- Is she **in the back yard**? (Place)/¿Está en el patio trasero?
5- Are they **chemists** or **teachers**? (Occupation)/¿Son químicos (as) o maestros (as)?

Short answer/Respuesta corta	Long answer/Respuesta larga
1R- Yes, I am. 1R-Si, estoy.	**1R- Yes, I am studying at school.** 1R-Si, estoy estudiando en la escuela.
No, I am not (I'm not) No, no estoy.	**No, I am not studying at school.** No, no estoy estudiando en la escuela.
2R-Yes, I am. 2R-Si, soy.	**2R-Yes, I am married.** 2R-Si, soy casado (a).
No, I am not (I'm not) No, no soy.	**No, I am not (I'm not) married.** No, no soy casado (a).
3R-Yes, she is 3R-Si, es.	**3R- Yes, she is happy.** 3R- Si, ella es feliz.
No, she is not (isn't). No, no es.	**No, she is not (isn't) happy.** No, ella no es feliz.
4R- Yes, she is. 4R-Si, está.	**4R- Yes, she is in the back yard.** 4R- Si, está en el patio trasero.
No, she is not (isn't). No, no está.	**No, she is not in the back yard.** No, no está en el patio trasero.
6- Yes, they are. 5R-Si, son.	**7- Yes, they are teachers.** 5R-Si, son maestros.
No, they are not. No, no son.	**No, they are not teachers.** No, no son maestros.

Exercise/Ejercicio

Create your questions in present tense with "to be" plus another
verb, adjective, family member, place, profession.

1- _____

2- _____

3- _____

4- _____

Crea sus preguntas en tiempo presente con **"To be"** (ser/estar) más otro verbo, adjetivo, miembro de familia, lugar, profesión.

1- _____

2- _____

3- _____

4- _____

5- _____

How to make simple questions in past tense with **"To be" (ser/estar) plus another verb.**
Cómo hacer preguntas simples con **"To be"** (ser/estar) más otro verbo.

"To work" (Trabajar), **"To travel"** (Viajar)

Formula: was or were + Pronoun + verb with "ing"

Was I working? **¿Estaba trabajando?**	Was I traveling? **¿Estaba viajando?**
Were You working? **¿Estabas trabajando?**	Were You traveling? **¿Estabas viajando?**
Was He working? **¿Estaba trabajando?**	Was He traveling? **¿Estaba viajando?**
Was She working? **¿Estaba trabajando?**	Was She traveling? **¿Estaba viajando?**
Was It working? **¿Estaba trabajando?**	Was It traveling? **¿Estaba viajando?**
Were We working? **¿Estabamos trabajando?**	Were We traveling? **¿Estabamos viajando?**
Were You working? **¿Estaban trabajando?**	Were You traveling? **¿Estaban viajando?**
Were They working? **¿Estaban trabajando?**	Were They traveling? **¿Estaban viajando?**

Example/Ejemplo

1-Was she **eating** the same thing yesterday? (Verb)/¿Estaba comiendo la misma cosa ayer?

2-Were you **skinny** when you were young? (Adjective)/¿Estabas delgado(a) cúando eras jóven?

3-Was your **father** a doctor? (Family member)/¿Tu padre fue doctor?

4-Were they **in the house**? (Place)/¿Estaban en la casa?

5-Were you **a nurse**? (Occupation)/¿Fuiste enfermera?

Short answer/Respuesta corta	Long answer/Respuesta larga
1R- Yes, she was. 1R- Si, estaba.	**1R- Yes, she was eating the same thing.** 1R- Si, estaba comiendo la misma cosa.
No, she was not (wasn't) No, no estaba.	**No, She wasn't eating the same thing.** No, no estaba comiendo la misma cosa.
2R-Yes, I was. 2R-Si, estaba.	**2R-Yes, I was skinny.** 2R- Si, estaba delgado (a).
No, I was not (wasn't). No, no estaba.	**No, I was not skinny.** No, no estaba delgado (a).
3R- Yes, he was. 3R-Si, era.	**3R-Yes, he was a doctor.** 3R- Si, era doctor.
No, he was not (wasn't). No, no era.	**No, he was not a doctor.** No, no era doctor.
4R-Yes, they were. 4R- Si, estaban.	**4R- Yes, they were in the house.** 4R-Si, estaban en la casa.
No, they were not. No, no estaban.	**No, they were not in the house.** No, no estaban en la casa.
6- Yes, I was. 5R-Si, yo fui	**5R-Yes, I was a nurse.** 5R-Si, fui enfermero (a)
No, I was not. No, no fui.	**No, I was not a nurse.** No, no fui enfermero (a).

Exercise/Ejercicio

Create your questions in the past tense with "to be" plus another
verb, adjective, family member, place, profession.

1- _____

2- _____

3- _____

4- _____

5- _____

Crea sus preguntas en tiempo pasado con **"to be"** (ser/estar) más
otro verbo, adjetivo, miembro de familia, lugar, profesión.

1- _____

2- _____

3- _____

4- _____

5- _____

How to make simple questions in future and conditional tense with "to be" (ser/estar) plus another verb.

Cómo hacer preguntas simples en tiempo future y condicional con "to be" (ser/ estar) más otro verbo.

"**To dance**" (Bailar), "**To sing**" (Cantar)

Formula: **Will + Pronoun + be + verb with (ing) / would + pronoun + be + verb with (ing)**

Will I be dancing? **¿Estaré bailando?**	Would I be singing? **¿Estaría cantando?**
Will You be dancing? **¿Estarás bailando?**	Would You be singing? **¿Estarías cantando?**
Will He be dancing? **¿Estará bailando?**	Would He be singing? **¿Estaría cantando?**
Will She be dancing? **¿Estará bailando?**	Would She be singing? **¿Estaría cantando?**
Will It be dancing? **¿Estará bailando?**	Would It be singing? **¿Estaría cantando?**
Will We be dancing? **¿Estaremos bailando?**	Would We be singing? **¿Estaríamos cantando?**
Will You be dancing? **¿Estarán bailando?**	Would You be singing? **¿Estarían cantando?**
Will They be dancing? **¿Estarán bailando?**	Would They be singing? **¿Estarían cantando?**

Example / Ejemplo

1- Will I be **watching** the novel? (Verb)/¿Estaré viendo la novela?
2- Would you be **happy** going to Asia? (Adjective)/¿Estarías feliz viajando a Asia?
3- Will she be **my sister**? (Family member)/¿Será mi hermana?
4- Would they be **in Italy**? (Place)/¿Estarían en Italia?
5- Will you be **an Engineer**? (Profession)/¿Serás Ingeniero?

Short answer/Respuesta corta	Long answer/Respuesta larga
1R- Yes, I will be. 1R-Si, estaré.	**1R- Yes, I will be watching the novel.** 1R-Si, estaré viendo la novela.
No, I will not (won't) be No, no estaré.	**No, I won't be watching the novel.** No, no estaré viendo la novela.
2R-Yes, I would be. 2R-Si, estaría.	**2R-Yes, I would be happy going to Asia.** 2R-Si, estaría feliz viajando a Asia.
No, I would not be. No, no estaría.	**No, I would not be happy going to Asia.** No, no estaría feliz viajando a Asia.
3R- Yes, she will be. 3R-Si, será.	**3R- Yes, she will be my sister.** 3R-Si, será mi hermana.
No, she will not (won't) be. No, no será	**No, she won't be my sister.** No, no será mi hermana.
11- Yes, they would be. 4R-Si, estarían.	**13- Yes, they would be in Italy.** 4R-Si, estarían en Italia.
No, they would not be No, no estarían.	**No, they would not be in Italy.** No, no estarían en Italia.
12- Yes, I will be. 5R-Si, seré. **No, I will not be** No, no seré.	**14- Yes, I will be Engineer.** 5R-Si, seré Ingeniero. **No, I will not be Engineer.** No, no seré Ingeniero

Exercise/Ejercicio

**Create your questions in future and conditional tense with "to be" plus
another verb, adjective, family member, place or profession.**
Crea sus preguntas en tiempo futuro y condicional con **"to be"** (ser/estar) más
otro verbo, adjetivo, miembro de familia, lugar o profesión.

1- _____

2- _____

3- _____

4- _____

5- _____

There are eight prepositions that must be memorized. These eight words are obligatory because it is impossible to understand any other questions without them. Those prepositions can be combined with "do", "does", "did", "will", "would", "is", "are", "was", "were", "will be", "would be". What we need to do is selecting one of them to complete the question.

However, this rule is not necessary in Spanish. To make questions in Spanish we must use the base form of the conjugated verb after the prepositions and that is the same rule for present tense, past tense, future and conditional tense. There is a few exception.

Hay ocho preposiciones que deben ser memorizadas. Estas ocho palabras son obligatorias, ya que es imposible entender cualquier otra pregunta sin ellas. Esas preposiciones se pueden combinar con **"do", "did", "will", "would", "is", "are", "was", "were", "will be", "would be."** Lo único que tenemos que hacer es seleccionar una de ellas para completar la pregunta.

Sin embargo, esta regla no es necesaria aplicarse en Español. Para hacer preguntas en Español debemos usar la forma base del verbo conjugado después de las preposiciones, y esa es la misma regla para todos los verbos en tiempo presente, pasado, futuro y condicional. Hay poca excepción.

Who (hu) = ¿Quién?

What = ¿Qué? lo que

When = ¿Cuándo?

Where (wer) ¿Dónde?

Why (wai) = ¿Porqué?

Which = ¿Cuál?

With = Con

How = ¿Cómo? Que!

How do you do?/When does it happen?
Who did their homework?

¿Cómo estás?/¿Cuándo paso esto?
¿Quíen hacía (hizó) su tarea?

What will you do tomorrow?
Where would you go after class?

¿Qué harás mañana?
¿Dónde irías despúes de clase?

When is your birthday?
Why are you staring at me?

¿Cúando es tu cumpleaños?
¿Porqué estás mirándome?

With whom was she married?
Where were they in town?

¿Con quién estaba casada?
¿Dónde estaban en la cuidad?

Example/ Ejemplo: **Present tense**/Tiempo presente

Questions with: Where/ Why/Which/How + Do or does + Pronoun + Verb
Negative Questions: Where/Why/Which/How + don't or doesn't + Pronoun + Verb

1- Where do they go after the ceremony?/Where does she go after class?
1- ¿Adónde van despúes de la ceremonia?/¿Adónde va despúes de clase?

2- Why don't you want to go there anymore?/Which dress fits her?
2- ¿Porqué ya no quieres ir allá?/¿Qué vestido le queda?

3- Where does she choose to live?/How do they feel about it?
3- ¿Dónde elíge vivir?/¿Cómo se sienten a cerca de eso?

THE EASIEST WAY TO LEARN AND TEACH ENGLISH/SPANISH

Example/ Ejemplo: **Past tense**/Tiempo pasado

Questions with: What/Who + did + Pronoun + Verb

1- What did we study last night?/Who did you see last night?
1- ¿Qué estudiabamos anoche?/¿A quien viste anoche?

2- Who did she call last night?/What informations did they ask?
2- ¿A quíen llamó anoche?/¿Qué información pedían?

Example/Ejemplo: **Future tense**/Tiempo futuro

Formula: Who+Will+Pronoun+Verb

1- Who will you see tonight?/Who will you invite to her secret birthday party?
1- ¿A quíen verás esta noche?/¿A quíen invitarás a su fiesta sorpresa de cumpleaños?
2- Who will be nominated for president?/¿Quíen será nominado para president?

Example/ Ejemplo: Condicional/Tiempo condicional

With whom+would+Pronoun+Verb

1- Who would you like to go on vacation with?/With whom should we eat dinner tonight?
1- ¿Con quíen te gustaría ir de vacación?/¿Con quíen deberíamos cenar esta noche?

Exercise/Ejercicio

Create your questions in present, past, future and conditional tense using the prepositions where, why, when etc...

Crea sus preguntas en tiempo presente, pasado, futuro y condicional usando las preposiciones dónde or adónde, cuándo, porqué etc...

1- _____

2- _____

3- _____

4- _____

5- _____

6- _____

7- _____

8- _____

9- _____

10- _____

SOME COMMON QUESTIONS TO LEARN AND TO ANSWER
ALGUNAS PREGUNTAS COMÚNES PARA APRENDER Y CONTESTAR

1-Do you have children?/How many children do you have?
¿Tiene (es) hijos?/¿Cúantos hijos tienes (tiene)?

2-Do you feel sick?/Are you allergy to certain medications?
¿Estás enfermo (a)? ¿Eres alérgico (a) a ciertos medicamentos?

3- Do you have an e-mail address?/What`s your e-mail address?
¿Tiene (s) un correo electrónico?/¿Cúal es su correo electrónico?

4-What`s your profession or what do you do for living?
¿Cúal es su profesión? o ¿A qué se dedica?

5- Do you study?/Where do you study?/what do you study?
¿Estudias?/¿Dónde estudias?/¿Qué estudias?

6-What date is today?/What date is your birthday or when is your birthday?
¿Qué fecha es hoy?/¿Qué fecha es su cumpleaños? o ¿Cúando es su cumpleaños?

7-What`s your daily routine?/At what time do you wake up in the morning?
¿Cúal es su rutina diaria?/¿A qué hora se levanta en la mañana?

8- At what time do you go to bed?/at what time do you go to work?
¿A qué hora se acuesta?/¿A qué hora va a trabajar?

9-How do you go to work?/What do you do in your spare time or free time?
¿Cómo va a trabajar?/¿Qué hace (s) en su tiempo libre?

10- How do you see yourself in ten years?/What is your goal?
¿Cómo se ve en diez años?/¿Cúal es su meta ?

11-What is your perception of the world?/What would you do to change it?
¿Cúal es su percepción del mundo?/¿Qué harías para cambiarlo?

12-What`s your favorite hobby?/Do you have any hobbies you don't like?
¿Cúal es su distración favorita?/¿Tiene algúna distración que no le gusta?

LESSON VI

LECCIÓN VI

VOCABULARY: A-B	VOCABULARIO: A-B
Able(ebol)	Capaz
About(abaut)	Acerca de, más o menos
Above(abov)	Arriba, encima
Absence(absens)	Ausencia
Account(akaont)	Cuenta, informe
Accurate(akiuwet)	Exacto, preciso
Ache(ek)	Dolor
Across(acros)	A través, otro lado de
Add	Sumar
Address	Dirección, dirigir
Admit	Confessar, permitir
Advertise(advertays)	Anunciar
Advice(advays)	Consejo
Advise(advayss)	Aconsejar
Affair(afer)	Asunto, relación de romance
Afraid(efred)	Tener miedo
After	Despúes
Ago(ego)	Hace(de un tiempo)
Agree	Acuerdo
Ahead(eherd)	Delante, dirigir hacia un lugar
Aim(eim)	Puntería, apuntar
Alike(elayk)	Parecidas
Alive(elayv)	Vivo(de estar con vida)
Allow(elow)	Permitir
Alone(elon)	Solo
Amount(amont)	Cantidad
Ancient(engent)	Antigüo
Bag	Bolsa(plastic bag in a store)
Balance(balens)	Equilibrio, saldar cuentas
Ballot	Votación, lista de candidatos

Bankrupt(benkropt)	Quebrado(de dinero)
Baptism(baptissm)	Bautismo
Bar	Cantina,obstáculo
Bare(ber)	Desnudo,escaso
Bargain	Regatear,oferta,negociar
Barn	Granja
Basket	Canasta
Belong(bilon)	Pertenecer
Belt	Cinto
Bet	Apostar
Between(bituin)	En medio de
Beware(biwer) Beware of dog	Tener cuidado Cuidado con el
Beyond(biyon)	Más allá
Bill	Billete,cuenta,pico de pájaro
Birth(bert)	Nacimiento
Bit	Bocado,broca,un poquito,
Bite(bait)	Picar,mordisco
Bitter	Amargo
Bleed(blid)	Sangrar
Bless	Bendecir,salud(estornudar)
Blind(blaind)	Ciego
Blink	Parpadear
Blister	Ampolla
Blow	Soplar
Board(bord)	Embarcarse,subir a bordo de tabla
Boil	Hervir
Bone(bon)	Hueso

Reading comprehension (Vocabulary A-B):
Cover the reading comprehension below and translate in Spanish
Lectura de comprensión (Vocabulario A-B):
Cubre la lectura de comprensión abajo y traduce en Español

1- The president of France addressed a letter of sympathy to the families who have been victimized in the Paris terrorist attack in 2015.

_____

2- Since the economic crisis has been declared in 2008, it has been very difficult for small business and big companies to move ahead.

_____

3- She was afraid to answer the question because she did not want to get involve.

_____

4- To start a business, you need a certain amount of money in your personal bank account.

_____

5- Loaded or not, it is not recommended to aim a rifle at another person.

_____

6- Across the street is the historical monument known as the house of Abraham Lincoln.

_____

Reading comprehension (Vocabulary A-B):
Cover the reading comprehension above and translate in English
Lectura de comprensión (Vocabulario A-B):
Cubre la lectura de comprensión arriba y traduce en Inglés

1- El presidente de Francia envió una carta de condolencia a las familias que han sido víctimas en el atentado terrorista en París en el año 2015.

_____

2- Desde que se declaró la crisis económica en el año 2008, ha sido muy difícil para las pequeñas y grandes empresas de salir adelante.

_____

3- Ella tenía miedo de contestar la pregunta porque no quería involucrarse.

_____

4- Para iniciar un negocio, se necesita una cierta cantidad de dinero en su cuenta bancaria.

_____

5- Cargado o no, no es recomendado apuntar un rifle a otra persona.

_____

6- Al otro lado de la calle está el monumento histórico conocido como la casa de Abraham Lincoln.

Exercise/Ejercicio
Create your phrases in English using the vocabularies A-B.
Crea sus frases en Inglés usando los vocabularios A-B.

1- _____

2- _____

3- _____

4- _____

5- _____

6- _____

Exercise/Ejercicio
Create your phrases in Spanish using the vocabularies A-B.
Crea sus frases en Español usando los vocabularios A-B.

1- _____

2- _____

3- _____

4- _____

5- _____

6- _____

Answer the question in English/Contesta las preguntas en Inglés.

1- When someone dies, what's more common: burial or cremation?

2- Do you think bragging about yourself is an act of humility?

3- Why do people avoid being alone when they become older?

4- Where would it be wiser to give birth: at home or in the hospital?

5- Why is a duty of every citizen to pay their taxes?

6- Don't you ever feel the urge to take a little vacation sometimes?

Answer the question in Spanish/Contesta las preguntas en Español.

1- Cuando alguien muere, ¿qué es lo más común: entierro o cremación?

2- ¿Crees presumiéndose es un acto de humildad?

3- ¿Porqué las personas evitan de estar solo cuando llegan a edad mayor?

4- ¿Dónde sería más sabio de dar nacimiento: en casa o en el hospital?

5- ¿Porqué es el deber de cada ciudadano de pagar sus impuestos?

6- ¿No tienes ganas a veces tomar una pequeña vacación?

LESSON VII

LECCIÓN VII

VOCABULARY: C-D-E   **VOCABULARIO: C-D-E**

Call(col)	Llamada, visita
Candle(kendel)	Vela
Cane(ken)	Bastón
Canvas(kenvas)	Lona
Cap	Tapar, gorra
Card	Baraja, tarjeta
Care(ker)	Atención, cargo, cuidado
Carry(kerwi)	Llevar, traer
Catch	Agarrar
Cattle(kadel)	Ganado(de animales)
Certain	Cierto, particular, seguro
Chain	Cadena
Challenge(chalench)	Desafío
Chance(chens)	Casualidad, oportunidad, riesgo
Charge(charch)	Acusación, carga, cargo, costo
Charm	Atractivo, encanto
Chase(cheis)	Persecución
Cheat(chit)	Estafa, fraude, tramposo
Chest	Baúl, pecho
Choice(chois)	Opción
Claim	Reclamación
Claw	Garra
Collect	Cobrar
Comfort	Cómodo, consuelo
Commit	Cometer, comprometerse
Complain(complent)	Queja
Compromise	Arreglo, solución intermedia
Conceit(concit)	Vanidad
Congratulate	Felicitar
Creek(crik)	Arroyo

Cripple(cripel)	Cójo,lisiado
Crook(cruk)	Estafador,ladrón
Crooked(cruked)	Chueco
Crop	Cultivo
Crowd(crawd)	Multitud
Crowded(crawdid)	Atestado,lleno
Curse(kers)	Hechizo,maldición,palabrota
Curtain(kertain)	Cortina
Dairy	Establo,diario
Damage(dameich)	Dañar
Damp(demp)	Húmedo
Dare(der)	Desafío
Date(deyt)	Cita,fecha
Dawn(dan)	Amanecer
Deal(dil)	Pacto,trato
Dear(dir)	Querido
Debt(dert)	Deuda
Decrease(dicruiss)	Reducción,decremento
Deep(dip)	Profúndo
Defeat(difit)	Derrota
Devil	Diablo
Devoted(divotid)	Fíel
Dig	Excavar
Dirt(dert)	Tierra,suciedad
Disgust(disgost)	Repugnancia
Dismiss	Despedir
Display(displei)	Exposición
Ditch	Zanja
Dot	Punto
Dozen	Docena
Drag(yuag)	Arrastrar
Drain(druen)	Drenar
Draw	Dibujar,sacar
Drop	Caer, gota,dejar caer
Dry(druai)	Seco
Due(du)	Pagadero
Dust(dost)	Polvo

Duty(duti)	Deber,obligación
Eager(iger)	Entusiasta
Edge(edch)	Borde,orilla
Effort	Esfuerzo,intento
Embarras	Apenar,avergonzar
Embrace(embrues)	Abrazo,abrazar
Employ	Emplear
Employee(employi)	Empleado
Engaged(engueichd)	Prometido
Equal(iqual)	Igual
Expand(expend)	Ampliar
Expense(expens)	Gasto

Reading comprehension (Vocabulary C-D- E):
Cover the reading comprehension and translate in Spanish
Lectura de comprensión (Vocabulario C-D-E):
Cubre la lectura de comprensión y traduce en Español

1- He dropped his gold ring into the drain and it was disgusting to pull it out.

_____

2- She claimed that the man cheated her when she purchased the ring at the jewelry store.

_____

3- She returned from her date at dawn and her parents were very concerned about her.

_____

4- Complaining doesn't do any good but searching for a solution helps.

_____

5- It was a cloudy day and the mist of the ocean was all over the street.

_____

6- It is unusual to see dairy workers return home clean and neat after a workday.

Reading comprehension (Vocabulary C-D-E):
Cover the reading comprehension and translate in English
Lectura de comprensión (Vocabulario C-D-E):
Cubre la lectura de comprensión y traduce en Inglés

1- Él dejó caer su anillo de oro en el drenaje y era repugnante sacarlo.

_____

2- Ella reclamaba que el hombre la engañó cuando compró el anillo en la joyería.

_____

3- Ella regresó de su cita en la madrugada y sus padres estaban muy preocupados por ella.

_____

4- No sirve de nada quejarse, pero búscando una solución ayuda.

_____

5- Fue un día nublado y la niebla del océano estaba por toda la calle.

_____

6- Es raro ver a los trabajadores del establo regresar a casa, limpios y ordenados después de un día de trabajo.

Exercise/Ejercicio
Create your phrases in English using the vocabularies C-D-E
Crea sus frases en Inglés usando los vocabularios C-D-E

1- _____

2- _____

3- _____

4- _____

5- _____

6- _____

Exercise/Ejercicio

Create your phrases in Spanish using the vocabularies C-D-E
Crea sus frases en Español usando los vocabularios C-D-E

1- _____

2- _____

3- _____

4- _____

5- _____

6- _____

Answer the question in English/Contesta las preguntas en Inglés.

1- How can a lady be certain if a man is committed to another woman?

2- People say that men and women are not equal, do you agree with that statement?

3- Would you feel embarrassed to go on a date with a crippled woman?

4- Why is it not recommended to carry too much cash in Mexico City?

5- Was the light bulb the first invention to replace the candle or the lamp?

6- If you had a blister on your hand, what would you do to get rid of it?

Answer the question in Spanish/Contesta las preguntas en Español.

1- ¿Cómo una mujer puede estar segura de que un hombre está comprometido con otra mujer?

2- La gente dice que hombres y mujeres no son iguales, ¿estás de acuerdo con esa declaración?

3- ¿Ústed sentiría avergonzado de ir a una cita con una mujer lisiada?

4- ¿Porqué no se recomienda llevar mucho dinero en efectivo en la Ciudad de México?

5- ¿Fue el foco la primera invención que reemplazó la vela o la lámpara?

6- Si tuvieras una ampolla en la mano, ¿qué harías para deshacerse de él?

LESSON VIII

LECCIÓN VIII

VOCABULARY: F-G-H-I	VOCABULARIO: F-G-H-I
Fact	Hecho
Fail(ferl)	Fallar,fracasar
Failure	Fracaso
Fair(fer)	Feria,justo
Faith(feit)	Creencia,confianza,fe,doctrina
Faithful(feitful)	Fíel
Fall	Caída
Fashion(fashon)	Moda
Fasten(fasen)	Abrochar,sujetar
Fate(feit)	Destino
Fault(falt)	Culpa,defecto
Fear(fir)	Miedo
Feather(feder)	Pluma(de pajáro)
Fence(fens)	Valla o cerca
Few(fiu)	Pocos
Field(fild)	Campo
File(fail)	Carpeta
Fill	Llenar
Find(faind)	Encontrar
Fine(fain)	Bien, multa,excelente,fino
Fist	Puño
Flag	Bandera
Flat	Llano,plano
Flatter(flader)	Adular,halagar
Flood(flod)	Inundación
Flow	Corriente
Fold	Doblar
Follow	Seguir
Force(fors)	Fuerza,forzar
Forget(forguet)	Olvidar

Free(fri)	Gratis,liberar,libre
Freeze(friss)	Congelar,helar
Frighten(frayten)	Asustar,tener miedo de algo
Fun(fan)	Diversión
Funny(fanni)	Gracioso
Furniture	Muebles
Gain(gen)	Aumento
Gamble(gembel)	Apostar
Game(geim)	Juego
Gang(geng)	Banda,pandilla
Garbage(garbeich)	Basura
Glad	Contento
Goal(gol)	Gol,meta
Gossip	Chismear
Grave(grueiv)	Grave,tumba
Grease(gruis)	Grasa
Greed(grid)	Avaricia
Greet(grit)	Saludar
Ground(graond)	Tierra,suelo
Grow	Crecer
Guess	Suposición,adivinar
Guilty	Culpable
Gun(gan)	Pistola,revólver
Half	Medio
Handle(hendel)	Manejar
Handsome(hendsom)	Guapo
Hang(heng)	Ahorcar
Happen	Ocurrir
Hard	Duro,dificil
Harm	Daño,dañar
Hate(heit)	Odiar
Health(helf)	Salud
Heat(hit)	Calor
Heaven	Cielo
Heavy(hevi)	Pesado
Height(hait)	Altura,estatura
Hell	Infierno

Hesitate(hessiteit)	Vacilar
Hidden	Escondído
Hide(haid)	Esconder
Hill	Colina
Hire(haier)	Contratar
Hit	Éxito,golpe
Hold	Agarrar,contener,ocupar
Ill	Enfermo,mal
Improve(impruv)	Adelantar,mejorar
Include(includ)	Incluir
Income(incom)	Ingresos
Increase(incruiss)	Aumentar
Injure	Herir,lesionar
Inquire(incuaier)	Preguntar
Inquiry(incuary)	Interrogante,pregunta
Insane(insein)	Demente,loco
Irritate(irriteit)	Fastidiar,molestar
Issue(ishu)	Asunto,cuestión
Itch	Picazón
Item(aitem)	Artículo

Reading comprehension (Vocabulary F-G-H- I):
Cover the reading comprehension below and translate in Spanish
Lectura de comprensión (Vocabulario F-G-H-I):
Cubre la lectura de comprensión abajo y traduce en Español

1- The harmful effect of pollution caused by industry has affected our planet for years.

_____

2- It's not funny to laugh at a disable person, on contrary we need to support them.

_____

3- Many people were injured when the twin towers were collapsed on September 11th in NY.

_____

4- She hoped she would be able to pass the job interview to start over a new life.

_____

5- It was a grave mistake to let them work in the mine without asking permission.

_____

6- A compulsive gambler is someone addicted to risking whatever he owns.

_____

Reading comprehension (Vocabulary F-G-H-I):
Cover the reading comprehension above and translate in English
Lectura de comprensión (Vocabulario F-G-H-I):
Cubre la lectura de comprensión arriba y traduce en Inglés

1- El efecto nocivo de la contaminación causada por la industria ha afectado nuestro planeta durante años.

_____

2- No es divertido reírse de una persona con discapacidad, al contrario, tenemos que apoyarlos.

_____

3- Muchas personas resultaron heridas cuando las torres gemelas se derrumbaron el 11 de Septiembre en la ciudad de Nueva York.

_____

4- Ella esperaba pasar la entrevista de trabajo para volver a empezar una vida nueva.

_____

5- Fue un grave error dejarlos trabajabar en la mina sin pedir permiso.

_____

6- Un jugador compulsivo es una persona adicta en arriesgar todo lo que posee.

Exercise/Ejercicio

Create your phrases in English using the vocabularies F-G-H-I
Crea sus frases en Inglés usando los vocabularios F-G-H-I

1- _____

2- _____

3- _____

4- _____

5- _____

6- _____

Exercise/Ejercicio

Create your phrases in Spanish using the vocabularies F-G-H-I
Crea sus frases en Español usando los vocabularios F-G-H-I

1- _____

2- _____

3- _____

4- _____

5- _____

6- _____

Answer the question in English/ Contesta las preguntas en Inglés.

1- Which family member inspires you to do well?

2- What is your favorite item on a Chinese food menu?

3- How can we protect our planet and prevent industry from harming nature?

4- If you had an itch in public would it be polite to scratch your body?

5- What issue in the world today can only be improved by the government?

6- What kind of hat would you wear to a Halloween party?

Answer the question in Spanish/ Contesta las preguntas en Español

1- ¿Qué miembro de tu familia te inspira en hacer buenas cosas?

2- ¿Cuál es tu platillo favorito en un menú de comida china?

3- ¿Cómo podemos proteger nuestro planeta y evitar que la industria daña la naturaleza?

4- Si tuvieras un picazón en público sería de buena educación rascar su cuerpo?

5- ¿Qué problema en el mundo hoy puede ser mejorado solamente por el gobierno?

6- ¿Qué tipo de sombrero llevarías puesto a una fiesta de Halloween?

LESSON IX

LECCIÓN IX

Jail(yel)	Cárcel
Jar(yar)	Bote
Jealous(yelous)	Celoso
Jewel	Joya
Joke(yok)	Broma
Journey(yerni)	Viaje
Joy(yoy)	Alegría
Judge	Juez, juzgar
Jump(yamp)	Brinco, salto
Junk(yank)	Desperdicios
Jury(yori)	Jurado
Just(yost)	Exactamente, justo, solamente
Key(kiy)	Llave
Kick	Patada
Kidnap	Secuestrar
Killer	Asesino
Kind(kaind)	Amable, tipo
King	Rey
Kiss	Beso
Kitchen	Cocina
Kitten	Gatito
Knife(naïf)	Cuchillo
Knit(nit)	Tejer
Knob(nob)	Botón
Knock(nock)	Golpe
Knot(not)	Nudo
Knuckle(nockol)	Nudillo
Label(leibol)	Etiqueta
Lack	Faltar
Ladder	Escalera
Lady(leidi)	Dama
Lake(leik)	Lago
Lamb(lemb)	Cordero

Lame(lem)	Cójo
Land(lend)	Agrícola,tierra,aterrizar
Large(larch)	Grande
Last	Último,durar
Laugh(laf)	Risa
Law	Ley
Lazy(leissi)	Perezoso
Lead(lid)	Delantera
Lead(lerd)	Plomo
Length(lenc)	Duración,longitud,extensión
Less	Menos
Let	Dejar,permitir
Level	Nivel
Lie(lai)	Mentir,acostarse
Life(laif)	Vida
Lift	Levantar
Limb	Rama
Little(lidel)	Chico
Loan(lon)	Préstamo
Lock	Candado, chapa
Lonely(lonli)	Solo
Look(luk)	Aparencia
Loose(lus)	Flojo
Lose(luss)	Perder
Loss	Pérdida
Lot	Lote
Loud(laud)	Alto(de densidad,fuerte)
Low	Bajo
Luck(lock)	Suerte
Luxury	Lujo
Mad	Enojado, loco
Mail(mel)	Correo
Main	Central,principal
Manage	Administrar,manejar
Maintain	Mantener
Mark	Huella
Marriage(merich)	Matrimonio
Master	Amo(de dueño)
Match	Cerillo,juego,pareja,
Mate(meit)	Compañero

Matter	Materia,cuestión
Meal(mil)	Comida
Mean(min)	Malo,significar,víl
Measure	Medída
Meet(mit)	Encontrarse
Melt	Derretir
Merchant(merchent)	Comerciante
Middle(midel)	En medio
Mind(maid)	Mente, tener inconveniente
Miss	Perder,fallar,señorita
Mistake(misteik)	Error
Mix	Mezcla
Moist	Húmedo
Mood(mud)	Humor,carácter
Motto	Lema
Mourn(morn)	Estar de luto
Mud(mord)	Barro, lodo
Must(most)	Deber, tener que
Narrow(nerow)	Angosta
Neat(nit)	Ordenado
Neglect(niglect)	Descuidado
News(niuss)	Noticias
Nice(nais)	Amable
Noise(nois)	Ruido
None(non)	Nada,ninguno
Nothing(nofing)	Nada
Now(nau)	Ahora
Nowhere(nower)	En ninguna parte
Occupation(ocupeishon)	Empleo,profesión,ocupación
Often(ofen)	Amenudo
Once(wons)	Una vez
Only	Solo, único
Operate(opereit)	Hacer funcionar,manejar,operar
Opposite(opossit)	Contrario
Ordinary(ordineiri)	Corriente,normal
Orphan(orfen)	Huerfano
Ought(ort)	Deber
Owe(ou)	Deber

Reading comprehension (Vocabulary J-K-L-M-N-O):
Cover the reading comprehension below and translate in Spanish
Lectura de comprensión (Vocabulario **J-K-L-M-N-O**):
Cubre la lectura de comprensión abajo y traduce en Español

1- It is recommended to knock on the door before entering someone's room.

_____

2- Before applying for a loan it is important to have a budget plan.

_____

3- When someone is rude to you, pay them back with kindness.

_____

4- Loneliness can be a serious problem, if it gets the best of you.

_____

5- Life in a little town can be irritating at times because of the same routines.

_____

6- Kidnapping is an act of cowardice and a violation of human rights.

Reading comprehension (Vocabulary J-K-L-M-N-O):
Cover the reading comprehension above and translate in English
Lectura de comprensión (Vocabulario J-K-L-M-N-O):
Cubre la lectura de comprensión arriba y traduce en Inglés

1- Se recomienda tocar la puerta antes de entrar en la habitación de alguien.

_____

2- Antes de solicitar un préstamo es importante contar con un plan de presupuesto.

_____

3- Cuando alguien es grosero con ústed, págale de vuelta con amabilidad.

_____

4- La soledad puede ser un serio problema, si lo dejas tomar lo mejor de ti.

_____

5- La vida en una pequeña ciudad a veces puede ser irritante, debido a las mismas rutinas.

_____

6- El secuestro es un acto de cobardía y una violación a los derechos humanos.

_____

Exercise/Ejercicio

Create your phrases in English using the vocabularies J-K-L-M-N-O
Crea sus frases en Inglés usando los vocabularios J-K-L-M-N-O

1- _____

2- _____

3- _____

4- _____

5- _____

6- _____

Exercise/Ejercicio

Create your phrases in Spanish using the vocabularies J-K-L-M-N-O
Crea sus frases en Español usando los vocabularios J-K-L-M-N-O

1- _____

2- _____

3- _____

4- _____

5- _____

6- _____

Answer the question in English/Contesta las preguntas en Inglés.

1- What kind of reply is polite if someone says, "thank you "?

2- How can we prevent kids from consuming junk foods?

3- Why is not recommended to listen to loud music?

4- Where do you think the advances in technology lead us?

5- If you had to choose an occupation, what would it be?

6- What color would you get if you mixed white and red?

Answer the question in Spanish/Contesta las preguntas en Español.

1- ¿Qué tipo de respuesta sería amable si alguien te dice "gracias"?

2- ¿Cómo podemos evitar que los niños consuman comida chatarra?

3- ¿Porqué no es recomendable escuchar música a alto volumen?

4- ¿Dónde cree ústed que los avances de la tecnología nos llevan?

5- Si tuvieras que elegir una ocupación, ¿cuál sería?

6- ¿Qué color obtendrías si mezclas blanco y rojo?

LESSON X
LECCIÓN X

VOCABULARY: P-Q	VOCABULARIO: P-Q
Pain(pein)	Dolor
Pale(peil)	Claro,pálido
Pan(pen)	Cazuela,cacerola
Parade(pareid)	Desfile
Pardon	Perdonar
Pasture(pascher)	Pasto
Patch	Parche
Pattern	Diseño,molde
Peak(pik)	Cima,cumbre,pico
Peek(pik)	Ojeada
Penalty	Castigo
Perform	Representar,realizar
Performer	Actor, actriz,interprete
Perish	Deteriorarse
Pet	Mascota
Pick	Eligir,escabar,pico
Pile(pail)	Montón
Pillar	Columna
Pillow	Almojada,cojinete
Pin	Seguro,horquilla
Pipe(paip)	Conducto,pipa,tubería
Pit	Hoyo
Pitch	Echada,lanzamiento
Pitcher	Cantaro,jarro, pitcher
Pity	Compasión
Plain(plein)	Claro
Plea(pli)	Petición,súplica
Pleased(plisd)	Contento,satisfecho
Pleasure(pleyer)	Gusto,placer
Pledge	Prenda,promesa

Plenty	Abundancia
Plus(plos)	Más,positivo
Pocket	Bolsillo
Poison(poisson)	Veneno
Polish	Brillo,cera
Poor	Pobre
Pot	Cazuela,puchero
Pour	Echar
Poverty	Pobreza
Powder(porder)	Polvo
Power(pawer)	Fuerza,poder
Praise(preiss)	Alabanza,elogio
Prayer(preier)	Oración
Prejudice(preyudis)	Prejuicio
Prescription	Receta(de medicamento)
Preserve(prisserv)	Conservar
Press	Apretar,prensa,presionar, pulsar
Pretend(pritend)	Fingir,pretender
Pretty(pridi)	Bonita
Prevent(privent)	Impedir
Pride(praid)	Orgullo
Priest(prist)	Sacerdote
Prize(praiss)	Premio
Profit	Ganancia
Proof(pruf)	Prueba
Proposal	Propuesta
Prove(pruv)	Probar
Pull	Jalar,tirar de
Purchase(percheis)	Compra
Quarrel	Pelea
Quality	Calidad
Quantity	Cantidad
Quarter	Cuarto
Quit	Renunciar
Quiet	Quieto, tranquilo
Quite	Completo

Reading comprehension (Vocabulary P-Q):
Cover the reading comprehension below and translate in Spanish
Lectura de comprensión (Vocabulario **P-Q**):
Cubre la lectura de comprensión abajo y traduce en Español

1- Life is not predictable, that is what makes it amazing.

_____

2- Everyone needs to have an <u>occupation</u> to make our society <u>progress.</u>

_____

3- The real estate business is a secure and profitable investment.

_____

4- A respectable person prefers quality over quantity.

_____

5- Quiet places are prefered to achieve peace of mind.

_____

6- She quits smoking after making a new year's resolution.

Reading comprehension (Vocabulary P-Q):
Cover the reading comprehension above and translate in English
Lectura de comprensión (Vocabulario P-Q):
Cubre la lectura de comprensión arriba y traduce en Inglés

1- La vida no es predecible, es lo que hace que sea asombrosa.

_____

2- Todo el mundo tiene que tener una ocupación para hacer progresar nuestra sociedad.

_____

3- El negocio de bienes raíces es una inversión segura y rentable.

_____

4- Una persona respetable prefiere calidad sobre cantidad.

_____

5- Se prefieren lugares tranquilos para lograr la paz de la mente.

_____

6- Ella deja de fumar después de hacer una resolución de año nuevo.

_____

Exercise/Ejercicio

Create your phrases in English using the vocabularies P-Q
Crea sus frases en Inglés usando los vocabularios P-Q

1- _____

2- _____

3- _____

4- _____

5- _____

6- _____

Exercise/Ejercicio

Create your phrases in Spanish using the vocabularies P-Q
Crea sus frases en Español usando los vocabularios P-Q

1- _____

2- _____

3- _____

4- _____

5- _____

6- _____

Answer the question in English/ Contesta las preguntas en Inglés.

1- How often do you feel powerless to help a friend?

2- Would you quit your project if it had a negative impact?

3- Have you ever wondered why there are so many orphans suffering in our society?

4- Would you ever pardon someone who tried to hurt you in the past?

5- Do you think having riches and power can make a person's life better?

6- Is there a remedy for persons who refuse to deal with reality?

Answer the question in Spanish/ Contesta las preguntas Español

1-¿Con qué frecuencia se siente impotente para ayudar a un amigo?

2- ¿Renunciarías a su proyecto si tuviera un impacto negativo?

3- ¿Nunca se ha preguntado porqué hay tantos huérfanos que sufren en nuestra sociedad?

4- ¿Perdonaría a alguien que trató de hacerle daño en el pasado?

5- ¿Crees teniendo riquezas y poder pueden hacer la vida de una persona mejor?

6- ¿Hay remedio para las personas que se niegan aceptar la realidad?

VOCABULARY: R-S-T   **VOCABULARIO: R-S-T**

Rag	Trapo
Rage(rech)	Furia,rabia
Ragged(ragerd)	Andrajoso,sucio
Rainbow(renbo)	Mellado,Arco iris
Raise(reiss)	Alzar,levantar,educar
Range(rench)	Rango,subir
Rank(renk)	Cordillera,extension,sierra
Ransom(rensom)	Rescate
Raw	Crudo (alimento)
Reach(rish)	Alcance,llegar
Ready(redi)	Listo (de estar preparado)
Realize(rilaiss)	Darse cuenta de
Rear(rir)	Detrás
Recall(ricol)	Recordar
Recipe(recipi)	Receta
Recognize(reconaiss)	Reconocer
Recover(ricover)	Recuperar,reponerse
Refuse(rifiuss)	Rechazar
Release(riliss)	Estreno,liberación
Relief(rilif)	Alivio,descanso
Remain(rimen)	Quedarse,restar,sobrar
Remark(rimark)	Comentario
Remove(rimuv)	Quitar,llevarse
Reply(riplay)	Respuesta
Request(ricuest)	Petición,solicitud
Research(riserch)	Investigación
Response(rispons)	Respuesta
Revenge(rivench)	Venganza
Ride(raid)	Montar, paseo
Rise(raiss)	Ascenso,crecimiento,subida

Rock	Piedra
Roll	Lista,rodar,rollo
Rotten	Podrido,putrefacto
Round(raond)	Redondo
Row	Fila,remar
Rub (rob)	Frotar
Rubber	Goma
Rude	Brusco,grocero
Ruler	Gobernante,regla
Rush(rosh)	Prisa
Rust(rost)	Oxidación
Sack	Saco
Sad	Triste
Safe(seif)	Caja fuerte,seguro
Saint(sent)	Santo
Save(seiv)	Ahorrar,guardar,rescatar,salvar
Scare (sker)	Susto
Scatter(skader)	Desparramar,esparcir
Scene(sin)	Escena
Scent(sent)	Aroma,olor
Score(scor)	Marcar,tanteo
Scratch	Arañazo,rascarse
Screen(scrin)	Pantalla
Sea(si)	Mar
Search(serch)	Buscar
Season(sisson)	Estación,sazonar
Seat(sit)	Sentar,silla
Seed(sid)	Semilla
Seek(sik)	Buscar
Seem(sim)	Parecer
Self(by myself)	Mismo(por mi mismo)
Selfish	Egoísta
Send	Enviar,mandar
Sense(sens)	Juicio,sensación,sentido
Set	Asignar,juego
Settle	Colocar,resolver
Shade(sheid)	Pantalla,persiana,sombra

Shadow	Sombra(de persona)
Shake(sheik)	Agitar,mover,sacudir
Shallow	Poco profundo
Shame(sheim)	Pena,vergüenza
Shape(sheip)	Figura,forma
Share(sher)	Parte,porción
Sharp	Afilado,agudo,definido
Shave(sheiv)	Rasurar,afeitar
Schedule(skeryerl)	Horario,programa
Sheet(shit)	Sabána
Shift	Cambio,turno
Shine(shain)	Brillo
Shoot(shut)	Disparar,lanzar
Shop	Taller,tienda
Shoplifter	Ratero
Short	Bajo,corto,chaparro
Shout(shaut)	Grito
Show	Demostración,enseñar
Shower(shawer)	Aguacero,ducharse
Shrink(shruenk)	Encogerse
Shut(shot)	Cerrar
Shy(shai)	Tímido
Sight(sait)	Vista
Sign(sai)	Firma,seña,señal
Silly	Ridículo,tonto
Sin	Pecado
Since(sins)	Desde
Sink	Hundir,fregadero,lavado
Size(saiss)	Medida,talla,tamaño
Skin	Píel
Skirt(skert)	Falda
Slap	Palmada,cacheteada
Slender	Delgado
Slim	Delgado
Slow	Despacio,lento
Small	Chico,pequeño
Smart	Astuto,inteligente

Smell	Olfato, olor
Smooth(smut)	Liso
Soft	Suave
Some(som)	Algunos
Sour(sawer)	Agrio, amargo
Spare(sper)	De reserva, sobrante
Speed(spid)	Rapidez, velocidad
Spell	Deletrear, hechizo
Spin	Vuelta
Split	Hendidura(banana split), partir
Square(squer)	Cuadrado
Stage(steich)	Escenario, plataforma
Stamp(stemp)	Estampilla, sello
Start	Comenzar, empezar, principio
Status	Estado(no estado de países)
Steady(sterdi)	Constante, estable
Steer(stir)	Conducir, manejar
Step	Escalón, paso
Stick	Adherir, palo, pegar, picar
Staff(stef)	Rigido
Still	Aún
Stone(ston)	Piedra
Straight(streit)	Recto
Straw	Popote
Stream(strim)	Arroyo
String	Cordón, cuerda
Struggle(strogol)	Lucha(no con la gente)
Track(chruaik)	Huella, vía, rastro
Trade(chrueid)	Comercio, industría, oficio
Trail(chrueil)	Cambiar, estela, pista, rostro
Train(chuein)	Estrenar, formar, tren
Transfer(transfer)	Traslado, traspaso
Translate(transleit)	Traducir
Trap(chuap)	Trampa
Trash(chruash)	Basura

Travel(chuavel)	Viajar
Treasure(chueyer)	Tesoro
Treatment	Trato
Trial(chruail)	Juicio,proceso,prueba,sufrimiento
Tribute(chruibiut)	Homenaje,tributo
Trick(chruick)	Broma,travesura,truco
Trip(chruip)	Viaje
Trouble(chuorbol)	Dificultad,problema
True(chru)	Cierto
Trunk(chruank)	Baúl,tronco
Trust(chruost)	Confianza
Truth(chruf)	Verdad
Try (chruay)	Intento,probar,tentativa
Tune(tun)	Melodía
Turn(tern)	Cambiar,transformarse,turno,vuelta
Twice(chruais)	Dos veces
Twist	Rollo,torcer,torsión,trenza
Type(taip)	Escribir a maquina,tipo

Reading comprehension (Vocabulary R-S-T):
Cover the reading comprehension below and translate in Spanish
Lectura de comprensión (Vocabulario **R-S-T**):
Cubre la lectura de comprensión abajo y traduce en Español

1- Taking teenagers off the street will protect them from drug addiction.

_____

2- Copyright was established to protect the content of the original work of a writer.

_____

3- Small Business Administration (SBA), has been created to support small business owners to achieve their company goals in the marketplace.

_____

4- The US Government tries to send bulletins to prepare the population in the event of a sudden natural disaster.

_____

5- Mount Everest has the highest peak <u>than</u> any other mountain in the world.

_____

6- Kids were impressed by the magician and wondered how he did the trick.

_____

Reading comprehension (Vocabulary R-S-T):
Cover the reading comprehension above and translate in English
Lectura de comprensión (Vocabulario R-S-T):
Cubre la lectura de comprensión arriba y traduce en Inglés

1- Quitando los adolescentes de la calle los protegerán de la adicción de droga.

_____

2- Derechos de Autor fue establecido para proteger el contenido de la obra original de un escritor.

_____

3- Small Business Administration (SBA), ha sido creado para apoyar a pequeños empresarios para lograr el objetivo de sus empresas en el mercado.

_____

4- El gobierno de Estados Unidos trata de enviar boletines para preparar a la población en caso de un repentino desastre natural.

_____

5- Monte Everest tiene el pico más alto que cualquier otra montaña en el mundo.

_____

6- Los niños estaban impresionados con el mago y se preguntaban cómo hizo el truco.

_____

Exercise/Ejercicio

Create your phrases in English using the vocabularies R-S-T-listed above.
Crea sus frases en Inglés usando los vocabularios R-S-T listado arriba.

1- _____

2- _____

3- _____

4- _____

5- _____

6- _____

Exercise/Ejerciccio

Create your phrases in Spanish using the vocabularies R-S-T listed above.
Crea sus frases en Español usando los vocabularios R-S-T listado arriba.

1- _____

2- _____

3- _____

4- _____

5- _____

6- _____

Answer the question in English/Contesta las preguntas en Inglés.

1- If your child misbehaves, what else can you do besides spanking him?

2- What is a better way to settle a fight instead of arguing?

3- When you were a kid your parents always told you a fairy tale before going to bed, so why grown up people always said: I don't believe in fairy tales?

4- When somebody compliments you by saying, "you look stunning," how do you usually answer?

5- If you had a tear in your coat, how would you mend it?

6- Which of these wild animals can be tamed; a shack, a crocodile, a horse?

Answer the question in Spanish/Contesta las preguntas en Español

1- ¿Si su hijo se porta mal qué más se puede hacer, a parte de darle unas nalgadas?

2- ¿Cúal es la mejor manera de resolver un pleito en vez de discutir?

3- Cuando ústed era niño sus padres siempre le contaba un cuento de hadas antes de ir a dormir, entonces ¿porqué la gente adulta siempre dice: Yo no creo en cuentos de hadas?

4- Cuando alguien te complimenta diciendo: " te ves genial," ¿Cómo sueles responder?

5- Si ústed tuviera un desgarro en su abrigo, ¿Cómo lo arreglaría?

6- ¿Cuál de estos animales salvajes pueden ser domesticados; un tiburón, un cocodrilo, un caballo?

LESSON XII

LECCIÓN XII

VOCABULARY: U-V-W-X-Y-Z   **VOCABULARIO: U-V-W-X-Y-Z**

Upset(opset)	Fastidiado,malestar
Useful	Útil
Urge	Animarse,ánimo
Upon	Encima
Valuable(valuebol)	Valioso
Value	Valor
Vast	Immenso
Verge(verch)	Borde
Vicious	Malicioso,atroz
Vine(vain)	Parra
Voice(vois)	Voz
Wave(weiv)	Ola,onda,señal
Wild(waild)	Salvaje
Wedding	Boda
Wide(waid)	Amplio
Wheel(wil)	Rueda
Wheel of fortune	Rueda de fortuna
Weight	Pesa
Wrestler(wesel)	Luchador
Wool(wul)	Lana
X-ray	Rayos x
Xylophone	Xilófono
Xenophobia	Xenofobia
Youth	Juventud
Young	Jóven
Yell	Gritar
Zoo	Zoológico
Zone	Zona
Zipper	Cierre
Zip code	Código postal

Reading comprehension (Vocabulary U-V-W-X-Y-Z):
Cover the reading comprehension below and translate in Spanish
Lectura de comprensión (Vocabulario U-V-W-X-Y-Z):
Cubre la lectura de comprensión abajo y traduce en Español

1- Sometimes we need to stop giving priority to useless things that prevent us from making progress.

_____

2- They were lost in the valley and were yelling to be rescued.

_____

3- All human inventions were based on nature as the wings of birds inspired men to fly.

_____

4- It was a sunny day and the weather was great, so they went to the beach.

_____

5- They usually take an x-ray before performing surgery.

_____

6- Urban people are not always interested in travelling to the wilderness.

_____

Reading comprehension (Vocabulary U-V-W-X-Y-Z):
Cover the reading comprehension above and translate in English
Lectura de comprensión (Vocabulario U-V-W-X-Y-Z):
Cubre la lectura de comprensión arriba y traduce en Inglés

1- A veces hay que dejar de dar prioridad a las cosas inútiles que nos impide avanzar.

_____

2- Ellos se perdieron en el valle y gritaban para ser rescatados.

_____

3- Todos los inventos humanos se basan en la naturaleza, como las alas de los pájaros que inspiraron a los hombres a volar.

_____

4- Fue un día soleado y el clima era genial, así que ellos fueron a la playa.

_____

5- Por lo general se toma una radiografía antes de realizar una cirugía.

_____

6- Personas urbanas no siempre están interesados en viajar al desierto.

_____

Exercise/Ejercicio

Create your phrases in English using the vocabularies U-V-W-X-Y-Z
Crea sus frases en Inglés usando los vocabularios U-V-W-X-Y-Z

1- _____

2- _____

3- _____

4- _____

5- _____

6- _____

Exercise/Ejercicio
Create your phrases in Spanish using the vocabularies U-V-W-X-Y-Z
Crea sus frases en Español usando los vocabulario U-V-W-X-Y-Z

1- _____

2- _____

3- _____

4- _____

5- _____

6- _____

Answer the question in English/Contesta las preguntas en Inglés.

1- Do you prefer zipper or buttons?

2- What would a virtuous person do if he witnessed a violent crime?

3- Why is recommended to warm up before starting your daily exercise routine?

4- Beside the zoo where else could we possibly see a zebra?

5- Is there another way besides verbal warning to effectively discipline children?

6- Do you have a solution to global warming?

Answer the question in Spanish/Contesta las preguntas en Español.

1- ¿Prefieres cremallera o botones?

2- ¿Qué haría una persona virtuosa si fuese testigo de un violento crimen?

3- ¿Porqué es recomendable calentarse antes de comenzar su rutina diaria de ejercicio?

4- A parte del zoológico dónde más posiblemente podríamos ver una cebra?

5- ¿Hay otra manera a parte de la advertencia verbal para disciplinar eficazmente a los niños?

6- ¿Tiene una solución para el calentamiento global?

LESSON XIII
LECCIÓN XIII

POSSESSIVE ADJECTIVES: My, your, etc...

ADJETIVOS POSESIVOS: My, your, etcétera

We use possessive adjectives to show the possession; possessive adjectives are always followed by a noun, whether it is singular or plural.

Utilizamos adjetivos posesivos para demostrar la posesión; adjetivos posesivos siempre van seguidos de un sustantivo, ya sea singular o plural.

Personal pronouns	Possessive adjectives
Pronombres personales	Adjetivos posesivos
I (yo)	My (mí)
You (tu)	Your (tu)
He (él)	His (su)
She (ella)	Her (su)
It (esto)	Its (su)
We (nosotros)	Our (nuestro (a)
You (ustedes)	Your (su)
They (ellos o ellas)	Their (sus)

- Note we use **its** when the possessor is an animal, or a thing.
- Tenga en cuenta que utilizamos " **Its (su)"** cuando el posesor es un animal o una cosa.

Example/Ejemplo:

1- I love **my family** like no other in the world/Amo a **mi familia** como ninguna otra en el mundo.

2- Did he paint **his house** for Christmas?/¿Pintó **su casa** para la Navidad?

3- They like **their grandmother** so much/Les gusta tanto a **sus abuelas**.

Exercise/Ejercicio
Create your phrases with "My, yours etc.."/Crea sus frases con **"Mí, su etcétera..."**.

1- _____

2- _____

3- _____

POSSESSIVE PRONOUNS: Mine, yours, etc...

PRONOMBRES POSESIVOS: Mío, suyo(a) etcétera.

We must use the possessive pronouns when it is not necessary to repeat a noun, no matter if it's singular or plural (Example: **This is my book/it's mine or it is mine**).

Debemos utilizar los pronombres posesivos cuando no es necesario repetir un sustantivo, no importa si es singular o plural. (Ejemplo: **Es mi libro/es mío**).

Personal pronouns Pronombres personales	Possessive adjectives Adjetivos posesivos
I (yo)	**Mine (mío)**
You (tu)	**Yours (tuyo)**
He (él)	**His (suyo)**
She (ella)	**Hers (suya)**
It (esto)	**No possessive pronouns**
We (nosotros)	**Ours (nuestro(a)**
You (ústedes)	**Yours (vuestro (a)**
They (ellos o ellas)	**Theirs (suyos o suyas)**

Example/Ejemplo:

1- This is my book. **It's mine**/Es mi libro. **Es mío.**
2- This is your notebook. **It's yours**/Es tu cuaderno. **Es suyo.**
3- This pen did belong to him. **It was his**/Esta pluma pertenecía a él. **Era o Fue suyo**.
4- These houses belongs to them. **They are theirs**/Esas casas les pertenece.
Son suyos o son suyas.

OTHER WAY TO SHOW THE POSSESSIVE FORM

OTRA FORMA DE MOSTRAR LA FORMA POSESIVA

We can demonstrate that something belongs to someone by adding an apostrophe plus "s" after the person, animal or thing's name. In Spanish, this rule does not apply, the whole phrase needs to be translated literally.

Podemos demostrar que algo pertenece a alguien al adiciónar un apóstrofo más una "s" después de la persona, animal o el nombre de cosa. En Español, esta regla no se aplica, toda la frase debe ser traducida literalmente.

Example/Ejemplo:

1- **This book belongs to Mike**/Este libro pertenece a Mike.
This is **Mike's book**/Es el libro de Mike.
2- **This house belongs to Joe**/Esta casa pertenece a Joe.
This is **Joe's house**/Es la casa de Joe.
3- **This pen belongs to Ricky**/Esta pluma pertenece a Ricky.
This is **Ricky's pen**/Es la pluma de Ricky.

LESSON XIV

LECCIÓN XIV

ADVERBS OF MANNER/ADVERBIOS DE MANERA

We usually use the adverbs of manner to describe how we do something. All we have to do is adding **"ly"** to the adjectives. In Spanish, the **"ly"** should be replaced by **"mente"**.

Utilizamos generalmente los adverbios de manera para describir la forma en que hacemos algo. Todo lo que tenemos que hacer es agregar **"ly"** despúes del adjetivo. En Español, el **"ly"** debe sustituirse por **"mente"**.

Formula: Pronouns + Verbs +Adjectives"**ly**"

Example/**Ejemplo**

1- **They listened to the lesson <u>careful</u>ly**/Ellos escuchaban la lección cuidadosa**mente.**
2- **He taught <u>patient</u>ly**/Él enseñaba paciente**mente.**
3- **Did she answer <u>polite</u>ly?**/¿Contestaba gentíl**mente?**
4- **Did they walk <u>slow</u>ly?**/¿Caminaban lenta**mente?**

ADVERBS OF DEGREE/ADVERBIOS DE GRADOS

We usually used the adverbs of degree to describe something we cannot count.
Por lo general, utilizamos los adverbios de grado para describir algo que no podemos contar.

Formula: Pronouns + Verbs + Adverbs (of degree) + Adjectives

Example/**Ejemplo**

1- They were <u>extremely</u> interested about the idea.
Estaban extremada**mente** interesados acerca de la idea.
2- They talked about the rules <u>clearly</u>/Platicaron a cerca de las reglas clara**mente**.

EXERCISE: Put in adverbs/Ponga en adverbios.

1- Vanessa was_____interested in traveling. (clear)

2-They_____did not go to church. (definite)

3- We wanted to arrive at school_____. (quick)

4-_____I haven't seen her. (late)

5- They worked all day_____.(hard)

EJERCICIO: Ponga en adverbios.

1R - Vanessa estaba_____interesada en viajar. (clara)

2R -_____no fueron a la iglesia. (definitiva)

3R-Queríamos llegar a la escuela_____(rápida)

4R-_____, no he visto a ella. (última)

5R- Ellos_____trabajaron todo el día. (dura)

ADVERBS OF FREQUENCY/ADVERBIOS DE FRECUENCIAS
It is not always possible to give precise rules about the position of adverbs in the sentence, the examples below will show us how to place them.
No siempre es posible dar reglas precisas sobre la posición de los adverbios en la oración, los ejemplos a continuación nos mostrarán cómo colocarlos.
List of some adverbs of frequency:
Often or frequently, sometimes or occasionally, rarely or seldom, usually or normally or generally.

Lista de algunos adverbios de frecuencia:
A menudo o frecuentemente, a veces o ocasionalmente, rara vez, usualmente o normalmente o generalmente.
Example/Ejemplo
1- **When you travel across France, do you usually visit Paris?**
¿Cúando viajas a Francia, usualmente visitas París?
2- **People are often frightened to talk about matters of life or death.**
La gente a menudo tiene miedo de platicar sobre los asuntos de vida o muerte.
3- **He had never sent her so many lovely flowers.**
Él nunca le envíaba tantas lindas flores.

ADVERBS OF TIME AND PLACE/ADVERBIOS DE LUGAR Y TIEMPO

Adverbs can be placed in the end, middle, or beginning position of the sentence: Again, now, then, recently, immediately, finally, suddenly, afterwards, today, once, nowadays, early, late, yesterday, tomorrow.

Los adverbios se pueden colocar al final, en medio, o al principio de las frases: Otra vez, ahora, entonces, recientemente, inmediatamente, finalmente, de repente, después, hoy, una vez, hoy en día, temprano, tarde, ayer, mañana.

Example/Ejemplo

1- **Now we can get some rest**/Ahora podemos descansar.
2- **You can now go take a nap**/Puedes ir ahora a tomar un descanso.
3- **They can go out, then have coffee**/Pueden salir, despúes tomar un café.

Exercise: Transform the adjectives in adverbs in English, then find the meaning of each of them in Spanish.

Adjectives	Adverbs	meanings
Sad...		
Successful..		
Nice...		
Respectful..		
Quick...		
Honorable..		
Hard..		
Soft..		
Passionate..		
Miserable...		
Exact...		
Honest...		
Thankful..		
Aparent..		

Ejercicio: Transforma los adjectivos en adverbios en Español, despúes encuentra el significado en Inglés.

Adjetivos	Adverbios	Significados
Triste		
Exitosa		
Linda		
Respetuosa		
Rapida		
Honorable		
Difícil		
Suave		
Apassionada		
Miserable		
Exacta		
Honesta		
Agradecida		
Aparente		

The word "Still" (aún/todavía) is often used in affirmative or negative sentences and questions to talk about a situation that is longer than we expected. While "Yet" is used in negative sentences and questions when we talk about something that has not happened, but that we expect to happen. It is recommended to put "Yet" (aún/todavía) at the end of the sentences. There is an exception to this rule (**Example**: The best is yet to come). **In Spanish this rule does not apply, we can use "Still or Yet"** (aún/todavía) **either way.**

La palabra "Still" aún/todavía se utiliza a menudo en oraciones afirmativa y preguntas o frases negativas, para hablar de una situación que es más largo de lo que esperábamos. Mientras que "Yet" se usa en oraciones negativas y preguntas cuando hablamos de algo que no ha sucedido, pero esperamos que suceda en un futuro. Se recomienda poner "Yet" al final de las frases. Hay una excepción a esta regla (**Ejemplo**: "The best is yet to come" lo mejor aún está por llegar). En Español esta regla no se aplica podemos utilizar "Still/Yet" (aún/todavía) en cualquier forma.

STILL/YET: AÚN / TODAVÍA
Example/Ejemplo

1- **Is he still engaged to her?**/¿**Aún o todavía** está comprometido con ella?
2- **I am still in Washington, D.C**/ **Aún o todavía** estoy en Washington, D.C.
3- **I still haven't found a good job**/No he encontrado **aún o todavía** un buen trabajo.
4- **Have they arrived yet?**/ ¿Han llegado **Aún o todavía**?
5- **They haven't made a decision yet**/ **Aún o todavía** no han tomado una decisión.

SOME/ANY

We use "Some" and "Any" for uncountable nouns or alone without a noun, but it is right to use "Some" in affirmative sentences & any in questions and negative sentences. In Spanish the words "Some" alguno (a), algunos (as), algo – "Any" algunos (as) algo, cualquier (a) , ninguno (a), are used to make a statement in affirmative, negative, questions depend on the sentence.

Utilizamos **"Some"** alguno (a), algunos (as), algo – **"Any"** algunos (as) algo, cualquier (a), ninguno (a) para cosas incontables o solo sin un sustantivo, sin embargo es correcto usar **"Some"** en oraciones afirmativas y **"Any"** en preguntas y oraciones negativas. En Español **"Some"** alguno (a), algunos (as), algo, **"Any"** ninguno (a), ningunos (as), algunos (as), algo, cualquier (a), se utiliza para hacer una confirmación en frases afirmativas, negativas, preguntas depende de la frase.

"Some" alguno (a), algunos (as), algo – **"Any"** algunos (as) algo, cualquier (a), ninguno (a)

Example/Ejemplo

1- **I have <u>some</u> questions**/Tengo <u>**algunas**</u> preguntas.
2- **Have you got <u>any</u> cooking oil?**/¿Has conseguido <u>**algo**</u> de aceite de oliva?
3- **We can find <u>some</u> in the bag**/Podemos hallar <u>**algo**</u> en la bolsa.
4- **Have they got <u>any</u> chance?**/¿Han tenido <u>**algo**</u> de suerte?
5- **No, they didn't get any**/No, no han tenido <u>**ninguna**</u>.
6- **Have we got <u>any</u> gas left?**/¿Ha quedado <u>**algo**</u> de gas?

LESSON XV

LECCIÓN XV

Anymore is always used in negative sentences to explain that the past situation has ended. We must use anyone in singular sentences. We usually use "anyone" in questions and in negative sentences. Somewhere can be used in affirmative sentences, and questions or to make a suggestion. Anywhere can be used in affirmative sentences and in questions. Anything means it doesn't matter what is used. In Spanish, this rule does not apply, we can use them either way, in affirmative, negative, questions singular or plural.

Anymore siempre se usa en oraciones negativas para explicar que la situación pasada ha terminado. Debemos usar "**Anyone**" (cualquier persona, alguien, nadie) en oraciones singulares. Utilizamos generalmente "**Anyone**" (cualquier persona, alguien, nadie) en las preguntas y en oraciones negativas. "**Somewhere**" (algún lugar) se puede utilizar en frases afirmativas y preguntas o para hacer una sugerencia. "**Anywhere**" (cualquier lugar) se puede utilizar en frases afirmativas y preguntas. **Anything** significa lo que sea o algo. En Español, esta regla no se aplica, podemos usarlos de cualquier forma en frases afirmativas, negativas, preguntas en singular o plural.

Anymore = Ya no - No más

1- **They don't bring flowers anymore**/Ya no traen Flores.
2- **She doesn't love him anymore**/Ella ya no lo quiere.

Anyone = Cualquier persona, alguien

1- **Is anyone upstairs?**/¿Alguien esta arriba?
2- **If you find anyone tell them the story.**
Si encuentras a alguien cuentale la historia.
3- **I haven't seen anyone down here**/No he visto a nadie aqui.

Somewhere = Algún lugar

1- **Would you like to go for a walk somewhere?**
¿Te gustaría ir algún lugar de paseo?
2- **He must be somewhere**/Él debe estar en algún lugar.

Anywhere = Cualquier lugar/Algún lugar

1- **They can go anywhere they want.**
Ellos pueden ir cualquier lugar que quieren.
2- **Where is my pen? Have you seen it anywhere?**
¿Dónde está mi pluma? ¿Lo has visto algún lugar?

Anything: Lo que sea, algo

1- **Did you find anything at the store?**
¿Encontraste algo en la tienda?
2- **He will do anything to save his mother's life.**
Hará lo que sea para salvar la vida de su madre.

Exercise/Ejercicio
Create your phrases with "anymore, anyone, somewhere, anywhere, and anything".
Crea sus frases con "ya no o no más, cualquier persona o
cualquiera, algún lugar, cualquier lugar, y lo que sea, algo."

1- _____

2- _____

3- _____

4- _____

5- _____

6- _____

7- _____

8- _____

How to use: This – That – These – Those
Cómo usar: Esto – Esta - Estos – Estas – Ese - Esos – Esa – Esas - Aquel – Aquella – Aquellos – Aquellas

"This" is always used as a singular noun for something that is near the speaker. The plural form is "These." That" is used as a singular noun for something further away. The plural form is 'Those."

"This" es siempre usado como un sustantivo singular por algo que esta cerca del hablante, su forma plural es "These." "That" es usado como sustantivo por algo alejado del hablante, su forma plural es "Those."

Example/Ejemplo

1- **This** napkin/**Esta** servilleta.
2- **These** napkins/**Estas** servilletas
3- **That** bull/**Ese** toro.
4- **Those** bulls/**Esos** toros.
5- **This** girl/**Esa** muchacha.
6- **These** girls/**Esas** muchachas.

In Spanish, **This "Aquel"** is used when the singular noun is masculine and not specific to proximity.
These "Aquellos" is used with a masculine plural noun and not specific to proximity.
That **"Aquella"** is used with a feminine singular noun and not specific to proximity.
Those **"Aquellas"** is used with a feminine plural noun and not specific to proximity.

En Español This **"Aquel"** es usado cuando el sustantivo es masculino y no específica a la proximidad.
These **"Aquellos"** es usado con un sustantivo masculino plural y no específica a la proximidad.
That **"Aquella"** es usada con un sustantivo femenino y no específica a la proximidad. Those **"Aquellas"** es usada con un sustantivo femenino plural y no específica a la proximidad.

Example/Ejemplo
1-In this time/**En aquel tiempo.**
2-In these times/**En aquellos tiempos.**
3-That cow/**Aquella vaca.**
4-Those cows/**Aquellas vacas.**

Exercise/Ejercicio
Create your phrases with "This – That – These – Those".
Crea sus frases con **"Esto – Esta - Estos – Estas – Ese – Esa – Esas – Esos – Aquel – Aquella Aquellos – Aquellas"**.

1- _____
2- _____
3- _____
4- _____
5- _____
6- _____

7- _____

8- _____

9- _____

10- _____

TOO: TAN/DEMASIADO

TOO MUCH: DEMASIADO

TOO MANY: DEMASIADOS

"**Too**" is sometimes used before an adjective. "**Too much**" with an uncountable noun (in singular) and "**Too many**" with a countable noun (in plural).

"**Too**" Tan/Demasiado a veces se usa delante de un adjetivo. También utilizamos "**Too much**" Mucho, con un sustantivo incontable (en singular) y "**Too many**" Demasiados con un sustantivo contable (en plural).

Example/Ejemplo

1- **They are <u>too</u> proud to confess it (adjective).**
1- Están **<u>tan</u>** orgulloso de confesarlo (adjetivo).
1- Están **<u>demasiado</u>** orgulloso de confesarlo (adjetivo).

2- **They have wasted <u>too</u> much money drinking (uncountable).**
2- Ellos gastaron **<u>demasiado</u>** dinero bebiendo (sustantivo incontable).

3- **We made <u>too many</u> mistakes on the exam (countable noun).**
3- Cometemos **<u>demasiados</u>** errores en el examen (sustantivo contable).

Exercise/Ejercicio
Complete the sentences with too/too much/too many.
Complete las frases con tan/demasiado/demasiados.

1- **It's not recommended to drink_____coffee.**
No es recomendable beber_____café.

2- **They are_____proud of their new house.**
Ellos están_____orgulloso de sus nuevas casas.

3- She drops_____**tears, for her husband's death.**

Ella deja caer_____lágrimas, por la muerte de su esposo.

4- She is getting fat because she is eating_____

Ella está engordando porque ella está comiendo_____

SO MUCH/SO MANY

TANTO (A)/TANTOS (AS)

We use **"So much"** to talk about a big quantity (in singular) and **"So many"** to talk about a large number of nouns (in plural).

Utilizamos **"So much"** <u>Tanto (a)</u> para hablar de una gran cantidad (en singular) y **"So many"** <u>Tantos (as)</u> para hablar de gran número de sustantivos (en plural).

Example/Ejemplo

1- Benjamin loves his family so much.

1- Benjamin quiere tanto a su familia.

2- There are so many nice things to see in Paris.

3- Hay tantas cosas bonitas de ver en París.

3- There was so much money wasted on this competition.

3- Hubo tanto dinero desperdiciado en esta competencia.

Exercise/Ejercicio
Complete the sentences with so much/so many.

Complete las frases con tanto (a)/ tantos (as).

1- They spend_____**time searching for this information.**

1- Ellos pasaron_____tiempo búscando esta información.

2- Nowadays_____**people don't have a place to live.**

2- Estos días_____gente no tienen un lugar para vivir.

3-_____**orphan children need to be adopted by someone.**

3- _____huérfanos necesitan ser adoptado por alguien.

MUCH/MANY
MUCHO (A)/MUCHOS(AS)

The plural form of **"Much"** is **"Many"**. Much can be used with uncountable nouns to talk about a quantity of something and Many for countable nouns. We can use both of them in questions and negative sentences, except sometimes we can use **"Many"** in affirmative sentences at the beginning of a sentence.

La forma plural de **"Much"** <u>Mucho (a) (masculino, feminino singular)</u> es **"Many"** <u>Muchos (as) (masculino, feminino plural).</u> **Much** puede ser usado con sustantivos incontables para mencionar la cantidad de algo y **Many** para sustantivos contables. Ambos pueden ser utilizados en preguntas y oraciones negativas, excepto que a veces podemos usar **"Many"** <u>Muchos (as) (masculino, feminino plural)</u>en oraciones afirmativas al principio de una frase.

Example/Ejemplo
1- **Does she cook <u>much </u>food?**/¿Ella cocina **<u>mucha </u>**comida?
2- **No, she does not cook <u>much </u>food**/No, ella no cocina **<u>mucha</u>** comida.
3- **We don't have <u>many</u> students this year**/No tenemos **<u>muchos</u>** estudiantes este año.

Exercise/Ejercicio: **Use much or many**/Utiliza mucho (a) o muchos (as)

1-_____of them are victims in this accident.
1- _____de ellas son víctimas en este accidente.

2- We didn't sleep_____last night.
2- No dormímos_____anoche.

HOW MUCH/HOW MANY: CUÁNTO (A)/ CUÁNTOS (AS)

We use "How much" to ask for a price or something unccountable and "How many" in plural form to ask for several countable things

Utilizamos **"How much"** <u>cuánto (a) (masculino, feminino singular)</u> para pedir un precio o algo incontable y **"How many"** <u>cuántos (as) (masculino, feminino plural)</u> para pedir cosas contables.

Example/Ejemplo

1- **How much is that cost?**/¿Cúanto cuesta?
2- **How much sugar did you put in the coffee?**/¿Cúanto azúcar pusiste en el café?
3- **How many houses do you have in that country?**/¿Cúantas casas tienes en este país?

1- _____

2- _____

PREPOSITIONS + VERBS + ING FORM

PREPOSICIÓNES + VERBOS + FORMA GERUNDIO (ANDO)

List of some prepositions/Lista de algunas preposiciones:
Without: Sin-**After**: Después de-**Before**: Antes de-**By**: Por-**In**: En- **Of**: de

To understand how to use the **"Ing"**form is very easy to do, what we need to know is that after each preposition we must add a verb in the **"Ing"**form. **In Spanish, this rule does not apply. If the preposition is followed by a verb, it will always come in infinitive form.**

Para comprender cómo utilizar la forma **"Ing"** gerundio (ando) es bastante fácil de hacerlo, lo que tenemos saber es, después de cada preposición hay que añadir un verbo en forma gerundio **"Ing"** ando. **En Español está regla no se aplica. Si una preposición sigue por un verbo, este verbo siempre viene en forma infinitiva.**

Example/Ejemplo
1-**They went to take the exam <u>without</u> studying.**
1-Ellos fueron a tomar el examen **<u>sin estudiar</u>**.
2-**<u>Before starting</u> let´s talk about your adventure.**
2-**<u>Antes de empezar</u>** vamos hablar sobre su adventura.
3-**By drinking a lot he lost his job.**
3-**<u>Por beber</u>** mucho el perdío su trabajo.
4-**She is not interested in studying anymore.**
4-Ella ya no está **<u>interesada en estudiar</u>**.

Exercise/Ejercicio:
Add a preposition before the verb/Agrega una preposición antes del verbo.

1- **Edith was very happy**_____visiting **Paris.**
1- Edith estaba muy feliz_____visitar París.

2-_____leaving he left a letter to apologize.

2-_____partir dejó una carta para disculparse.

3- Are you interested_____**studying astrology?**

3- Estás interesada_____estudiar astrología?

HOW TO USE OBJECT PRONOUNS/CÓMO USAR PRONOMBRES ACUSATIVOS

Sometimes students made a lot of mistakes applying: "me", "you"," him", "her", "us", "them". To make it easier to understand how to apply those object pronouns try to use them after the verbs and prepositions.

A veces los estudiantes cometen muchos errores en aplicar: "**Me**"me - "**You**"te/le - "**Him**"le -"**Her**" le - "**Us**" nos - "**Them**"los. Para que sea más fácil de entender cómo aplicar esos pronombres acusativos trata de usarlos después de los verbos y preposiciones.

Example with object pronouns/Ejemplo con pronombres acusativos

Me = me	(**tell me**: dime o digame)
You = te/le	(**tell you**: te digo o le digo)
Him = le	(**tell him**: dile o digale)
Her = le	(**tell her**: dile o digale)
Us = nos	(**tell us**: dinos o diganos)
Them = los	(**tell them**: dilos o digalos)

Exercise: Create your phrases with "me", "you", "him", "her", "us", "them" in English then translate in Spanish.

Ejercicio: Crea sus frases con "me", "te" or "le", "nos", "los" en Inglés después traduce en Español.

1- _____

2- _____

3- _____

4- _____

5- _____

6- _____

WHAT/WHICH: QUÉ/CÚAL

We use "What" and "Which" when there are choices to be made. "What" if we ask for an object that is not part of a group and "Which" if we ask for something located in a group.

Utilizamos "What" (Qué) y "Which" (Cúal) cúando hay diferentes opciones para elegir. "What" (Qué) se usa cúando no es parte de un grupo específico y "Which" (Cúal) se usa cúando hace parte de un grupo.

Example/Ejemplo
1- **What** are you going to do?/¿**Qué** vas hacer?
2- In **which** house do you live?/¿En **cúal** casa vives?
3- **Which** dress are you going to wear?/¿**Qué** vetido vas a poner?
4- **What** time are you leaving?/¿**A qué** hora te vas?

Exercise/Ejercicio
Create your phrases with "What" or "Which"/ Crea sus frases con "Qué" o "Cúal

1- _____

2- _____

3- _____

4- _____

AGO: HACE

"**Ago**" can be used to describe when something happened in the past. In Spanish is reversing comparing to English (Example: "**Two days ago**" hace dos días).

"**Ago**" puede ser usado para describir algo que sucedió en el pasado. En Español se invierte comparátivamente al Inglés (Ejemplo: "**Two days ago**" hace dos días).

Exercise/Ejercicio: **Use "Ago" in your answers**/Utiliza **Ago** "**Hace**" en sus respuestas.
1- **How long ago did you see your sister?**
2- ¿Hace cúanto viste a tu hermana?
3- **When did you start to study at the University?**
4- ¿Cúando empezaste a estudiar en la universidad?

3-When did you go to the hospital with her?/ ¿Cúando fuiste al hospital con ella?
4- **At what time do they get up?**/ ¿A qué hora se despiertan?

Little=poco(a)-**Very little**=muy poco(a)-**Few**=pocos(as)-**Very few**=muy pocos(as)

Little and very little is used with uncountable nouns in singular to talk about a small quantity. Few and very few are used with plural nouns to talk about a small quantity.

Poco y **muy poco** se usa con sustantivos incontables en singular para hablar de una pequeña cantidad. **Pocos** y **muy pocos** son utilizados con nombres en plural para hablar de una pequeña cantidad.

Example/Ejemplo
1- **I drank a <u>little</u> water this morning**/Bebí un <u>**poco**</u> de agua está mañana.
2- **She had <u>very little</u> exercise last night**/Ella tenia **<u>muy poco</u>** ejercicio anoche.
3- **She ate <u>few</u> vegetables yesterday**/Ella comío **<u>pocas</u>** verduras ayer.
4- **They had <u>very few</u> songs on the disc**/Tenian **<u>muy pocas</u>** canciónes en el disco.

Exercise/Ejercicio
Complete the sentences with: Little/Very little/Few/Very few
Complete las frases con: Poco(a)-Muy poco(a)-Pocos(as)-Muy pocos(as)

1- They have been gone for a_____days.
1- Ellos se han ido por_____días.

2- They spent_____days on vacation.
2- Ellos pasaron_____días de vacación.

3- After the accident he wanted to drink_____water.
3- Despúes del accidente él quiso beber_____agua.

4- They brought_____water with them to go camping.
4- Ellos traeron_____agua con ellos para ir a campar.

LESSON XVI
LECCIÓN XVI

COMPARATIVE/SUPERLATIVE
COMPARATIVO/SUPERLATIVO

Comparative is used to compare people or things and superlative is used to show the superiority of both (people and things).

Comparativo se usa para comparar gente o cosas y superlativo se usa para mostrar la superioridad de ambas (gente y cosas).

Formula#1: **More + Long adjective + Than**
Formula#1: Más + Adjetivo largo + Que
Formula#2: **Short adjective + Er + Than**
Formula#3: **Adjective which end in "Y" change in "Ier" + Than**
Formula#2 and 3 does not apply in Spanish
La formula# 2 y 3 no se aplica en Español

List of some long adjectives: Important - Intelligent - Pleasant - Horrible - Available - Difficult
Lista de adjetivos largos: Importante - Inteligente - Agradable - Horrible - Disponible - Dificíl

List of some short adjectives: Short -Tall - Big - Fast - Quick - Slow
Lista de adjetivos cortos: Corto (a) - Alto (a) - Grande-Rápido (a) -Lento (a)

List of adjectives that end in "Y": Funny - Easy - Tricky
Lista de adjetivos que terminan con "Y": "Funny" divertido(a)-"Easy"Fácil-"Tricky"Engañoso (a)

Some exceptions in English for comparative and superlative
Algunas excepciones en Inglés para comparativo y superlativo:
Good-better-best/Bad-worse-worst/Fat-fatter-fattest/Far-farer-farest/Poor-poorer-poorest

COMPARATIVE/COMPARATIVO
Example/Ejemplo
1- Edith is **more beautiful than** her sister Myriam/Edith **es más bonita que** su hermana Myriam.
2- Socorro's house **is bigger than** Joe's/La casa de Socorro **es más grande que** la de Joe.
3- English **is easier than** Chinese/Inglés **es más fácil que** Chino.

Formula#1: The most + Long adjective
Formula#2: Short adjective + Est
Formula#3: Adjective which end in "Y" change in Iest
In Spanish none of these are used, only we need to add at the end of the adjective "ísimo (a)"
En Español esas formulas no se aplican, sólo se agrega al final del adjetivo "ísimo(a)"
(Masculino, feminino).

Example/Ejemplo
1- **Edith is <u>the most beautiful</u>**/Edith es <u>bonitísima.</u>
2- **Socorro's house is <u>the biggest</u>**/La casa de Socorro es <u>grandísima</u>.
3- **English is <u>the easiest</u>**/Inglés es <u>facilísimo.</u>

Past Participle/Participio Pasado

We use "Have" plus the verb in past participle to explain an event that happened or had not happened in the past. We can use it in affirmative, negative and questions into a sentence.
Example: I have been in New York.

Usamos **"Have"**(Tener), más el verbo en participio pasado para explicar una situación que ocurrió o no había ocurido en el pasado. Podemos utilizarlo en afirmativa, negativa y preguntas en una frase.
Ejemplo: He estado en Nueva York.

Formula: Have +Verb (Past participle) – Negative: Haven't or Hasn't +Pronoun + Verb (Past.p)

Exercise: Complete your sentences in affirmative form
using the right-hand column
Ejercicio: Complete sus frases en forma afirmativa usando la columna derecha

I have + been.../He estado	**I have been in London** He estado en Londres
You have + done.../Has hecho	
He has + become........................../Ha llegado a ser	
She has + gone.................................... /Ha ido	
It has + felt../Ha sentido	
We have + got..................................../Hemos tenido	
You have + kept..................................../Ha guardado	
They have + known .... /Han sabido	

Exercise: Complete your sentences in negative form using the right-hand column

Ejercicio: Complete sus frases en forma negativa usando la columna derecha

I haven't + seen ..../No he visto	**I haven't seen the movie** No he visto la película
You haven't + eaten........................../No has comido	
He hasn't + come.................................../No ha llegado	
She hasn't + left...................................../No ha dejado	
It hasn't + had ..../No ha tenido	
We haven't + heard........................../No hemos oído	
You haven't + held........................../No ha sostenido	
They haven't given ..../No han dado	

Exercise: Complete your sentences making questions using the right–hand column

Ejercicio: Complete sus frases haciendo preguntas usando la columna derecha

Have I + read ..../¿He leído?	**Have I read the book?** ¿He leído el libro?
Have you + sold..................................... /¿Has vendido?	
Has he + shown..................................... /¿Ha mostrado?	
Has she + slept ..../¿Ha dormido?	
Has it + sat../¿Ha sentado?	
Have we + spoken ..../¿Hemos hablado?	
Have you + spent ..../¿Ha gastado?	
Have they written ..../¿Han escrito?	

FOR/SINCE: DESDE

"For" is used for a period of unspecified time with the present, past, or future tense and **"Since"** is used for a specified time with the present, past, or future tense. **In Spanish both can be used for specified and unspecified time.**

"For" (desde) se utiliza durante un período de tiempo no especificado en tiempo presente, pasado o futuro **"Since" (desde)** se utiliza por un tiempo especificado en tiempo presente, pasado o futuro. **En español ambos pueden ser utilizados por un tiempo especificado y no especificado.**

Example/Ejemplo
1-**They lived in Paris since 1977**/Vivieron en París desde 1977.
2- **I've been working on this for 3 years**/He estado trabajando en eso desde hace 3 años.
3-**We haven't eaten since yesterday**/No hemos cómido desde ayer.
4-**She stopped exercising for years**/Ella dejó de hacer ejercicio desde hace años.

Exercise/Ejercicio
Use "For" and "Since" in your answer/Utiliza desde en su respuesta.

1- **How long have you studied biology at school?**
1- ¿Hace cúanto que estudiaste biología en la escuela?

2- **How long did they live in Paris?**
2- ¿Hace cúanto vivían en París?

3- **How long will you continue working on this?**
3- ¿Por cúanto tiempo continuarás trabajando en eso?

Reading comprehension

Ask the students to read the story. After reading, ask if they understood. When "yes" pick a student to explain what he/she understood. If "no" give them a summary of the story to explain what happened. Later double check by asking all the students if they understood the story. Then get to the teacher's final questions.

On August 6th,1945 the second world war has started in Japan after the Japanese attacked the US Navy at pearl harbor, many Americans have left their homes to defend the country, and their families. To avoid thing getting worse, the US Air Force dropped an atomic bomb named **"Little boy"** over Hiroshima which killed one hundred forty thousand Japanese, including men, women, and children. After the first atomic bomb was dropped, there still remained more than a hundred thousand injured people who died soon after from the nuclear radiation. On August 9th the same year the second atomic bomb named **"Fat man"** was dropped over Nagasaki killing over 70,000 Japanese, and on the other side, a million Americans were saved. When the war was over in 1945 people in America celebrated the victory, and were happy that this war came to an end. Many American soldiers could not make it, they were killed in combat, and some of them barely made it home, the rest of them only their names were painted on the wall and on the heart of their beloved one. Most of the remaining American soldiers back home were enduring nightmares cause by the wounds of the war, not even a shrink could cure and take their pain away, but they did what they had to do to keep America and their families safe.

Teacher's part

1- What was the cause of the Second World War in 1945?
2- What should we do to stop war in the world?
3- Could the United States avoid the war against Japan in 1945?
4- What should we do to protect the national defense of our country?
5- Why the drop of the atomic nuclear bomb on Hiroshima has affected our planet?
6- According to the story, what title would be appropriate for the text?
7- If the second World War did not start with the Japanese which country started it?

Lectura de comprensión

Pide a los estudiantes de leer la historia. Después de leer, pregunte si entienden. Si entienden, elige un estudiante para explicar lo que él o ella entiende. Si no entienden, dé un resumen de la historia para explicar lo que pasó. Luego vuelva a comprobar si han captado la explicación de la historia. Después del debate de la historia usa las preguntas del profesor cuestionando a cada estudiante.

El 6 de agosto de 1945, la segunda guerra mundial empezó en Japón después del ataque de los Japoneses a la nave maritima de Estados Unidos en Pearl Harbor, Muchos Americanos han dejado sus hogares para defender el país, y sus familias. Para evitar que se empeore la situación, la Fuerza Aérea de Estados Unidos. Lanzó una bomba atómica llamada **"Little boy"** sobre Hiroshima, que mató a ciento cuarenta mil Japoneses, incluyendo hombres, mujeres y niños. Después de la caída de la primera bomba atómica, quedaron más de cien mil personas heridas los cuales murieron después de la radiación nuclear. El mismo año 9 de agosto la segunda bomba atómica llamada **"Fat man"** fue caído en Nagasaki matando a más de 70.000 japoneses y poniendo a salvo más de un millón Américanos. Cuando la guerra terminó en 1945 la gente en Estados Unidos celebraron la victoria, y estaban felices que la guerra ya habia llegado a su fin. Muchos soldados americanos no sobrevivieron, fueron matados en el combate, algunos de ellos apenas pudieron llegar a casa, el resto de ellos sólo sus nombres fueron pintados en la pared y el corazón de las personas queridas. La mayoría de los soldados estadounidenses sobrevivientes que han vuelto a casa sufrieron enormes pesadillas causado por las heridas de la guerra, y ni siquiera un psiquiatra podía curar y quitarles el dolor, sin embargo, ellos hicieron lo que tenían que hacer para mantener a Estados Unidos y sus familias a salvo.

Parte del profesor

1- ¿Cuál fue la causa de la segunda guerra mundial en 1945?
2- ¿Qué debemos hacer para detener la guerra en el mundo?
3- ¿Podría Estados Unidos evitar la guerra contra Japón en 1945?
4- ¿Qué debemos hacer para proteger la defensa nacional de nuestro país?
5- ¿Porqué la caída de la bomba nuclear en Hiroshima ha afecto nuestro planeta?
6- ¿Según la historia ¿qué título podría ser mejor para la lectura de comprensión?
7- ¿Si la segunda guerra mundial no se inició con los Japoneses, qué país la inició?

Reading comprehension

Ask the students to read the story. After reading, ask if they understood. When "yes" pick a student to explain what he/she understood. If "no" give them a summary of the story to explain what happened. Later double check by asking all the students if they understood the story. Then get to the teacher's final questions.

A mass devastation of seven magnitudes was caused by Tuesday's earthquake in Haiti. The presidential palace in Port-Au-Prince and a thousand schools, and houses lay in ruins. For most of the countries, January 12th, 2010 has been a time of hope, to face to the economic crisis, but for the island it just has been a nightmare. The earthquake has caused 100.000 deaths, and 1.5 million people have become homeless. After suffering a hurricane in 2008, that took 800 lives, the population never expected the worst was about to come. Can humanity be saved when Mother Nature is in a fury? Since February 7th, 1986 we have never experienced such a lost. The earthquake has caused a 15% destruction of the abrupt production of the country, as well as the lack of jobs. To support, the UN has offered millions of dollars which have been given by different organizations to help the population. The period of reconstruction of such damaging destruction may take 3 or 5 years, Pablo Ruiz Hiebra, the specialist prevention, and recovering disaster (PNUD), has declared. After that tragedy, experts estimated a rise of 3% for the economy system, which will start to attract the tourist sector again, in spite of the world economic crisis.

Teacher's part

1-What is the difference between seismology and an earthquake?
2-How many people who have been victimized by the earthquake?
3-What would you recommend to prevent people getting hurt before having a natural disaster in your country?
4-What does the UN do to keep the people calm and avoid killing for survival and food?
5-What should the government do to get the economy back on track again?
6-According to the story, what title would be appropriate for the text?

Lectura de comprensión

Pide a los estudiantes de leer la historia. Después de leer, pregunte si entienden. Si entienden, elige un estudiante para explicar lo que él o ella entiende. Si no entienden, dé un resumen de la historia para explicar lo que pasó. Luego vuelva a comprobar si han captado la explicación de la historia. Después del debate de la historia usa las preguntas del profesor cuestionando a cada estudiante.

Una devastación masiva de siete puntos de magnitud, causó el terremoto del martes en Haití, el palacio presidencial en Puerto Príncipe y miles de escuelas y casas cayeron en ruinas. Para la mayoría de los países 12 de enero, 2010 ha sido un tiempo de esperanza frente a la crisis económica, pero para la isla sólo ha sido una pesadilla. El terremoto ha causado 100.000 muertos, y 1.5 millones de personas han quedado sin hogar. Después de sufrir un huracán en 2008, que cobró 800 vidas, la población nunca esperaba lo peor estaba por venir. ¿Se puede salvar la humanidad cuando la madre naturaleza está en furia? Desde el 7 de febrero del año 1986 nunca se ha experimentado tal perdida. El terremoto ha causado una destrucción del 15% de la producción abrupta del país, también la falta de empleo. Para apoyar la ONU ha ofrecido millones de dólares que se han dado a distintos organizaciónes para ayudar a la población. El período de reconstrucción de una destrucción tan dañino puede durar de 3 o 5 años, ha declarado Pablo Ruiz Hiebra, especialista en prevención y recuperación de desastres (PNUD). Después de la tragedia, los expertos estiman un aumento del 3% del sistema económico que comenzará a atraer de nuevo al sector turístico, a pesar de la crisis económica.

Parte del profesor

1- ¿Cuál es la diferencia entre sismología y un terremoto?
2- ¿Cuántas personas han sido víctimas por el terremoto?
3- ¿Qué recomendaría para evitar que se lastime la gente antes que pase un desastre natural en su país?
4- ¿Qué hizó la ONU para mantener a la gente tranquila y evitar que se maten por la supervivencia de comida?
5- ¿Qué debe hacer el gobierno para poner en marcha de nuevo la economía?
6- ¿Según la historia ¿qué título podría ser mejor para la lectura de comprensión?

Reading comprehension

Ask the students to read the story. After reading, ask if they understood. When "yes" pick a student to explain what he/she understood. If "no"give them a summary of the story to explain what happened. Later double check by asking all the students if they understood the story. Then get to the teacher's final questions.

During the last past years, 2008 and 2009, the U. S Government has suffered a terrible economic crisis. They believed that illegal Latinos could be a threat to the United States society. From 2009 to 2014, 1 million Mexicans and their families, including U. S born children left the U.S to Mexico.According to the data from the Mexican Survey of the Demographic Dynamics (ENADID). On the other hand, U. S census data for the same period has shown that 870.000 Mexican nationals left Mexico to enter the U. S. Most of the families deported to Mexico cannot adapt to the country system due to the period of time they have been away from home. 99 percent of kids born or raised in the United States do not speak the language, where their parents were born, and to adapt to the Mexican educational system across the country will be very difficult. Prior to 2000 till 2007 Mexicans have never been told to request a visa to enter Canada, on July 13ᵗ 2009 visa restrictions were introduced for Mexican citizens to travel to Canada. As the result of the keystone oil pipeline disagreement, on April 22nd, 2015, the Canadian government has announced in its annual budget that visa will no longer exist for Mexican national and that the new rule will be applied in 2016. Mexico is one of the largest oil producers in Central America, that is rich in natural resources, such as oil, copper, silver and agricultural crops, that can make it very prosperous and to become like any other prominent countries, until today its population is wondering why it still considered a sub-developing country?

Teacher's part

1- What did cause the economic crisis in the United States 2008 and 2009?
2- What should Mexicans do to help Mexico to become a prominent country?
3- What difference would that make for its people, if Mexico has had the same level of life like Canada and the United States?
4- What was the disagreement between the U. S and Canada?
5- What solution is required in public schools to help Mexicans children who lived in the U.S to adapt to the educational system in Mexico?
6- According to the story, what title would be appropriate for the text?

Lectura de comprensión

Pide a los estudiantes de leer la historia. Después de leer, pregunte si entienden. Si entienden, elige un estudiante para explicar lo que él o ella entiende. Si no entienden, dé un resumen de la historia para explicar lo que pasó. Luego vuelva a comprobar si han captado la explicación de la historia. Después del debate de la historia usa las preguntas del profesor cuestionando a cada estudiante.

Durante los últimos años, 2008 y 2009, el Gobierno de los Estados Unidos ha sufrido una terrible crisis económica. Ellos creían que los Latinos ilegales podrían ser una amenaza para la sociedad de los Estados Unidos. Del año 2009 a 2014, 1 millón de mexicanos y sus familias, incluyendo los niños nacidos en Estados Unidos salieron del país a México. Según los datos de Encuesta Mexicana por la demográfia dinámica (ENADID). Por otro lado, los datos de Estados Unidos revelaron por el mismo periodo que 870.000 ciudadanos mexicanos dejaron México para entrar en los Estados Unidos. La mayoría de las familias deportadas a México no pudieron adaptar con el sistema del país debido al largo período de tiempo que han estado fuera de casa. 99 por ciento de los niños nacidos o criados en los Estados Unidos no hablan el idioma, dónde nacieron sus padres, y será muy difícil adaptarse al sistema educativo mexicano. Antes del año 2000 hasta el año 2007 nunca han pedido a los mexicanos de solicitar una visa para entrar a Canadá, el 13 de julio, 2009 introdujeron restricciones de visado para los ciudadanos mexicanos que viajarán a Canadá. Como resultado del desacuerdo de la pipa de petróleo de Keystone, el 22 de abril, 2015, el Gobierno de Canadá anunció en su presupuesto anual que la visa ya no existirá para los mexicanos y que esta nueva regla se aplicará en 2016. México es uno de los países considerado cómo más grande productores de petróleo de Central América, que es rico en recursos naturales, como el petroleo, el cobre, la plata y los cultivos agrícolas, que pueden hacerlo muy prospero y transformarlo como cualquier otros países poderosos, hasta hoy su población se pregunta ¿Porqué sigue considerando un país subdesarrollado?

Parte del profesor

1- ¿Cuál fue la causa de la crisis económica en los Estados Unidos del 2008 y 2009?
2- ¿Qué deben hacer los Méxicanos para ayudar a México convertirse en un país potencial?
3- ¿Qué diferencia México tendría para su pueblo si ha tenido el mismo nivel de vida como Canadá y los Estados Unidos?
4- ¿Cuál fue el desacuerdo entre USA y Canadá?
5- ¿Qué solución se requiere en escuelas públicas para ayudar a niños mexicanos que vivieron en Estados Unidos a adaptarse al sistema de educación en México?
6- Según la historia ¿qué título podría ser mejor para la lectura de comprensión?

Reading comprehension

Ask the students to read the story. After reading, ask if they understood. When "yes" pick a student to explain what he/she understood. If "no" give them a summary of the story to explain what happened. Later double check by asking all the students if they understood the story. Then get to the teacher's final questions.

For thousands of years, astronauts have been searching for another similar earth planet in the universe. Are there other planets similar to ours? In 1995, Suisse investigators found an extrasolar planet & later, another group found a second one, located in the Virgo constellation. However, all of those are in extreme condition to live, some of them have a low temperature, and others a high temperature. Still none has our planet's weather condition. Among, them we noticed Jupiter, Venus, & some other pulsar planets formed from the supernova explosion that could destroy our planet. In that case visiting those planets is not recommended because of the radiation they emit. Our planet is only a dot in an expanding universe. There are many powerful things that can cause a disaster to humanity. The meteorites and the supernova explosion are one of them. If scientists would find a similar planet like ours, would there be survivors? How would we communicate with them? Millions of planets are surrounding us, to get to them will take us a million years, but scientists invented a new way of communication, the BLA radio satellite emits into the universe a signal that will give us a chance to be contacted by some other creatures. Finally, in 2010 NASA has confirmed the existence of five other planets bigger than ours, called KEPLER 4B, 5B, 6B, 7B, 8B, with a temperature of $1.200°c$ till $1.65°c$, and they don't have the same atmosphere as our planet, but scientists are still hoping to find another planet to make a living on it.

Teacher's part

1- What is a supernova? /What is a meteorite?
2- If a supernova explodes near our planet, what would happen?
3- Why is our planet exposed to so many dangers?
4- What does the author mean when he refers to a low and high temperature?
5- What is the difference between a star, a satellite, and a planet?
6- According to the story, what title would be appropriate for the text?

Lectura de comprensión

Pide a los estudiantes de leer la historia. Después de leer, pregunte si entienden. Si entienden, elige un estudiante para explicar lo que él o ella entiende. Si no entienden, dé un resumen de la historia para explicar lo que pasó. Luego vuelva a comprobar si han captado la explicación de la historia. Después del debate de la historia usa las preguntas del profesor cuestionando a cada estudiante.

Miles de años, astronautas buscaron en el universo otro planeta tierra. ¿Hay otros planetas similares al nuestro? En 1995, los investigadores Suizos descubrieron un planeta extrasolar y más tarde, otro grupo ha encontrado una segunda, situada en la constelación de Vigo. Sin embargo, todos ellos están en condiciones extremas para vivir, algunos de ellos tienen una baja temperatura, y otros una alta temperatura. Aún, ninguno tiene todavía nuestra condición meteorológica. Entre, ellos notificamos a Júpiter, Venus y algunos otros planetas púlsar que se forman de la explosión de supernova que podría destruir nuestro planeta. En este caso visitar a esos planetas no sería recomendable debido a la radiación que emiten. Nuestro planeta es solamente un punto en un universo en expansión. Hay muchas cosas poderosas que pueden causar un desastre para la humanidad. Los meteoritos y la explosión de supernova son uno de ellos. Si los científicos encontrarían un planeta similar como lo nuestro, ¿Habría sobrevivientes? ¿Cómo podemos comunicarnos con ellos? Millónes de planetas nos rodean y para llegar a ellos nos llevarán millónes de años, pero los científicos inventaron una nueva forma de comunicación por señales, el radio satélite BLA emite en el universo una señal que nos dará la oportunidad de ser contactado por otras criaturas. Finalmente, en el año 2010 la NASA ha confirmado la existencia de otros cinco planetas más grandes del nuestro, llamado Kepler 4B, 5B, 6B, 7B, 8B, con una temperatura de 1.200 ° C hasta 1,65 ° C, y todavía no tienen la misma atmósfera como nuestro planeta, pero los científicos aún tienen la esperanza de encontrar otro planeta para vivir.

Parte del profesor

1- Qué es una supernova?/¿Qué es un meteorito?
2- Si una supernova occure cerca de nuestro planeta, ¿qué pasaría?
3- ¿Porqué nuestro planeta está expuesto a tantos peligros?
4- ¿Qué quiere decir el autor cuando se refiere a una temperatura baja y alta?
5- ¿Cuál es la diferencia entre una estrella, un satélite y un planeta?
6- Según la historia ¿qué título podría ser mejor para la lectura de comprensión?

Reading comprehension

Ask the students to read the story. After reading, ask if they understood. When "yes" pick a student to explain what he/she understood. If "no"give them a summary of the story to explain what happened. Later double check by asking all the students if they understood the story. Then get to the teacher's final questions.

The last past year has been difficult for everyone. The world has endured a global economic crisis, and now this year, 2009 a global flu epidemic has invaded most of the countries, between them, we count the United States, Mexico, & the Europe continent. **Where did the flu epidemic come from?** The International Health Care Organization (OMS) has proved the original source of that kind of epidemic came from the birds migrated in Mongolia and Siberia, which has been transmitted to the pets resided in all parts of the world. This biological bomb is similar to the epidemic called Spanish Influence which showed up in 1918 and the epidemic named the Nile Occidental which appeared in Manhattan in New York in 1999. At that time, research showed that it was coming from the mosquitos. This period of time, Government did not have a control mosquitos program. Because of that 62 people have been sick and seven died, among them we recalled Mr. Harro Marsh. The virus expanded in 30 states, Louisiana was the most affected. 80 people got the Nile virus and finally the same epidemic got started in California in 2002. Now schools, airports, and other road transportation has been controled to forbid the virus to be expanded. All the people that have traveled to United States and Mexico have been put under control until the medical care makes sure they don't have the flu symptom. Wallace's families from Auckland New Zealand and others have been put in quarantine to avoid the extension of the virus in the rest of the country. Consider the information given by the responsible Health Care in Mexico 152 people nearly died because of the typical pneumonia and twenty have been victimized by the virus **A H1N1** in Tlalpan, Magdalena, and other cities. **Did he really tell the truth about the amount of victims?** The community health care has been informing the people the damage the virus can cause and the maximum cautions they must take to prevent this serious problem. All work together to find a vaccine cure to make everyone feel secure.

Teacher's part

1- According to the text which virus are we talking about?
2- After all the previous epidemic in 1918, 1999 and 2002, why the International Health Care Organization could not prevent the death of seven people and other victims from the virus?
3- Where did the virus get started? Was it a threat to National Security?
4- Closing the main economic source for instance: airports, schools, and others, was it good decision making by the Mexican Government?
5- Does Mexico have efficient medical resources to combat any virus? If not, what should they do to improve their medical resource conditions, to protect the nation?
6- How can an epidemic,collapse the global economic system of a country?
7- What was the virus name that appeared in 1999?
8- If you were the Mexican president, what values would you promote related to virus prevention?
9- Even they found a cure for the virus, what should we do to protect our family from it?
10- What can we do to prevent the loss of lives caused by epidemics?
11- Who was the first to invent a vaccine cure for tuberculosis epidemic?
12- In Africa more than a million children are dying due to a lack of medicine, what do you suggest to stop that continuing to happen?
13- Sometimes people are not well attended in public hospitals and forced to go to private ones. What is your point of view?
14- What difference would it make having surgery in a public hospital in a developing country or in a sub-developing country?
15- According to the story, what title would be appropriate for the text?

Lectura de comprensión

Pide a los estudiantes de leer la historia. Después de leer, pregunte si entienden. Si entienden, elige un estudiante para explicar lo que él o ella entiende. Si no entienden, dé un resumen de la historia para explicar lo que pasó. Luego vuelva a comprobar si han captado la explicación de la historia. Después del debate de la historia usa las preguntas del profesor cuestionando a cada estudiante.

El último año pasado ha sido difícil para todos. El mundo ha sufrido una crisis económica mundial, y ahora este año, 2009 una epidemia de gripe ha invadido la mayoría de los países, entre ellos contamos los Estados Unidos, México, y el continente europeo. ¿De dónde vinó la epidemia? La Organización Internacional de Salud (OMS) ha demostrado la fuente original de ese tipo de epidemia que provenía de las aves que migraron en Mongolia y Siberia, esa epidemia ha sido transmitida a los animales domésticos viviendo en todas partes del mundo. Esta bomba biológica es similar a la epidemía llamada influencia española aparecida en 1918 y la epidemia llamada Nilo Occidental que apareció en Manhattan, Nueva York en 1999. En este tiempo las investigaciones mostraron que esa epidemia venía de los mosquitos. En este período de tiempo, el Gobierno no tenía un programa de control de mosquitos. A causa de eso 62 personas han estado enfermas y siete murieron, entre ellas recordamos el señor Harro Marsh. El virus se expandió en 30 estados, Louisiana fue la más afectada. 80 personas contrajeron el virus del Nilo y por último la misma epidemia comenzó en California en el año 2002. Ahora escuelas, aeropuertos, y otros medios de transporte vial han estado bajo control para prohibir que se expanda el virus. Todas las personas que han viajado a los Estados Unidos y México han sido puestas bajo control médica asegurando que no tienen el síntoma de gripe. La familia Wallace desde Auckland Nueva Zelanda y otros han sido puestos en cuarentena, para evitar la extensión del virus en el resto del país. Según la información dado por el responsable de atención de salud en México casi 152 personas murieron a causa de una neumonía típica y veinte han sido víctimas por el virus **A H1N1** en Tlalpan, Magdalena, y otras ciudades. ¿Realmente ha dicho la verdad sobre la cantidad de víctimas? El centro de salud de la comunidad ha informado a la gente el daño que el virus puede causar y las precauciones máximas que deben tomar para evitarlo. Todos trabajando en conjunto para encontrar una cura que harían sentir a todos seguros.

Parte del profesor

1- De acuerdo con el texto de que virus estamos hablando?

2- Después de todas las epidemias previas en 1918, 1999 y 2002, porqué la Organización Internacional de Salud no podría evitar la muerte de las siete personas y otras víctimas del virus?

3- ¿Dónde comenzó primero el virus? ¿Fue una amenaza para la Seguridad Nacional?

4- Cerrando las fuentes económicas principales como ejemplo: aeropuertos, escuelas, y otros, ¿fue una buena decisión tomada por parte del Gobierno Mexicano?

5- ¿Tiene México recursos médicos eficaces para combatir cualquier virus? Si no es así, ¿qué deben hacer para mejorar sus condiciones médicas para proteger a la nación?

6- ¿Cómo una epidemia puede colapsar el sistema económico de un país?

7- ¿Cómo se llama el virus que apareció en 1999?

8- Si ústed fuera el presidente de México, que valores promovieras para la prevención de virus?

9- A pesar que encuentraron una cura para el virus, ¿qué debemos hacer para proteger a nuestra familia de ella?

10- ¿Qué podemos hacer para evitar la pérdida de vidas causado por epidemias?

11- ¿Quién fue el primero inventor de la vacuna contra la epidemia de tuberculosis?

12- En África, más de un millón de niños mueren por falta de medicina, ¿qué sugieres para evitar que eso siga pasando?

13- A veces las personas no están bien atendidas en hospitales públicos y son obligados a ir a hospital privado. ¿Qué opinas?

14- ¿Cuál es la diferencia de tener una cirugía en un hospital público en un país desarrollado y un país subdesarrollado?

15- Según la historia ¿qué título podría ser mejor para la lectura de comprensión?

Reading comprehension

Ask the students to read the story. After reading, ask if they understood. When "yes" pick a student to explain what he/she understood. If "no" give them a summary of the story to explain what happened. Later double check by asking all the students if they understood the story. Then get to the teacher's final questions.

Human inventions have been the success key in the growth of our civilization. It started 200,000 years ago with human evolution named by scientist **"Homo Sapiens"**, which means **"wise man,"** the species as a human being that we belong to today. How did they survive? According to some research, we discovered that they created tools to hunt animals and wore the animal skins to protect them from the variation of the climate seasons, and other challenges of an unstable environment. Today the world has turned a new leaf from a primitive epoch to a modern one. **"Thomas Elva Edison"** 1847-1931, his first great invention was a phonograph, in that he displayed a way to record and play back sound. **"Benjamin Franklin"** 1706-1797 invented an iron furnace named Franklin Stove that allowed people to heat their homes while using less wood, not to forget the others, such as **Leonardo Da Vinci, Nikola Tesla, Alexander Graham Bell, James Watt, Albert Einstein and recently William Henry Gates III** known as **Bill Gates** who invented Microsoft, started on April 4th, 1975. The idea of creating Microsoft was to replace the typing machine for a new era of technology. As any history of humanity, inventions have always been created not only to improve our quality of life, but to make our lives easier. An invention is something that is new and useful created for the human being; however, most of the idea of an invention was inspired by our Mother Nature. For instance, the airplane has been invented to facilitate a faster transportation; its design was based on the bird spreading its wing to fly across from one distance to another. Not all inventions have benefited our society, some of them have made a dramatic change in it, but no matter where the idea of an invention came from, we must appreciate those inventors who tried to help the world become a better place to live.

Teacher's part

1-Who would you consider the pioneer of inventions?
2-Why should we have a festive day in memory of all inventors?
3-How does the invention of technology transform our planet?
4-If you had to come up with an invention, what would that be?
5-Why not all inventions have benefited our society?
6-According to the story, what title would be appropriate for the text?

Lectura de comprensión

Pide a los estudiantes de leer la historia. Después de leer, pregunte si entienden. Si entienden, elige un estudiante para explicar lo que él o ella entiende. Si no entienden, dé un resumen de la historia para explicar lo que pasó. Luego vuelva a comprobar si han captado la explicación de la historia. Después del debate de la historia usa las preguntas del profesor cuestionando a cada estudiante.

Los inventos humanos han sido la clave del éxito en el crecimiento de nuestra civilización. Iniciado hace 200,000 años con la evolución humana nombrado por los científicos **"Homo Sapiens"**, que significa **"hombre prudente"**, la especia de ser humano que todos pertenecemos hoy. ¿Cómo sobrevivieron? Según algunas investigaciones, hemos descubierto que crearon herramientas para cazar animales y llevaban puestos las pieles de animales para protegerse de las variaciones climáticas, y otros desafíos de un ambiente inestable. Hoy el mundo se ha cambiado de una época primitiva a moderna. **"Thomas Edison Elva"** 1847-1931, su primera gran invención fue un fonógrafo, en el que él mostró una manera de grabar y reproducir sonido. **"Benjamin Franklin"** 1706-1797 inventó un horno de acero llamado Estufa de Franklin que permitió a la gente calentar sus hogares al utilizar menos madera, no hay que olvidar los otros, tal como: **Leonardo Da Vinci, Nikola Tesla, Alexander Graham Bell, James Watt, Albert Einstein y recientemente, William Henry Gates III** conocido como **Bill Gates**, quien inventó Microsoft iniciándolo el 4 de abril 1975. La idea de creer Microsoft fue de sustituir la máquina de escribir por una nueva era de tecnología. Como cualquier historia de la humanidad, las invenciones siempre se han creado no sólo para mejorar nuestra calidad de vida, sino también para hacer la vida más fácil. Una invención es algo que es nuevo e útil, creado para el ser humano, sin embargo, la mayor parte de invenciónes fue inspirado por nuestra madre naturaleza. Por ejemplo, el avión ha sido inventado para facilitar más rápido el transporte, su diseño se basó en las aves que extienden sus alas para volar de una distancia a otra. No todos los inventos han beneficiado nuestra sociedad, algunos de ellos han hecho cambios dramáticos en ella, sin embargo, no importa dónde fue inspirada la idea de una invención, hay que apreciar aquellos inventores que trataron de contribuir para que el mundo sea un mejor lugar para vivir.

Parte del profesor

1- ¿A quién usted considería el pionero de invenciones?
2- ¿Porqué debería tener un día festivo en memoria de todos los inventores?
3- ¿Cómo la invención de la tecnología transforma nuestro planeta?
4- Si tuviera que inventar algo, ¿qué sería?
5- ¿Porqué no todas las invenciones beneficiaron nuestra sociedad?
6- Según la historia ¿qué título podría ser mejor para la lectura de comprensión?

Reading comprehension

Ask the students to read the story. After reading, ask if they understood. When "yes" pick a student to explain what he/she understood. If "no" give them a summary of the story to explain what happened. Later double check by asking all the students if they understood the story. Then get to the teacher's final questions.

Even after two hundred years volcano eruptions remain a threat to humanity. Western Europe, North America, & South America have been notified. A seismic activity in 2009 severely increased and shook the Eyjafjallajökull volcano in 2010, and erupted in Iceland and caused enormous disruption in the air across Western and Northern Europe for six following days in April 2010. To avoid major problems, 20 countries closed their airspace to commercial flights. As the result of that, thousands of travelers were affected. Finally, the government in Europe made this problem official in October 2010, when they noticed the snow on the glacier did not melt. In America, there are 10 eminent danger volcanoes listed by the U.S Geological Survey (USGS) that can erupt at any time. The Craker Lake in Oregon is one of them, since Mount St Helens erupted 30 years ago; the future is not predictable anymore. South America has more than 200 volcanoes; the most active are located in Peru, Argentina, Colombia and Equator. Lately in Chile on May 2nd, 2008 Chaitén volcano has made its eruption right after the earthquakes on April 30th, 2008. A rescue plan immediately was led by SERNAGEOMIN to evacuate the area as soon as possible. Thanks to the heavy rain after the eruption, the population was out of danger. Base on research it is not frequent to see a volcano eruption. In fact, there are many factors that must come together in order to provoke a volcano explosion. One of the elements is the earthquake which does not occur very often because the earth is made of a series of large tectonic plates, and those plates are not moved with frequency to stimulate a volcano disaster. Since the earth exist volcanoes have been, and still remain a potential danger for our planet, however, each government is doing the best they can to stay alerted in the event one of those volcanoes will erupt.

Teacher's part

1- What should we do in the event a volcano erupts near our city?
2- How serious is the threat of volcanos in the world?
3- How often does a volcano erupt? Should we be worried about it?
4- What factors must be put together in order to activate a volcano?
5- What happened in Western and Northern Europe in 2010?
6- According to the story, what title would be appropriate for the text?

Lectura de comprensión

Pide a los estudiantes de leer la historia. Después de leer, pregunte si entienden. Si entienden, elige un estudiante para explicar lo que él o ella entiende. Si no entienden, dé un resumen de la historia para explicar lo que pasó. Luego vuelva a comprobar si han captado la explicación de la historia. Después el debate de la historia usa las preguntas del profesor cuestionando a cada estudiante.

Desde hace dos cientos años las erupciones volcánicas han sido una amenaza para la humanidad. Europa Occidental, América del Norte y América del Sur han sido notificadas. Una actividad sísmica en el año 2009 se incrementó severamente y sacudió el volcán Eyjafjallajökull en 2010 y entró en erupción en Islandia y causó enormes trastornos en el aire a través del Oeste y el Norte de Europa durante seis días consecutivos, en abril 2010. Para evitar más problemas 20 países cerraron su espacio aéreo a vuelos comerciales. Como resultado miles de viajeros fueron afectados. Finalmente, el gobierno Europeo ha hecho oficial ese problema en octubre 2010, cuándo se dieron cuenta que la nieve en el glaciar no se derritaba. En Estados Unidos, hay 10 volcanes con eminente peligro enumerados por el Servicio Geológico de Estados Unidos (USGS) que pueden entrar en erupción en cualquier momento. El Lago Craker en Oregon es uno de ellos, ya que el Monte Santa Helena entró en erupción hace 30 años, el futuro no es predecible. América del Sur tiene más de 200 volcanes, los más activos se encuentran en Perú, Argentina, Colombia y Ecuador. Últimamente, en Chile el 2 de mayo, 2008 el volcán Chaitén ha hecho su erupción justo después del terremoto el 30 de abril del año 2008. Un plan de rescate de imediato fue dirigido por SERNAGEOMIN para evacuar la zona lo pronto posible. Gracias a la fuerte lluvia después de la erupción, la población estaba fuera de peligro. Según investigadores no es frecuente ver una erupción volcánica. De hecho, hay muchos factores que deben de poner en conjunto para provocar una explosión volcánica. Uno de los elementos es el terremoto que no se produce con frecuencia porque la tierra se ha hecho de una serie de grandes placas tectónicas y esas placas no se mueven con frecuencia para estimular un desastre volcánico. Desde que existe la tierra los volcanes han sido y sigue siendo un peligro potencial para nuestro planeta, sin embargo, cada gobierno está haciendo lo mejor que pueda para mantenerse alerta en caso que uno de esos volcanes entrará en erupción.

Parte del profesor

1- ¿Qué debemos hacer en caso de una erupción volcánica cerca de nuestra ciudad?
2- ¿Qué tan grave es la amenaza volcánica en el mundo?
3- ¿Con qué frecuencia entró en erupción un volcán? Deberíamos estar preocupados por ello?
4- ¿Qué factores deben de ponerse en conjunto para activar un volcán?
5- ¿Qué ocurrió en el Norte y Oeste de Europa en 2010?
6- Según la historia ¿qué título podría ser mejor para la lectura de comprensión?

Reading comprehension

Ask the students to read the story. After reading, ask if they understood. When "yes" pick a student to explain what he/she understood. If "no" give them a summary of the story to explain what happened. Later double check by asking all the students if they understood the story. Then get to the teacher's final questions.

Companies in the U.S are spending millions of dollars to be covered by insurance associations. That is required by law, all across the country to get your company license and insurance. However, some people rather have an online business, others have become book writers to make a living and avoid certain requirements by acquiring a company. Recently stress has become a very serious problem in company expenses. According to the injury and illness prevention program, every year, more than 4.1 million workers suffer a serious job injury or illness, and the total costs are needed to be paid by employers for workers, and it has been estimated over 1 billion per week spent for direct worker's compensation. So there are many challenges companies are facing beside of trying to be productive. Today things have changed, on July 30, 1953, Congress set up Small Business Administration to aid, counsel and assist companies. More than ever, business owners have become smarter running their businesses. Most of them rather hire an independent employee or people for a part-time job instead of a full-time job. Whatever business owners are doing to protect their companies, the goal will always be to keep America prospering by promoting a nation of winners, for the winners and by the winners.

Teacher's part

1- According to the story how serious is the problem of stress in companies?
2- How important is job creation for the U.S economy?
3- How important is for a business owner to cut off expenses?
4- Running a business has never been easy, if you had to choose to be a business owner or an employee, which would you pick?
5- Why is wise to plan for your future by making a retirement plan at an early age?
6- According to the story, what title would be appropriate for the text?

Lectura de comprensión

Pide a los estudiantes de leer la historia. Después de leer, pregunte si entienden. Si entienden, elige un estudiante para explicar lo que él o ella entiende. Si no entienden, de un resumen de la historia para explicar lo que pasó. Luego vuelva a comprobar si han captado la explicación de la historia. Después del debate de la historia usa las preguntas del profesor cuestionando a cada estudiante.

Empresas en los Estados Unidos han gastado millones de dólares para ser cubiertos por asociaciones de seguro. Es requerido por ley, en todo el país obtener su licencia y un seguro para su compañía. Sin embargo, algunas personas prefieren tener un negocio en línea, otros se han convertido en escritores de libros para ganarse la vida y evitar ciertos requisitos por la adquisición de una empresa. Recientemente el estrés se ha convertido en un serio problema en gastos de las empresas. Según el programa de prevención de enfermedad y lesiones, cada año, más de 4.1 millones de trabajadores sufren una lesión o contraen una enfermedad grave en el trabajo, y se necesitan altos ingresos para pagar los empleadores, y se ha estimado más de 1 billón de dólares de gastos por semana para la compensación directo a trabajadores. Así que hay muchos desafíos que las empresas se enfrentan a parte de tratar de ser productivo. Hoy las cosas han cambiado, el 30 de julio, 1953 El Congreso ha establecido (SBA) Administración de Pequeños Negocios para ayudar y aconsejar a las empresas. Más que nunca, los propietarios de negocios se han convertido más astutos en gestión de sus negocios, la mayoría de ellos prefieren contratar a un empleado independiente o contratar a la gente por tiempo parcial en lugar de tiempo completo. No importa lo que los dueños de negocios están haciendo para proteger a sus empresas, el objetivo será siempre de mantener a Estados Unidos prospero para los ganadores y por los ganadores.

Parte del professor

1- ¿Según la historia que tan serio es el problema del estrés en empresas?
2- ¿Qué tan importante es la creación de empleo para la economía de Estados Unidos?
3- ¿Qué tan importante es el corto de gastos para los dueños de negocio?
4- Gestiónar una empresa nunca ha sido fácil, si tuvieras que elegir entre ser dueño de un negocio o ser empleado, ¿cuál escogerías?
5- ¿Por qué es aconsejable planificar su futuro haciendo un plan de jubilación en edad temprana?
6- ¿ Según la historia ¿qué título podría ser mejor para la lectura de comprensión?

Reading comprehension

Ask the students to read the story. After reading, ask if they understood. When "yes" pick a student to explain what he/she understood. If "no" give them a summary of the story to explain what happened. Later double check by asking all the students if they understood the story. Then get to the teacher's final questions.

America is the most amazing country in the whole world. John D Rockefeller, Cornelius and Vanderbilt, Andrew Carnegie, Henry Ford and J.P Morgan built America from the darkness to a modern nation that could be distinguished from other countries. Those entrepreneurs were the giants of the industry. John D Rockefeller constructed the railroad and Thomas Edison invented Electricity. **What would be America without the innovators and business creators?** America is well known as a country full of opportunities. Talented athletes, singers, filmakers writers, innovators are earning billions when nowhere in the world has the same opportunity to do so. People do believe in the American dreams for the reason, if they work hard and believe in themselves, they can achieve anything. The U. S government is involved in his population and their activities, many programs have been planted for people, to help them have a better life. However, not everybody understands the government's efforts to keep active the country. The society is a system created by government based on moral values to make people live better and in order to live in it, every single individual need to be productive by taking and giving something in return to keep it running. That is why today schools and Jobs have been created. Years ago, living a primitive life was not offering the life we all have today; there were almost nothing people wished to own. Lately, the country was crossing a rough time because of the opposition forces against the principles that have been regulated and the government is forced to keep it in the right direction, which is worthy because losing those principles, will be wasting all the good values that have been built to keep this great country.

Teacher's part

1- Why is America considered the most amazing country to live in?

2- What is the U.S government doing to keep America great?

3- As a citizen, living in the country, what is your obligation?

4- Why doesn't everybody want to play by the rules set up by government?

5- Why should the government give the opportunity to those making an effort to run a business in America?

6- According to the story, what title would be appropriate for the text?

Lectura de comprensión

Pide a los estudiantes de leer la historia. Después de leer, pregunte si entienden. Si entienden, elige un estudiante para explicar lo que él o ella entiende. Si no entienden, dé un resumen de la historia para explicar lo que pasó. Luego vuelva a comprobar si han captado la explicación de la historia. Después del debate de la historia usa las preguntas del profesor cuestionando a cada estudiante.

América es el país más asombroso en todo el mundo. John D Rockefeller, Cornelius Vanderbilt, Andrew Carnegie, Henry Ford y J. P Morgan construyeron America de la oscuridad a una nación moderna que podía distinguirse de otros países. Esos empresarios eran los gigantes de la industria. John D Rockefeller construyó el ferrocarril y Thomas Edison inventó la electricidad. ¿Qué sería América sin los innovadores y creadores de empresas? Estados Unidos es conocido como un país lleno de oportunidades. Atletas talentuosos, cantantes, actores de películas, escritores, innovadores etc, están ganando miles de millones de dólares cuando en ninguna parte del mundo tienen la misma oportunidad de hacerlo. Las personas creen en el sueño Americano por una razón, si trabajan duro y creen en sí mismos, pueden lograr cualquier cosa. El gobierno de los Estados Unidos está involucrado en su población y sus actividades, muchos programas han sido planteados para la gente con el fin de ayudarlos a tener una mejor vida. Sin embargo, no todo el mundo entiende los esfuerzos del gobierno para mantener activo el país. La sociedad es un sistema creado por el gobierno basado sobre los valores morales para que la gente viva mejor y para vivir en ella, cada individuo debe ser productivo para tomar y dar algo a cambio, para que siga el país funcionando. Es por eso que hoy en día se han creado escuelas y empleos. Hace años, viviendo una vida primitiva no ofrecía la vida que todos tenemos hoy en día, no había casi nada que deseábamos poseer. Últimamente, el país estaba atravesando un mal momento debido a fuerzas opuestas en contra de los principios que han sido regularizados y el gobierno se ve obligado a mantenerlo en la dirección correcta, ya que vale la pena, porque perder esos principios es perder todos los buenos valores que han sido construidos para mantener este gran país.

Parte del profesor

1- ¿Porqué los Estados Unidos se consideran el país más asombroso para vivir?

2- ¿Qué hace el gobierno para mantener Estados Unidos grandiosos?

3- ¿Cómo ciudadano que vive en el país, cúal es su obligación?

4- ¿Porqué no todos quieren jugar con las reglas establecidas por el gobierno?

5- ¿Porqué el gobierno debería dar la oportunidad a los que hacen un esfuerzo de abrir un negocio en los Estados Unidos?

6- ¿Según la historia ¿qué título podría ser mejor para la lectura de comprensión?

Reading comprehension

Ask the students to read the story. After reading, ask if they understood. When "yes" pick a student to explain what he/she understood. If "no" give them a summary of the story to explain what happened. Later double check by asking all the students if they understood the story. Then get to the teacher's final questions.

Emotional distress has been considered as a disorder brain stem. Sometimes people who have been through it barely noticed it. Young people besides, adults, and kids, are not excluded from getting this emotional disorder. What is emotional distress and how would we know we suffer from it? According to Substance Abuse and Mental Health Services Administration SAMHSA an emotional distress is an anxiety suffered in response to a sudden, severe and saddening incident of mass violence. Including Shooting, bombing not to mention an everyday crime in a neighborhood where violence is part of the daily life activity. Those incidents may affect our collective sense. People who suffered from an emotional distress might feel nothing matters to them anymore, sometimes they might feel helpless or hopeless, feeling guilty for no specific reason. Drinking, smoking or using drugs in excess is the bottom edge of it said researchers. For instance, 9/11 has impacted negatively many people's senses after the twin towers collapsed in New York City. The towers destruction took about 3,000 innocent lives and another 10,000 injured, until today this horrible act could not be forgotten. Based on experts, symptoms may manifest in everyone's life differently, and that can take days, weeks, months, or even years after the incident occured. Doctors estimate that children are more affected than grown up people, & that event may cause them a serious psychological problem. To protect our children, we are all required to work together with the government to prevent those awful scenes to take place in our neighborhood or our community.

Teacher's part

1-Why did 9/11 have a terrible impact on many families?
2-What should we do if we have been in a terrible disaster like this?
3- If our children are the most exposed, what should we do to protect them?
4-How can we prepare ourselves and family for such chaos like 9/11?
5- If a disaster happens, and you have five minutes to leave, what would you take with you?
6-According to the story, what title would be appropriate for the text?

Lectura de comprensión

Pide a los estudiantes de leer la historia. Después de leer, pregunte si entienden. Si entienden, elige un estudiante para explicar lo que él o ella entiende. Si no entienden, dé un resumen de la historia para explicar lo que pasó. Luego vuelva a comprobar si han captado la explicación de la historia. Después del debate de la historia usa las preguntas del profesor cuestionando a cada estudiante.

La angustia emocional ha sido considerada como un trastorno cerebral. A veces, las personas que han pasado por ello casi no la notaron. Los jóvenes a parte de los adultos, y los niños, no están excluidos en adquirir esta angustia emocional. ¿Qué es la angustia emocional y cómo podríamos saber que padecemos de ella? De acuerdo a la organización de Abuso de Sustancias y Servicios de Salud Mental (SAMHSA), una angustia emocional es una ansiedad sufrido en respuesta a un súbito y severo y lamentables incidentes de violencia masiva, incluyendo disparo bombardeo, sin olvidar de mencionar el crimen cotidiana en un barrio dónde la violencia es parte de la actividad de la vida diaria. Esos incidentes pueden afectar nuestro sentido colectivo. Las personas que sufren de una angustia emocional pueden sentir que nada les importa, a veces pueden sentir impotentes y sin esperanza, sintiéndose culpable sin ninguna razón específica. Beber, fumar o tomar drogas en exceso es el tope, dijeron los investigadores. Por ejemplo, el once de septiembre ha impactado negativamente al sentido común de muchas personas después del colapso de las torres gemelas en la ciudad de Nueva York. La destrucción ocurrida tomó alrededor de 3000 vidas inocentes y otros 10,000 heridos, hasta hoy este acto horrible, no podía ser olvidado. Basado en los expertos, los síntomas pueden manifestarse en la vida de todos, de manera diferente y pueden tomar días, semanas, meses o incluso años después de que ocurre el incidente. Los médicos estiman que los niños son los más afectados que los adultos, y ese evento les pueden causar grave problema psicológico. Para proteger a nuestros hijos, todos estamos obligados a trabajar en conjunto con el gobierno para evitar que esas terribles escenas sucedan ya sea en nuestro barrio o nuestra comunidad.

Parte del profesor

1- Porqué el 11 de septiembre tiene un impacto negativo en muchas familias?
2- ¿Qué debemos hacer si estuviéramos en un terrible desastre como este?
3- ¿Si nuestros hijos son los más expuestos, ¿qué debemos hacer para protegerlos?
4- ¿Cómo podemos preparar nosotros mismos y nuestra familia de un desastre como el 11 de Septiembre?
5- ¿ Si ocurre un desastre y tienes cinco minutos para evacuar, ¿qué llevarías contigo?
6- ¿Según la historia ¿qué título podría ser mejor para la lectura de comprensión?

Reading comprehension

Ask the students to read the story. After reading, ask if they understood. When "yes" pick a student to explain what he/she understood. If "no" give them a summary of the story to explain what happened. Later double check by asking all the students if they understood the story. Then get to the teacher's final questions.

San Juan Nico, November 19, 1984, a date that will never be forgotten in Mexican history. The Mexican government reported the amount of people victimized in Pemex right after the explosion in the Federal industry. That explosion caused about 600 innocent people's lives, and another 7,000 suffering severe burns in Mexico City. What caused that terrible explosion? For morethan 50 years the government has never seen the necessity to make the reform in Pemex plant, until the day the tragic accident happened. **The disaster was provoked by a gas leak on a pipe rupture which caused the initiation of a massive series of explosions at a liquid petroleum gas (LPG) tank.** That explosion consumed 11,000 m^3 of LPG, representing one-third of mexicocity's entire liquid petroleum gas supply, said an expert, since the federal government has hired other foreign companies such as a Korean and German companies to reconstruct the industry. At that period, a few private Mexican sectors wanted to take responsibilities to participate in the reconstructions, not only because they did not count with the adequate technology to do the job, but as well for the fear to be sued by the government if something went wrong, damaging the federal industry. That year one of the areas which have been repaired by Bukuen Company has been sabotaged in the test process and the government sued Bukuen, the Korean company, over 20 million pesos. This is one of the reasons private Mexican companies are sometimes hesitant to accept such a job, for not being responsible for any damages or either assume the consequences given by the Federal Mexican Government, for damaging the industry. Since 1987, they have never figured out that it was necessary to make Pemex reconstruction until that year.

Teacher`s part

1- Why Pemex has always required, the service of foreign companies?
2- What was the cause of the explosion on November 19, 1984?
3- Why is not recommended keeping Pemex areas in the city?
4- Why is there a duty for every Mexican Citizen to help government protect pemex?
5- What caution needs to be taken to avoid this tragedy to happen again?
6- According to the story, what title would be appropriate for the text?

Lectura de comprensión

Pide a los estudiantes de leer la historia. Después de leer, pregunte si entienden. Si entienden, elige un estudiante para explicar lo que él o ella entiende. Si no entienden, dé un resumen de la historia para explicar lo que pasó. Luego vuelva a comprobar si han captado la explicación de la historia. Después del debate de la historia usa las preguntas del profesor cuestionando a cada estudiante.

San Juan Nico, 19 de noviembre, 1984, un día que nunca se olvidará en la historia de México. El Gobierno Méxicano ha informado la cantidad de personas víctimas en Pemex. Justo después de la explosión ocurrida en la industria Federal. Esta explosión causó alrededor de 600 vidas inocentes y otros, 7,000 que sufrieron quemaduras graves en la cuidad de México. ¿Qué ha causado esta terrible explosión? Durante más de 50 años, el Gobierno nunca ha visto la necesidad de hacer la reforma en la planta de Pemex, hasta el día en que ocurrió este trágico accidente. "El desastre fue provocado por una fuga de gas en una rotura de tubería que provocó el inicio de una serie masiva de explosiones en un tanque de gas (GLP). Esa explosión consumió 11.000 m3 de gas GLP, lo que representa un tercio de todo el suministro de gas licuado de petróleo de la Ciudad de México, dijo un experto. Desde entonces el Gobierno Federal ha contratado a otras empresas del extranjero tal como empresas de Corea y de Alemania para reconstruir la planta industrial. En ese periodo, casi ningunos de los sectores privados mexicanos querían tomar responsabilidades para participar en las reconstrucciones, no sólo porque no contaban con la tecnología adecuada para hacer el trabajo, sino también por el temor de ser demandado por el Gobierno en el evento que se daña la industria Federal. Ese año una de las zonas que reparó la empresa Bukuen ha sido saboteado en el proceso de prueba y el Gobierno demandó la compañía Coreana más de 20 millones pesos, esto es una de las razónes que las empresas Mexicanas privadas a veces dudan en aceptar el trabajo, para no ser responsable de los daños o bien asumando las consecuencias dadas por el Gobierno Federal, por dañar la industria. Desde 1987, nunca se han dado cuenta de que era necesario realizar la reconstrucción de Pemex hasta ese año.

Parte del profesor

1- ¿Porqué Pemex ha requerido siempre, el servicio de las empresas extranjeras?
2- ¿Cuál fue la causa de explosión de 19 de noviembre, 1984?
3- ¿Porqué no se recomienda mantener el area de Pemex en la ciudad?
4- ¿ Porqué es una obligación a cada ciudadano apoyar al gobierno para proteger Pemex?
5- ¿ Qué precaucion debe de ser tomada para evitar que sucede este tragedia?
6- ¿Según la lectura ¿qué título podría ser mejor para esta lectura de comprensión?

Reading comprehension

Ask the students to read the story. After reading, ask if they understood. When "yes" pick a student to explain what he/she understood. If "no" give them a summary of the story to explain what happened. Later double check by asking all the students if they understood the story. Then get to the teacher's final questions.

Today millions of women are facing infertility problems, the chances of having a baby have decreased by 3% to 5% per year after the age of 30. This reduction of fertility is noted to a much greater extent after age 40. Some women who have problems with ovulation are recommended to follow a specialist to guide and help them resolve that issue. About 10% of couples in the United States are affected by that, both men and women can be infertile. According to the Centers for Disease Control, 1/3 of the time diagnosis is due to female infertility, 1/3 of the time is linked to male infertility and the remaining cases of infertility are due to a combination of factors from both partners, for approximately 20% of couples. Many happy marriage couples desire to have kids and be sure that their family blood will not end and other categories do not want to get pregnant, but rather adopt a baby. Either way, private hospitals with special experts offer various possibilities or treatment to have a baby, besides government institutions also are giving the option to have a baby in adoption to couples who are seeking to adopt one. Doctors said the problem can be caused by the damage to the Fallopian tubes, which carry the eggs from the ovaries to the uterus; this can prevent the contact between the egg and the sperm. Another theory said that the hormone causes is another natural fact, some women are having problems with ovulation, though is not precise to determine the exact cause of this health problem, based on medical researchers. Each of these problems has a solution and experts are still working on helping couples who wish to have a baby on their own.

Teacher's part

1-What is your point of view about birth control?
2-What can cause the fertility problem in both men and women?
3-How can the birth control pill affect women's pregnancy?
4-What's your point of view concerning adoption?
5-Is there a solution for human infertility?
6-According to the story, what title would be appropriate for the text?

Lectura de comprensión

Pide a los estudiantes de leer la historia. Después de leer, pregunte si entienden. Si entienden, elige un estudiante para explicar lo que él o ella entiende. Si no entienden, dé un resumen de la historia para explicar lo que pasó. Luego vuelva a comprobar si han captado la explicación de la historia. Después del debate de la historia usa las preguntas del profesor cuestionando a cada estudiante.

Hoy en día millones de mujeres enfrentan problemas de infertilidad, las posibilidades de tener un bebé han disminuido de un 3% a 5% por año después de la edad de 30. Esta reducción de fertilidad se puede observar a un grado mucho mayor después de los 40. Algunas mujeres que tienen problemas de ovulación son recomendadas de seguir un especialista para orientar y ayudarlas a resolver ese problema. Alrededor del 10% de parejas en los Estados Unidos se ven afectados por esto, tanto los hombres como las mujeres pueden ser infértiles. Según los Centros de Control de Enfermedades, 1/3 de diagnóstico es debido a la infertilidad femenina, 1/3 está relacionado con la infertilidad masculina y el resto de los casos de infertilidad se deben a una combinación de factores de ambas partes, por aproximadamente 20% de las parejas. Muchas parejas casadas desean tener hijos y asegurarse de que la sangre de su familia se multiplique y otras categorías de personas no desean quedar embarazadas, sino adoptar un bebé. De cualquier manera, los hospitales privados con expertos especiales ofrecen diversas posibilidades de tratamiento para tener un bebé, a parte las instituciones gubernamentales también están dando la opción de tener un bebé en adopción a las parejas que tratan de adoptar uno. Los médicos dijeron que el problema puede ser causado por daños a las trompas de Falopio, que llevan los óvulos de los ovarios hasta el útero, esto puede impedir el contacto entre el óvulo y el esperma. Otra teoría dice que las causas de hormona es otro hecho natural, algunas mujeres tienen problemas con ovulación, aunque no es precisa de determinar la causa exacta de este problema de salud según los investigadores médicos. Sin embargo, cada uno de estos problemas tienen una solución y los expertos siguen trabajando para ayudar a las parejas que desean tener un bebé por su cuenta.

Parte del profesor

1- ¿Cuál es su punto de vista acerca del control de embarazo?
2- ¿Qué puede causar el problema de fertilidad en hombres y mujeres?
3- ¿Cómo las pastillas anticonceptivas pueden afectar el embarazo en las mujeres?
4- ¿Cuál es su punto de vista sobre la adopción?
5- ¿Hay solución para la infertilidad humana?
6- Según la historia ¿Qué título podría ser mejor para la lectura de comprensión?

Reading comprehension

Ask the students to read the story. After reading, ask if they understood. When "yes" pick a student to explain what he/she understood. If "no" give them a summary of the story to explain what happened. Later double check by asking all the students if they understood the story. Then get to the teacher's final questions.

For many decades, human cloning has stopped the audiences on radio and television. Why haven't we heard of it anymore? First, let's get started with its meaning. Human cloning is the creation of a genetical identical copy of a human. The term was generally used to refer to artificial human cloning, which is the reproduction of human cells and tissue, based on scientific researchers. This subject has raised a lot of concerns and controversy in human history and it has been prohibited by law to clone people due to the threat of losing our true identity. Based on how the world was created and how life has existed on this planet, there is no precise explanation of life, but it was saying that life has been designed in five steps: birth, nutrition, growth, reproduction, and death, which means as a human being we were born to be nourished, grow, reproduce and die. However, with the advance of technology scientists and researchers, metaphorically speaking, have tried to make mankind last forever. If modern science has found the key to clone humans, why they did not do so? That controversy has its pros and cons. The pros were when someone we loved very much died we could replace him by only cloning him to relief our pain. The cons were that we will lose our true identity. Imagine we have 3 or 5 identical persons with the same name how confusing that will be? On the other hand, some people believe that life is a circle that everyone must go through by following its process and die when it is time. Others believe that human beings have been re-incarnated for years in different bodies. Whatsoever our belief and the efforts scientists are making to change the course of human life, everything was created to come to an end.

Teacher's part

1- Why cloning has been considered an eminent threat in mankind's history?
2- According to the passage what is your point of view about human cloning?
3- If you had a chance to clone a person you loved very much that passed away would you do it?
4- What are the pros and cons raised for human cloning?
5- What are the 5 steps related to life?
6- According to the story, what title would be appropriate for the text?

Lectura de comprensión

Pide a los estudiantes de leer la historia. Después de leer, pregunte si entienden. Si entienden, elige un estudiante para explicar lo que él o ella entiende. Si no entienden, dé un resumen de la historia para explicar lo que pasó. Luego vuelva a comprobar si han captado la explicación de la historia. Después del debate de la historia usa las preguntas del profesor cuestionando a cada estudiante.

Desde hace muchas décadas, clonación humana ha dejado las audiencias en la radio y la televisión. ¿Porqué no hemos oído hablar de ella? En primer lugar, vamos a empezar con su significado. Clonación humana es la creación de una copia genética idéntica de un humano. El término se emplea generalmente para referirse a la clonación artificial humana, que es la reproducción de las células humanas y el tejido, basado en investigadores científicos. Este tema ha levantado muchas preocupaciones y controversia en la historia humana y ha sido prohibido por ley de clonar a las personas debido a la amenaza de perder nuestra verdadera identidad. Basado en cómo el mundo fue creado y cómo la vida ha existido en este planeta, no hay ninguna explicación precisa de la vida, pero se dice que la vida ha sido diseñado en cinco etapas: Nacimiento, nutrición, crecimiento, reproducción, muerte, lo que significa como ser humano nacimos para ser alimentados, crecer, reproducir y morir. Sin embargo, con el avance de la tecnología, los científicos e investiga -dores metafóricamente hablando, han tratado hacer que el ser humano viva por siempre. Si la ciencia moderna ha encontrado la clave para clonar humanos, ¿por qué no lo hicieron? Esa controversia tiene su por y contra. El por fue cuando alguien que queríamos mucho muere, pudiéramos sustituirlo por clonación y aliviar nuestro dolor. La contra era que íbamos a perder nuestra verdadera identidad. Imaginemos que tenemos 3 o 5 personas idénticas con el mismo nombre, ¿qué confundido sería? Por otro lado, algunas personas creen que la vida es un círculo que todo el mundo tiene que pasar siguiendo su proceso y morir cuando llegue su tiempo. Otros creen que el ser humano se ha reencarnado desde hace años en diferentes cuerpos. Lo que sea nuestra creencia y esfuerzos, los científicos están haciendo para cambiar el curso de la vida humana, todo lo que fue creado fue creado para llegar a su fin.

Parte del profesor

1- Por qué la clonación ha sido considerada como una amenaza eminente en la historia humana?
2- Según el texto ¿cuál es su punto de vista acerca de clonación humana?
3- Si tuviera la oportunidad de clonar una persona fallecida que amaba mucho ¿lo haría?
4- ¿Cuál es el por y la contra presentada a la clonación humana?
5- ¿Cúales son los 5 pasos relacionado a la vida?
6- Según la historia ¿qué título podría ser mejor para la lectura de comprensión?

Reading comprehension

Ask the students to read the story. After reading, ask if they understood. When "yes" pick a student to explain what he/she understood. If "no" give them a summary of the story to explain what happened. Later double check by asking all the students if they understood the story. Then get to the teacher's final questions.

Studies have shown exercise helps increase the immune system and release stress. Practice 3 or 6 days a regular exercise routine will make our bones stronger and support the circulation of the white blood cells faster. Those white blood cells are responsible for the body to detect any disease at an earlier age and fight the bacteria that will cause the illness to prevent the body turn to sick. However, we need to moderate, the days and the timing if we want to adapt to an exercise routine, not doing so the excessive exercise will decrease our white blood cells and make the body more vulnerable to disease. Not only exercise will help us feel better about ourselves, it will also help us to be healthier, but to be both healthy and energetic there are other requirements that should be followed after the exercise, that requirement is a good nutritional balance by taking what the body needs daily in order to strengthen the metabolism of our body. That is why vitamins and good nutrition play an important role in each person's life who wants to keep on exercising. It is more recommended to consume carbohydrate and natural vitamins that can be found in vegetables and fruits. There are many physical activities a person can adapt such as swimming, bicycling, walking, running, hiking, fitness, yoga, golf and other flexibility exercises are great for the body. The American Heart Association stated that walking 30 minutes a day can reduce the chances of heart disease, improve blood pressure and enhance mental well-being, research has proven that swimming can help get the human body fit better, the body burns 200 calories in half an hour every time we swim, in other words exercise increases our life expectancy. As they say" prevention is better than cure" It is our obligation to take care of ourselves to stay healthy, however, it is up to each person to pick which exercise they will feel more comfortable practicing.

Teacher's part

1- Why exercising, plays an important role in our daily lives?
2- What is the cell name that protects our organism system?
3- Why a nutrition balance should work together with exercise?
4- What will happen if we don't exercise?
5- If you had to choose a routine exercise, which one would you pick between those mentioned?
6- According to the story, what title would be appropriate for the text?

Lectura de comprensión

Pide a los estudiantes de leer la historia. Después de leer, pregunte si entienden. Si entienden, elige un estudiante para explicar lo que él o ella entiende. Si no entienden, dé un resumen de la historia para explicar lo que pasó. Luego vuelva a comprobar si han captado la explicación de la historia. Después del debate de la historia usa las preguntas del profesor cuestionando a cada estudiante.

Los estudios han demostrado que el Ejercicio ayuda a aumentar el sistema inmune y liberar el estrés. Prácticando de 3 a 6 días una rutina regular de ejercicio hará que nuestros huesos sea más fuertes, ayudando a la circulación del glóbulo blanco de la sangre y hacerlo funcionar más rápido. Esas células blancas de la sangre son responsables en el cuerpo para detectar cualquier enfermedad a edades muy tempranas y combatir las bacterias que causarán las enfermedades para evitar que el cuerpo se enferme. Sin embargo, necesitamos moderar, los días y el tiempo si queremos adaptarnos a una rutina de ejercicios, de no hacerlo el ejercicio resultará excesivo, disminuirá nuestras células blancas de la sangre y hará que el cuerpo sea más vulnerable a las enfermedades. No solamente el ejercicio nos ayudará a sentirnos mejor, sino que también nos ayudará a ser más saludable, pero para ser saludable y enérgico hay ciertos requerimiento que se debe seguir después del ejercicio y el requerimiento es un buen equilibrio nutricional que necesitamos todos los días para reforzar el metabolismo de nuestro cuerpo. Es por eso, las vitaminas y una buena nutrición juegan un papel importante en la vida de cada persona que quiere adaptarse a un ejercicio. Es recomendable consumir más carbo hidratos y vitaminas naturales que se pueden encontrar en las verduras y las frutas. Hay muchas actividades físicas que una persona puede adaptarse tales como: natación, ciclista, caminata, correr, yoga, golfo y otros ejercicios flexibles que son buenos para el cuerpo. *La Asociación American Heart* afirma que al caminar 30 minutos al día puede reducir las enfermedades del corazón, mejorando la presión arterial y el bienestar mental, informes ha demostrado que la natación puede ayudar a que el cuerpo humano se ajuste mejor, el cuerpo quema 200 calorías en media hora cada vez que nadamos, en otra palabra el ejercicio prolonga nuestra vida. Como suelen decir "es mejor prevenir que lamentar" Es nuestra obligación de cuidarnos para mantenernos saludable, sin embargo, es de cada persona elegir qué ejercicio se sentirá más cómodo para práticar.

Parte del profesor

1- ¿Porqué hacer ejercicio, juega un papel importante en nuestra vida diaria?
2- ¿Cuál es el nombre de célula que protege nuestro organismo?
3- ¿Porqué un balance nutricional debe de ir en conjunto con el ejercicio?
4- ¿Qué pasará si no hacemos ejercicio?
5- Si tuviera que elegir una rutina de ejercicio, ¿cuál elegirías entre las que hemos mencionado?
6- Según la historia ¿qué título podría ser mejor para la lectura de comprensión?

Reading comprehension

Ask the students to read the story. After reading, ask if they understood. When "yes" pick a student to explain what he/she understood. If "no" give them a summary of the story to explain what happened. Later double check by asking all the students if they understood the story. Then get to the teacher's final questions.

Nowadays climate change is not only one country concerns but the whole world. The United Nations held a conference in Paris, France from 30th of November to 12th of December to talk about how they can improve this. According to the organizing committee at the outset of the talks, there was an agreement to set a goal of limiting global warming to less than 2 degrees Celsius (°C) compared to the pre-industrial levels. Regarding the version of the Paris agreement, parties should put their effort together to limit the temperature increase to 1.5°C. What causes the global warming today? Scientists stated that it's primarily a problem of too much carbon dioxide (CO_2) in the atmosphere, which acts as a blanket, trapping heat and warming the planet. For years the world industries never noticed how serious the toxic fuel emitted into the air was going to be. Deforestation, which has been used to build houses and other needs, has never been replaced. By cutting the trees the atmosphere shield has been removed and the remaining trees were not enough to absorb the extra carbon dioxide flying to the atmosphere. In the late 1980s and early 1990s the first book on green marketing entitled Ecological Marketing inspired the world with the term of Going Green, according to researchers it means taking steps, whether big or small, to minimize the harm we do to the environment. To achieve that goal people, need to be educated to know why is so important to protect the environment and how to do so. Plants and animals have gone extinct by human action, as the result we have what is called the climate change, which is causing a dramatic issue on the earth planet, all including: earthquakes, tsunamis & so on. Mankind has become greedy pursuing the gain of materialism ignoring the damages they are causing to the earth. Though we need to take a stand now to make an improvement about the climate change by saving what is left, otherwise our children and grandchildren will live in an atmosphere full of pollution.

Teacher's part

1- What causes the changes we are having today on the planet?
2- If we are not conscious and take responsibility now, what would happen to the planet?
3- Why is it so important to protect the animals?
4- What are the steps people need to take to have an environment free of pollution?
5- Is climate change part of global warning?
6- According to the story, what title would be appropriate for the text?

Lectura de comprensión

Pide a los estudiantes de leer la historia. Después de leer, pregunte si entienden. Si entienden, elige un estudiante para explicar lo que él o ella entiende. Si no entienden, dé un resumen de la historia para explicar lo que pasó. Luego vuelva a comprobar si han captado la explicación de la historia. Después del debate de la historia usa las preguntas del profesor cuestionando a cada estudiante.

Hoy en día el cambio climático no es solamente una preocupación de algunos países sino de todo el mundo. Las Naciones Unidas llevaron a cabo una conferencia en París, Francia, del 30 de noviembre al 12 de diciembre para debatir sobre cómo se puede mejorar esto. De acuerdo al comité organizador al inicio de las conversaciones, hubo un acuerdo por establecer un objetivo para limitar el calentamiento global a menos de 2 grados Celsius ($^\circ$C) en comparación con los niveles pre-industriales. Con respecto a la versión del acuerdo de París, las partes deben poner su esfuerzo en conjunto para limitar el aumento de temperatura de 1,5 $^\circ$C. ¿Qué causa el calentamiento global hoy en día? Los científicos indicaron que es principalmente un problema de exceso de dióxido de carbono en la atmósfera, que actúa como una manta, atrapando el calor y produce el calentamiento del planeta. Durante años las industrias no se dieron cuenta de la gravedad de los combustibles tóxicos que han emitido en el aire. La deforestación, que ha sido utilizado para construir casas y otras necesidades, cortando los árboles nunca fueron reemplazados, cortando los árboles el escudo de atmósfera ha sido eliminado y los árboles restantes no fueron suficientes para absorber el dióxido de carbono extra que volaron al atmósfera. A finales de 1980 y principios de 1990 en la comercialización del primer libro titulado Marketing Ecológico inspiró al mundo con el término de Going Green, según el investigador significa tomar medidas, ya sea grande o pequeño, para reducir al mínimo el daño que hicieron al medio ambiente. Para lograr ese objetivo la gente necesita ser educado para saber porqué es tan importante proteger el medio ambiente y cómo hacerlo. Las plantas, y animales se han extinguidos por la acción humana, como resultado tenemos lo que se llama el cambio climático que está causando un problema dramático en el planeta, incluyendo: terremotos, tsunamis etc. Los seres humanos se han vuelto avaliciosos persiguieendo la ganancia del materialismo ignorando los daños que están causando a la tierra, Así tenemos que tomar una posición ahora para mejorar el cambio climático, de lo contrario nuestros hijos y nietos van a vivir en un ambiente lleno de contaminación.

Parte del profesor

1- ¿Qué ha causado los cambios que estamos teniendo hoy en el planeta?
2- Si no somos conscientes y asumir la responsabilidad ahora, ¿qué pasaría con el planeta?
3- ¿Por qué es tan importante proteger a los animales?
4- ¿Cuáles son los pasos que las personas necesitan tomar para tener un medio ambiente libre de contaminación?
5- ¿El cambio de clima, es parte del calentamiento global?
6- Según la historia ¿qué título podría ser mejor para la lectura de comprensión?

Reading comprehension

Ask the students to read the story. After reading, ask if they understood. When "yes" pick a student to explain what he/she understood. If "no" give them a summary of the story to explain what happened. Later double check by asking all the students if they understood the story. Then get to the teacher's final questions.

Drug abuse is the public number one enemy in the United States and the rest of the world. Since 1968 federal law enforcement started a war on drugs to stop multiple crimes on the streets. Till today this issue has not come to an end. The law in the United States is varied from state to state, meanwhile, prior presidents were making all efforts demolishing this toxic abuse other states had already acted to reduce criminal penalties for possession and use. If Congress had not let bills pending to reduce drug penalties, the society would have lost control on drugs and it could have been worst. Drug abuse has always been a serious threat to our society because not only it kills our children but as well destroys families, our moral values, and the government institutions. Losing control of it will plunge our nation into a deep, painful mess said President Ronald Reagan. Why the consummation of drugs so dangerous? There are many risks involving in the consummation of all types of drugs. First, it has a physical impact on the human body and limits our ability to know the difference between right and wrong. It weakens the immune system, keeping our organism defenseless, killing our IQ system, Including seizures, stroke and sudden heart attack. When someone uses drugs such as marijuana, cocaine, ecstasy amphetamines and heroin he/she will have less self-control and will become paranoid, aggressive, impulsive and even experiment hallucinations. An addicted woman in case of pregnancy can put at risk her baby with a birth defect. Many centers for rehabilitation are opened offering people who are going through a drug addiction, the possibility to recover their lives and live free from it. Some have 90 days program to be followed with special consultants, all available to help. The epidemic of drug abuse has been spread nationwide, it is hard to repair the damages that have been caused to so many households, but today the cure is preferably saying "No" when it comes to its consummation.

Teacher's part

1- How serious is the problem of drug abuse in our country?
2- Colorado legalized in 2012 the consummation of weeds, what is your point of view?
3- Why is important for each citizen to support the government in this fight?
4- What negative reactions drug will have on us if we consume it?
5- What will our society become if the government does not take steps to penalize drug possessions?
6- According to the story, what title would be appropriate for the text?

Lectura de comprensión

Pide a los estudiantes de leer la historia. Después de leer, pregunte si entienden. Si entienden, elige un estudiante para explicar lo que él o ella entiende. Si no entienden, dé un resumen de la historia para explicar lo que pasó. Luego vuelva a comprobar si han captado la explicación de la historia. Después del debate de la historia usa las preguntas del profesor cuestionando a cada estudiante.

El abuso de drogas es el enemigo público número uno en los Estados Unidos y el resto del mundo. Desde 1968 la ley federal inició una guerra contra las drogas para detener los crímenes múltiples en las calles, hasta hoy esta cuestión no ha llegado a su fin. La ley en los Estados Unidos se varía de estado a estado, mientras, los presidentes anteriores habían hecho todos los esfuerzos para destruir este abuso tóxico, otros estados han actuado para reducir las penas por uso y posesión de droga. Si el Congreso no había dejado las cuentas pendientes para reducir las penas por posesión de drogas, la sociedad pudiera perder el control y podría haber sido peor. El abuso de drogas ha sido siempre una amenaza grave en nuestra sociedad ya que no sólo mata a nuestros hijos, pero también la familia, nuestros valores morales, y las instituciones gubernamentales. Pérdiendo el control de la misma se hundirá nuestra nación en un lío profunda y dolorosa, dijo el presidente Ronald Reagan. ¿Por qué la consumación de drogas es tan peligrosa? Hay muchos riesgos que implican en el consumo de todo tipo de drogas. En primer lugar, tiene un impacto físico en el cuerpo humano y limitar nuestra capacidad de diferenciar entre el bien y el mal. Se debilita el sistema inmunológico, deja nuestro organismo indefenso, mata nuestro coeficiente intelectual (IQ), provoca convulsiones, derrame cerebral y un súbito ataque cardíaca. Cuando alguien usa drogas como la marihuana, cocaína, éxtasis, anfetaminas, heroína él/ella tendrá menos control de sí mismo(a) y se convertirá en paranoia, en agresividad e incluso experimentará alucinaciones. Una mujer adicta en caso de embarazo puede poner en riesgo a su bebé con defectos de nacimiento. Muchos centros de rehabilitación se abren ofreciendo a las personas que están pasando por una adicción de drogas para darles la posibilidad de recuperar sus vidas y vivir libre de ella. Algunos tienen 90 días de programa de seguimiento con consultores especiales, todos están disponibles para ayudar. La epidemia de abuso de drogas se ha extendido en todo el mundo, es difícil de reparar los daños que ha causado a tantas familias, pero hoy en día el mejor remedio es decir no a la droga cuando se trata de consumirla.

Parte del profesor

1- ¿Qué tan grave es el problema del abuso de drogas en nuestro país?
2- Colorado ha legalizado en 2012, la consumación de marihuana, ¿cuál es su punto de vista?
3- ¿Porqué es importante para los ciudadanos apoyar al gobierno en esta lucha?
4- ¿Qué reacciones negativas tendremos si consumimos drogas?
5- ¿En qué se convertirá nuestra sociedad si el gobierno no tomaba medidas para sancionar las posesiones de drogas?
6- Según la historia ¿qué título podría ser mejor para la lectura de comprensión?

Reading comprehension

Ask the students to read the story. After reading, ask if they understood. When "yes" pick a student to explain what he/she understood. If "no" give them a summary of the story to explain what happened. Later double check by asking all the students if they understood the story. Then get to the teacher's final questions.

Today research has demonstrated that certain people are more vulnerable to go through a nervous breakdown than others. What is a nervous breakdown? A nervous breakdown is a major depressive disorder, a mental illness caused by extreme stress in a very difficult situation that the person cannot take control anymore. Its symptoms include panic attack, fear, and feeling of worry, anxiety and confusion. We are all limited to cope with certain things but not everything. Some people may go through a nervous break due to a breakup, loss of fortune, or family matters. In the Rise and Fall of the Nervous Breakdown (2013), Edward Shorter, a professor of psychiatry argues that in the majority of the women half of them tend to be depressed due to hormonal changes. It is easier to detect a depressive sign in women because of a sudden radical change of mood than men. From that, major action can be taken to prevent collateral damage. Research has proved the percentage of men who looked for counseling when they feel depressed are minimized to 40%, the remaining lean on smoking and alcohol to escape the zone. However, a nervous breakdown can happen to anyone at any age, more likely if the person has an anxiety family disorder history or a high-stress period of time, it is considered more serious when it comes to suicidal behavior and thought of harming others. When someone is anxious and feels like he/she is going to have a nervous breakdown it is always recommended to search for a counselor assistance as soon as possible to deal with the problem.

Teacher's part

1-Define what is a nervous breakdown? What makes people go through it?
2-What's a person capable of doing when the breakdown is extremely serious?
3-Who might be more exposed to getting a nervous breakdown?
4-What are the symptoms of a nervous breakdown?
5-What is recommended when someone feels he/she is going to a nervous breakdown?
6-According to the story, what title would be appropriate for the text?

Lectura de comprensión

Pide a los estudiantes de leer la historia. Después de leer, pregunte si entienden. Si entienden, elige un estudiante para explicar lo que él o ella entiende. Si no entienden, dé un resumen de la historia para explicar lo que pasó. Luego vuelva a comprobar si han captado la explicación de la historia. Después del debate de la historia usa las preguntas del profesor cuestionando a cada estudiante.

Hoy en día la investigación ha demostrado que ciertas personas son más vulnerables para pasar por un ataque de nervios que otros. ¿Qué es un ataque de nervios? Un ataque de nervios es un trastorno depresivo mayor, una enfermedad mental causada por un extremo estrés en una situación muy difícil que la persona no puede tomar el control. Sus síntomas incluyen ataque de pánico, miedo y sentimiento de preocupación, ansiedad y confusión. Todos estamos limitados para confrontar ciertas cosas. Algunas personas pueden pasar por un ataque de nervios debido a una ruptura amorosa, pérdida de fortuna, problemas familiares. En el **"Rise and Fall"** de ataque de nervios publicado en (2013), Edward Shorter, profesor de psiquiatría sostiene que la mayoría de las mujeres, la mitad de ellas tienden a estar deprimidos debido a los cambios hormonales. Es más fácil detectar una señal de depresión en las mujeres, ellas se enfrentan a un cambio de estado radical repentino de ánimo diferente que los hombres. A partir de eso, una acción puede ser tomada para evitar daños colaterales. Investigación ha demostrado que el porcentaje de hombres que buscan consejo cuando se sienten deprimidos se reducen al mínimo 40%, los restantes se apoyan en el tabaquismo, el alcohol y otros hábitos para escapar la zona. Sin embargo, un ataque de nervios puede suceder a cualquier persona y a cualquier edad, más probable si la persona tiene una historia de trastorno de ansiedad de origen familiar o teniendo un período de tiempo de alto estrés, y se considera más grave precisamente cuando se trata de un comportamiento suicida y pensamiento de perjudicar a los demás. Cuando alguien está ansioso y sentir que está pasando por un ataque de nervios, siempre se recomienda buscar la asistencia de una especialista tan pronto posible para hacer frente al problema.

Parte del profesor

1- ¿Definir qué es un ataque de nervios? ¿qué puede provocarlo?
2- ¿Qué es capaz una persona cuando el ataque de nervios es extremadamente grave?
3- ¿Quién podría estar más expuesta a tener un ataque de nervios?
4- ¿Cuáles son los síntomas de un ataque de nervios?
5- ¿Qué es recomendable cuándo alguien se siente que esta pasando por un ataque de nervios?
6- Según la historia ¿qué título podría ser mejor para la lectura de comprensión?

Reading comprehension

Ask the students to read the story. After reading, ask if they understood. When "yes" pick a student to explain what he/she understood. If "no" give them a summary of the story to explain what happened. Later double check by asking all the students if they understood the story. Then get to the teacher's final questions.

Today's ocean pollution should be everyone's concern. It started from big companies thousand years ago. At that time corporations were made to extract all they can from the oil in order to facilitate a better living for human beings. From 42 gallon barrel of oil, industries could get 19.4 gallons of gasoline and the rest of the substance was used to make drinking cups, dishes, toothpaste, trash bags & so on. Why should we be concerned about the ocean's pollution? In November 30, 2016 investigators conducted a search on Midway Island to know the cause of death of hundreds of birds living in the area. As result; various plastic debri was found in them. Following that, a rescue plan was set up by U.S citizens to protect other animals being victimized by the same cause. Thousands of miles debri travels from different points in the ocean and to clean it up entirely, it might be almost impossible. If we take a stand to educate others about the problem, this could come someday to an end.

Teacher's part

1- Why ocean pollution should be everyone's concern?
2- What strategy should be used to keep the ocean clean?
3- Do you think the discovery of oil has played an important role in the development of our society?
4- What caused the bird's death on Midway Island?
5- What action has been taken by Midway citizens to prevent other animals getting hurt?
6- According to the reading, what title would be appropriate for the text?

Lectura de comprensión

Pide a los estudiantes de leer la historia. Después de leer, pregunte si entienden. Si entienden, elige un estudiante para explicar lo que él o ella entiende. Si no entienden, dé un resumen de la historia para explicar lo que pasó. Luego vuelva a comprobar si han captado la explicación de la historia. Después el debate de la historia usa las preguntas del profesor cuestionando a cada estudiante.

Hoy en día la contaminación del océano debería ser preocupación de todos. Inició desde la creación de grandes compañías hace miles de años. En este tiempo las compañías fueron creadas para extraer todo lo que pueden del petróleo para poder facilitar una vida mejor a los seres humanos. Desde 42 galones de barril de gasolina, las compañías podrían sacar 19.4 galones de gasolina y el resto de substancia se usaba para manufacturar vasos, platos, pasta de dientes, bolsa de basuras etc. ¿Porqué deberíamos preocuparnos de la contaminación del océano? El 30 de Noviembre 2016, investigadores hicieron una búsqueda en la Isla de Midway para saber el motivo de muerte de cientos de pájaros viviendo en el área. Como resultado, varios desechos de plásticos se encuentraban dentro de ellos. A continuación, un plan de rescate fue establecido por cuidadanos de Estados Unidos para prevenir que otros animales fueron victimas de lo mismo. Miles de desechos viajan de diferentes puntos al océano, y para limpiarlo completamente podria ser imposible. Si tomamos un paso para educar a otros a cerca del problema, tal vez esto podría llegar algún dia a un fin.

Parte del profesor

1- ¿Porque la contaminación del océano debería ser la preocupación de todos?
2- ¿Qué estrategia debería ser usado para mantener limpio el oceano?
3- ¿Piensas el descubrimiento de petróleo ha jugado un papel importante en el desarrollo de nuestra sociedad?
4- ¿Qué ha causado la muerte de los pájaros en la Isla de Midway?
5- ¿Qué acción debe ser tomada por los cuidadanos de Midway para prevenir que otros animales se lastiman?
6- Según la lectura ¿qué título podría ser mejor para esta lectura de comprensión?

Reading comprehension

Ask the students to read the story. After reading, ask if they understood. When "yes" pick a student to explain what he/she understood. If "no" give them a summary of the story to explain what happened. Later double check by asking all the students if they understood the story. Then get to the teacher's final questions.

Bipolar disorder is a phenomenon of a manic-depressive disease caused in a human brain that changes with a frequency the energy and the mood of the patient. Its attack can take complete control over the patient and make him/her lose all the ability to carry out an everyday activity. There are different types of bipolar disorders and it may come in many ways in the person's life. Those manic depressions can have results from a deterioration of a relationship which can end up self-harming (suicide). There is no specific proof that causes this health problem, there are speculations raised by scientists that people with relatives that have bipolar genes are more sensitive to inherit the disease, but this is a controversy. Many years ago a study was conducted on two twins born from the same mother with bipolar disease, even the kids had the identical genes, but no signs of bipolar disorder had been shown. In spite of the non-specific explanation to that disorder, researchers have launched "A Bipolar Disorder Phenome Database" funded in part by the National Institute of Mental Health (NIMH) to find a clear response to that phenomenon, as well another disease that has similar symptoms in the human body therefore, bipolar disorder symptoms have been divided into two categories according to scientists: an overly joyful state is called <u>manic episode</u> which comes with extreme irritability. The other one is when the patient feels completely sad and hopeless, it has been called <u>depressive episode</u>. As stated, behavioral changes for a manic episode are quite different from behavioral changes for a depressive episode. In order to know which episode, the patient is crossing, it is recommended to check with a specialist to determine it, but both can be controlled by medication prescription. No matter how serious bipolar behavior can be, this illness can be cured and allow anyone who has it to carry on a long productive life expectancy.

Teacher's part

1- According to the text, how can you describe a bipolar disorder?
2- How can a person take control of his life if he/she has a bipolar disorder?
3- Why a family member who has that disorder can't transmit it to another sibling?
4- What is the reaction of a manic episode and depressive episode?
5- What is different between a behavioral change for a manic episode and depressive episode?
6- According to the story, what title would be appropriate for the text?

Lectura de comprensión

Pide a los estudiantes de leer la historia. Después de leer, pregunte si entienden. Si entienden, elige un estudiante para explicar lo que él o ella entiende. Si no entienden, dé un resumen de la historia para explicar lo que pasó. Luego vuelva a comprobar si han captado la explicación de la historia. Después el debate de la historia usa las preguntas del profesor cuestionando a cada estudiante.

El trastorno bipolar es un fenómeno de una enfermedad maníaco-depresiva provoca en el cerebro humano que cambia con frecuencia la energía y el estado de ánimo del paciente. Su ataque puede tener un control completo sobre el paciente y él o ella puede perder toda la capacidad de llevar a cabo una actividad diaria. Hay diferentes tipos de trastorno bipolar, que aparece en diferentes formas en la vida de las personas. Esas depresiones maníacas pueden ser el resultado de una relación deteriorada que puede acabar en dañar a sí mismo (suicidio). No hay ninguna prueba que específica la causa de este problema de salud, hay especulaciones planteadas por los científicos que las personas con genes bipolares son más sensibles a heredar la enfermedad, pero hay una controversia. Hace muchos años se realizó un estudio de dos gemelos nacidos de la misma madre con trastorno bipolar, aunque los niños tenían los genes idénticos, no se han mostrado ningún signo de trastorno bipolar. No hay una explicación específica a ese trastorno, los investigadores han puesto en marcha **"un trastorno bipolar de base de datos"**, financiado por parte del Instituto Nacional de Salud Mental (NIMH) para encontrar una respuesta clara a los fenómenos bipolares, y así también otra enfermedad que tiene síntomas similares en el cuerpo humano. Los síntomas del trastorno bipolar se han dividido en dos categorías según los científicos: un estado demasiado alegre se llama **episodio maníaco** que viene con irritabilidad extrema, la otra es cuando el paciente se siente completamente triste y sin esperanza, eso se llama **episodio depresivo**. Como se ha indicado, los cambios de tamiento para el episodio maníaco son bastante diferentes de los cambios de comportamiento de episodio depresivo. Para saber qué episodio el paciente está cruzando, se recomienda consultar un especialista para determinarlo, pero ambos pueden ser controlados por pastillas recetadas. No importa la gravedad de la conducta bipolar, esta enfermedad puede ser curada y permitir que cualquier persona que lo tenga desarrolle una larga y productiva vida.

Parte del profesor

1- De acuerdo al texto, ¿cómo se puede describir un trastorno bipolar?
2- ¿Cómo una persona puede tomar el control de su vida si tiene un trastorno bipolar?
3- ¿Por qué un miembro de la familia que tiene el trastorno no puede transmitirlo a otro miembro?
4- ¿Cuál es la reacción de un episodio maníaco y episodio depresivo?
5- ¿Cuál es la diferencia entre un cambio de comportamiento para episodios maníacos y episodios depresivos?
6- Según la historia ¿qué título podría ser mejor para la lectura de comprensión?

Reading comprehension

Ask the students to read the story. After reading, ask if they understood. When "yes" pick a student to explain what he/she understood. If "no" give them a summary of the story to explain what happened. Later double check by asking all the students if they understood the story. Then get to the teacher's final questions.

A Caterpillar transformation into a butterfly is a great example of nature showing that nothing dies on earth, but only turn into a different matter. Since the planet existance there was always a symbiotic relationship between mankind and nature. That symbiotic relationship is defined as a mutual relationship in taking and giving back, one to another. Some symbiotic relationships are forced because of the fact that one cannot live without the other. Scientists, related that sometimes this relationship can be beneficial and at times very harmful. There are two types of symbiotic relationships. One called <u>defense symbiotic</u> and another one <u>cleaning symbiosis</u>. The cleaning symbiotic is for instance, when one organism is getting rid of parasites off another organism's body and turns them into a food process to feed the other. The defense symbiotic is clearly shown with the clownfish in a one-on-one relationship. The clownfish are protected from predators by living in the anemone's tentacles and the sea anemone not only feels protection by the clownfish from its predators, but as well flourishing because of its presence. Another clear example, once a caterpillar has finished its transformation process and turn into a butterfly, it has a symbiotic relationship with the flowers where both species benefit from one another. According to an article adult butterflies feast on the nectar provided by flowers, drawing it through a long straw-like proboscis. The caterpillar's transformation into a butterfly and its symbiotic generosity toward the flowers taught us a lesson of unity in working in a team, to live better in a society where all of us need to give something in return.

Teacher's part

1-According to the passage, what is a symbiotic relationship?
2-How does clownfish and the sea anemone work?
3-How do you explain the cleaning and the defense symbiotic process?
4-How beneficial is the activity of the butterfly from flowers to flowers?
5-According the passage what lesson can human being learn from mother nature?
6-According to the story, what title would be appropriate for the text?

Lectura de comprensión

Pide a los estudiantes de leer la historia. Después de leer, pregunte si entienden. Si entienden, elige un estudiante para explicar lo que él o ella entiende. Si no entienden, dé un resumen de la historia para explicar lo que pasó. Luego vuelva a comprobar si han captado la explicación de la historia. Después del debate de la historia usa las preguntas del profesor cuestionando a cada estudiante.

La transformación del gusano en mariposa es un gran ejemplo de la naturaleza que demuestra que nada muere en la tierra, pero sólo se convierte en diferente materia. Desde que el planeta existe siempre había una relación simbiótica entre el ser humano y la naturaleza. Esa relación simbiótica se define como una relación mutua en tomar y dar uno a otro. Algunas relaciones simbióticas son forzadas por el hecho de que uno no puede vivir sin el otro. Los científicos, estipulan que a veces esta relación puede ser beneficioso, pero a veces perjudicial. Hay dos tipos de relaciones simbióticas. Uno se llama defensa simbiótica y otra limpieza simbiótica. La limpieza simbiótica, por ejemplo, es cuando un organismo se deshace de los parásitos del cuerpo de otro organismo y los convierten en un proceso de comida para alimentar a la otra. La defensa simbiótica se muestra claramente con el pez payaso en una relación uno-a-uno. El pez payaso está protegido de los depredadores al vivir en los tentáculos de la anémona y la anémona de mar no sólo siente protección por el pez payaso de sus depredadores, pero también florece debido a su presencia. Otro ejemplo claro, un gusano una vez ha terminado su proceso de transformación y después de convertirse en mariposa, tiene una relación simbiótica con las flores dónde ambas especies se benefician de uno a otro. Según un artículo el banquete de mariposas adultas, el néctar proporcionado por flores, dibuja una larga trompa similar a una pajilla. La transformación del gusano en mariposa y su generosidad simbiótica hacia las flores nos enseña una lección de unidad para trabajar en equipo, y vivir mejor en una sociedad en la que todos tenemos que dar algo a cambio.

Parte del profesor

1- ¿Según el pasaje, qué es una relación simbiótica?
2- ¿Cómo el pez payaso y la anémona de mar trabajan?
3- ¿Cómo se explica el proceso de limpieza y defensa simbiótica?
4- ¿Cómo la actividad de la mariposa se beneficia de flor a flor?
5- ¿Según el pasaje de texto qué lección el ser humano puede aprender de la madre naturaleza?
6- Según la historia ¿qué título podría ser mejor para la lectura de comprensión?

Reading comprehension

Ask the students to read the story. After reading, ask if they understood. When "yes" pick a student to explain what he/she understood. If "no" give them a summary of the story to explain what happened. Later double check by asking all the students if they understood the story. Then get to the teacher's final questions.

Lately, more than 80% of people suffer from sleep apnea or sleep apnoea. It is a serious sleep disorder that breaks the breathing up and down continuously while the person falls asleep. Generally, people with sleep apnea have trouble sleeping at night and always feel tired during the daytime. After many years of research experts have found that there are at least 3 types of that disorder: **Obstructive sleep apnea** that occurs when the patient's throat muscles are relaxing. **Central sleep apnea,** which occurs when the patient's brain doesn't send the adequate signals to the muscles that control the breathing. **Complex sleep apnea syndrome** occurs when someone has both obstructive sleep apnea and central sleep apnea. According to the National Institute of Health, more than a million people have obstructive sleep apnea and another half ignored it. Who can be affected by it and why? Anyone can get sleep apnea, but mostly heavy set people with excessive weight are more vulnerable, because of the obstruction of the upper airway that has been blocked by fat deposit in the body. However, there are more elements that can cause it, such as abuse of alcohol, nasal congestion, smoking, heart disorder, and stroke. The neck circumference on the pillow can cause that problem as well, because of the narrowed air, but that case can be easily detected and correct when the person is having this trouble breathing. The continuous snoring he/she emits while sleeping can be automatically solved by moving or changing the person's position. In order to facilitate a relief in patients who want to be cured of sleep apnea, doctors have recommended wearing a continuous positive airway pressure (CPAP) or an automatic positive airway pressure (APAP) with a plastic face mask to allow the airflow with facility. Not every patient feels comfortable wearing a plastic mask while sleeping; some preferably accept the illustration of surgery on the mouth and throat to cease that annoying problem.

Teacher's part

1- How do you define sleep apnea?
2- How many types of sleep apnea exist?
3- If you had to choose one of the treatments recommended for sleep apnea, would you pick the use of a plastic face mask or would you rather go for the illustration of surgery?
4- Who is the most expose to it, and why?
5- What are the elements that can cause this problem?
6- According to the reading, what title will be appropriate for the text?

Lectura de comprensión

Pide a los estudiantes de leer la historia. Después de leer, pregunte si entienden. Si entienden, elige un estudiante para explicar lo que él o ella entiende. Si no entienden, dé un resumen de la historia para explicar lo que pasó. Luego vuelva a comprobar si han captado la explicación de la historia. Después del debate de la historia usa las preguntas del profesor cuestionando a cada estudiante.

Últimamente, más de ochenta porciento personas sufren de ronquidos apnea de sueño. El ronquido es un grave trastorno de sueño que rompe la respiración hacia arriba y abajo de forma continua mientras que la persona duerme. En general, las personas con ronquidos apnea de sueño tienen problemas para dormir en la noche y siempre se sienten cansados durante el día. Después de muchos años de investigación los expertos han encontrado que hay al menos tres tipos de trastornos de ronquidos apnea de sueño: **ronquidos obstructivos de sueño** que se produce cuando los músculos de la garganta del paciente son relajantes. **Ronquido central de sueño**, que se produce cuando el cerebro del paciente no envía las señales adecuadas a los músculos que controlan la respiración. El **síndrome de ronquido complejo de sueño** que ocurre cuando alguien tiene tanto el **ronquido obstructivo** y el **ronquido central de sueño**. Según el Institutos Nacional de Salud, más de un millón de personas tienen ronquidos obstructivos del sueño y la otra mitad lo ignoraron. ¿Quién puede ser afectado y porqué? Cualquier persona puede tener ronquido apnea de sueño, en mayoría las personas con exceso de peso son más vulnerables, debido a la obstrucción de vía aérea superior que ha sido bloqueado por el depósito de grasa en el cuerpo. Sin embargo, hay más elementos que puedan ocasionarlo, como el abuso de alcohol, la congestión nasal, el tabaquismo, trastornos del corazón, y derrame cerebral. La circunferencia del cuello en la almohada puede causar también este problema, debido a que el aire se redujo, pero ese caso puede ser fácilmente detectado y corregido cuando la persona está teniendo dificultad de respirar. Los ronquidos continuos que emite la persona pueden solucionarse automá -ticamente por mover o cambiar de posición a la persona. Para facilitar un alivio en los pacientes que quieren ser curados del ronquido apnea de sueño, los médicos han recomendado de llevar una presión de aire (CPAP) con una mascarilla plástico para permitir el flujo de aire con facilidad. No todos los pacientes se sienten cómodos usando una máscara de plástico mientras que duermen, algunos prefieren una ilustración de cirugía en la boca y la garganta para cesar la molestia.

Parte del profesor

1- ¿Cómo se puede definir la apnea del sueño?
2- ¿Cuántos tipos de apnea existen?
3- ¿Si tuviera que elegir uno de los tratamientos recomendados para el apnea del sueño ,¿cuál escogería?
4- ¿Quién es el más expuesto, y porqué?
5- ¿What are the elements that can cause this problem?
6- Según la historia ¿qué título podría ser mejor para la lectura de comprensión?

Reading comprehension

Ask the students to read the story. After reading, ask if they understood. When "yes" pick a student to explain what he/she understood. If "no" give them a summary of the story to explain what happened. Later double check by asking all the students if they understood the story. Then get to the teacher's final questions.

The Second World War in 1945 raised a lot of concerns in European countries. To stop the killing rose frequently for conflict of interest between neighboring countries located in the continent. In 1957 six countries took a step to be unified and set up an example for others that wished to be part of it. The six countries which started with the economic and political union to stop the bloodshed are called the founders of peace: France, Belgium, Germany, Italy, Luxembourg and Netherlands are the pioneers of the European peace. The cold war from East and West in the 1950s to 1956 had taken millions of lives, when the intervention of the soviet tanks put down the Hungarian protest against the communist regime.To face the need to remain strong in 1973 the United Kingdom (UK), Denmark and Ireland joined the union. Today the European Union is formed by twenty eight countries, those countries belonging to the Union have no migration restrictions and that union has wide benefits for whoever searching for opportunities to prosper.However, not every body has seen it this way. Many European citizens have left the continent traveling to North America looking for a new life; mostly they have traveled to the United States or Canada in order to make a living. On the other side immigrants moved from the United States to Europe seeking for a better living.In human history people always moved from East to West hoping to find a convenient place to live, but most of all is to be where they feel more comfortable.

Teacher's part

1- Why was the European Union agreement signed in 1957?
2- Why being a European citizen could be more beneficial than other countries?
3- What is the controversy raised by European citizens who left the continent?
4- How many countries today are parts of the Union?
5- How many countries started with the Unification?
6- If you had a chance to acquire a dual nationality which country in the union would you pick?

Lectura de comprensión

Pide a los estudiantes de leer la historia. Después de leer, pregunte si entienden. Si entienden, elige un estudiante para explicar lo que él o ella entiende. Si no entienden, dé un resumen de la historia para explicar lo que pasó. Luego vuelva a comprobar si han captado la explicación de la historia. Después el debate de la historia usa las preguntas del profesor cuestionando a cada estudiante.

La segunda guerra mundial en 1945 levantó muchas preocupaciones los países europeos. Para detener la matanza levantada frecuentemente por conflicto de interés entre los países vecinos localizados en el continente europeo. En 1957 seis países tomaron un paso para unificarse y dar un ejemplo a otros que desearon ser parte de ello. Los seis países que iniciaron con la unificación económica y política para detener el sangrado se llaman fundadores de paz: Francia, Belgica, Alemaña, Italia, Luxemburgo y los países bajos son los pioneros de la paz Europeo. La guerra fría del Este al Oeste en los años 1950 a 1956 habia tomado millones de vidas, cuando la intervención de los tanques Sovieticos dispersaron la protesta húngaro en contra del régimen comunista. Viendo la necesida de mantenerse fuerte en 1973 Reyno Unido (UK), Dinamarca e Irlanda alcanzaron la Union. Hoy la Unión Europea esta formado por 28 países, los países perteneciendo a la Unión no tienen restricciones migratorias y esta Unión tiene amplios beneficios a cualquiera que busca oportunidades de prosperar. Sin embargo, no todos lo han visto de esa manera. Muchos cuidadanos Europeos dejaron el continente viajando a Norte de America buscando una nueva vida, la mayoría viaja a los Estados Unidos o Canada para ganarse la vida. Por otra parte Imigrantes de Estados Unidos se mudaron a Europa buscando una mejor vida. En la historia de los seres humanos, la gente siempre se ha mudado del Este al Oeste con esperanza de encontrar un lugar conveniente para vivir, pero lo más importante es de estar dónde se sienten a gusto.

Parte del profesor

1- ¿Porqué fue firmado el acuerdo "Unión Europea" en 1957?
2- ¿Porqué siendo un cuidadano Europeo puede ser más beneficiado que otros países?
3- ¿Cuál fue la controversia por los cuidadanos Europeos que han dejado el continente?
4- ¿Cuántos países hoy hace parte de la Unión?
5- ¿Cuántos países empezaron con la unificación?
6- ¿Si tuviera la oportunidad de adquirir una doble nacionalidad ¿cuál de esos países europeos elegirías?

Reading comprehension

Ask the students to read the story. After reading, ask if they understood. When "yes" pick a student to explain what he/she understood. If "no" give them a summary of the story to explain what happened. Later double check by asking all the students if they understood the story. Then get to the teacher's final questions.

Telecommunication is one of the sustainable business which is having an incredible influence in peoples' lives today. It is very crucial in our society. Before, the telegraph was the only means that allowed people to communicate with each other at a long distance. Later the telegraph and the telephone (AT&T) service were provided to people. Today the technologies used for telecommunications have changed greatly over the last 50 years. Carlos Slim Helu born January 28, 1940, in Mexico City has been considered one of the richest men in the world from 2010-2013, as a chairman and chief executive of Telmex telecommunication. Slim had acquired his first wealth in Mexican industries at an early age. Having the monopoly with no direct competition the public had no other options but hiring telephone lines, whether to conduct business or relate to friends, and families. Later with the release of the new mobile phone named America's Movil in 2010, he had accumulated over 49 billion dollars. In November 3rd, 2015 he was nominated the #2 on the Forbes billionaires list, with a net worth estimated at 63.5 billion dollars. Telecommunication industry has overcome the past, such it was in 1968, now its offering multiple services such as software applications, cable system operators, the internet, satellite operators, and others. Without the enormous advance of telecommunication our civilization will be still considered primitive, but today it gives us the facility to communicate one to another at a long distance no matter the country we belong to. Considering the stories of other successful people who had become rich and powerful overnight, they all were inspired to make a major change in their country. Mostly their capital interests have been in education, healthcare, inventions, manufacturing, food and beverages, real estate, airlines, media, mining, oil, hospitality, entertainment, technology, retail, sports, financial services, etc. It does not matter which is our primary interest in life to become successful, the most important is doing always what we enjoy the most.

Teacher's part

1-Why should we enjoy what we are doing for a living?

2-What are the chances to succeed when it comes to inventing a non-competitive product?

3-Why do we need to discipline ourselves in what we are doing in order to succeed?

4-Which job activity are you interesting in doing to help you succeed?

5-Do you agree or disagree with the statement:"If you want to become wealthy, start at an early age"?

6-According to the story, what title would be appropriate for the text?

Lectura de comprensión

Pide a los estudiantes de leer la historia. Después de leer, pregunte si entienden. Si entienden, elige un estudiante para explicar lo que él o ella entiende. Si no entienden, dé un resumen de la historia para explicar lo que pasó. Luego vuelva a comprobar si han captado la explicación de la historia. Después del debate de la historia usa las preguntas del profesor cuestionando a cada estudiante.

Telecomunicaciones es uno de los negocios sostenible que está teniendo una influencia increíble en la vida de la gente hoy en día. Es muy crucial en nuestra sociedad. Antes, el telégrafo era el único medio que permite a las personas comunicarse uno a otro a larga distancia. Más tarde, el telégrafo y el teléfono (AT & T) fueron proporcionados a la gente como servicio. Hoy en día las tecnologías utilizadas para telecomunicaciones se han cambiado mucho en los últimos 50 años. Carlos Slim Helú nacido el veinti ocho de enero, de 1940 en la Ciudad de México ha sido considerado uno de los hombres más ricos del mundo en el año 2010 y 2013, como presidente y director ejecutivo de Telmex. Slim había adquirido su primera riqueza en la industria de México ico a una edad temprana. Teniendo el monopolio sin ninguna competencia directa, el público no tenía otra opción para contratar una línea telefónica, ya sea para hacer negocios o relacionarse con amigos y familiares. Más tarde, con el lanzamiento del nuevo teléfono móvil llamado America's Movil en 2010, Slim había acumulado 49 mil millones de dólares. El 3 de noviembre del año 2015 fue nombrado el # 2 en la lista de multimillonarios de Forbes, con una fortuna estimada en 63.5 millones de dólares. La industria de telecomunicación ha superado el pasado, como lo fue en 1968, ahora ofrece un servicio múltiple tales como aplicaciones de software, operadores de sistemas de cable, internet, operadores de satélites, y otros. Sin el enorme avance de telecomunicación nuestra civilización se considería todavía primitiva, pero hoy en día nos dio la facilidad de comunicarnos uno a otro a larga distancia sin importar el país que pertenecemos. Tomando en cuenta las historias de otras personas éxitosas que llegaron a ser ricos y poderosos de la noche a la mañana, todos ellos se inspiraron en hacer un cambio importante en sus países. Sobre todo sus capitales interés han sido: educación, la atención sanitaria, las invenciones, la manufactura, los alimentos y bebidas, los bienes raíces, las líneas aéreas, los medios de comunicaciónes, la minería, el petróleo, la hospitalidad, el entretenimiento, la tecnología, el comercio minorista, los deportes, los servicios financieros, etc no importa cúal será nuestro interés primordial en la vida para tener éxito, lo más importante siempre es hacer lo que más nos apasiona.

Parte del profesor

1- Por qué debemos disfrutar a lo que nos dedicamos para ganarse la vida?
2- ¿Cuáles son las posibilidades de éxito cuando se trata de inventar un producto no competitivo?
3- ¿Por qué tenemos que disciplinarnos en lo que estamos haciendo para tener éxito?
4- ¿Qué actividad de trabajo estás interesado en hacer para tener éxito?
5- ¿Estás de acuerdo con esta confirmación "Si tu quieres ser rico, empieza a edad temprana"?
6- Según la historia ¿qué título podría ser mejor para la lectura de comprensión?

Reading comprehension

Ask the students to read the story. After reading, ask if they understood. When "yes" pick a student to explain what he/she understood. If "no"give them a summary of the story to explain what happened. Later double check by asking all the students if they understood the story. Then get to the teacher's final questions.

Hong Kong is a main attraction center for commercialization. In 1842 after China has ceded from the United Kingdom(UK) a parcel of its territory, such as the <u>Hong Kong Island</u>, the <u>Kowloon</u> <u>Peninsula</u>, and the land between the Kowloon Peninsula, the <u>Sham Chun River,</u> and neighboring islands, citizen in Hong Kong have been allowed to carry a British passport with limited rights. In spite of the privilege granted to Hong Kongers having a British passport, People's Republic of China (PRC) did not recognize Hong Kongers with Chinese ancestry as British. Hong Kong passed all its rights to the UK after the Chinese lost the opium war, mostly it has been taken because of its location as the world's most important economic center, located between Japan and Singapore, it facilitates the shipping and air cargo of the western Pacific, connects with the major port of entry and trade of China, where investments were flowing. Base on commerce till today, Singapore, Hong Kong's neighbor remains the world largest container port. In 2010, China became the world's largest manufacturer. According to research it has 23.2% share of manufacturing that overpasses the U.S share in the world manufacturing activity. In 2008, the weakening U.S economy has forced most of the companies to move to China due to the cheap manufacturing and business opportunities offering by the Chinese government. In 1978 the country was considering very poor, but its market reform has given a rapid growth that made it overcome many other countries. Due not only to its history where the British have left most of their wealth after their sovereignty over Hong Kong for 156 years, but as well for the hard work and collaboration of every Chinese Citizen who understood how important it was to make a radical economic growth through manufacturing and commercialization. This example must be taken by other countries which have the natural resources to develop themselves, but not being capable of doing so because of the lack of collective agreement.

Teacher's part

1- Why did Hong Kong become a British colony?
2- What makes today China the world's largest manufacturer?
3- What was the benefit the British government offered to Hong Kongers in 1842?
4- What was the controversy raised between Hong Kongers and the People's Republic Of China?
5- Why could it have been a national treat for the UK if the British Citizen has been allowed to all Hong Kongers with no limited rights?
6- According to the story, what title will be appropriate for the text?

Lectura de comprensión

Pide a los estudiantes de leer la historia. Después de leer, pregunte si entienden. Si entienden, elige un estudiante para explicar lo que él o ella entiende. Si no entienden, dé un resumen de la historia para explicar lo que pasó. Luego vuelva a comprobar si han captado la explicación de la historia. Después del debate de la historia usa las preguntas del profesor cuestionando a cada estudiante.

Hong Kong es un centro de atracción principal para comercialización. En 1842, después que China ha cedido al Reino Unido (UK) una parcela de su territorio, como la isla de Hong Kong, la península de Kowloon, y la tierra entre la península de Kowloon, el río Sham Chun y las islas vecinas, se ha permitido a ciudadano de Hong Kong obtener un pasaporte Británico con derechos limitados. A pesar del privilegio otorgado a los habitantes de Hong Kong que tuvieron un pasaporte Británico, República Popular de China no reconoció los hongkoneses con ascendencia china como Británico. Hong Kong pasó todos sus derechos al Reino Unido después de que los chinos perdieron la guerra del opio, sobre todo se ha tomado debido a su ubicación como centro económico más importante del mundo que se encuentra entre Japón y Singapur, que facilita el transporte marítimo y aéreo del Pacífico oeste, conecta con el principal puerto de entrada del comercio de China, dónde las inversiones fluían. Basado en el comercio hasta hoy, Singapur, vecina de Hong Kong sigue siendo el puerto de contenedores más grande del mundo. En 2010, China se convirtió en el mayor fabricante del mundo. Basado en investigaciónes tiene el 23.2% de manufacturas que han rebasado a Estados Unidos en la actividad de fabricación en el mundo. En 2008, la economía de los Estados Unidos se debilitó y ha obligado a la mayoría de las empresas a trasladarse a China debido a la mano de obra barata y oportunidad de negocio ofrecido por el gobierno Chino. En 1978, el país se consideraba muy pobre, pero su reforma en el mercado le ha dado un rápido crecimiento que le hizo superar muchos otros países, esto es debido no solamente por su historia en el que los Británicos han dejado la mayor parte de su riqueza después de su soberanía sobre Hong Kong desde hace 156 años, sino por el duro trabajo y la colaboración de todos los cuidadanos Chinos que entendieron lo importante era de crecer económicamente a través de la fabricación y comercializaciones. Este ejemplo debe ser adoptado por otros países que tienen los recursos naturales para desarrollarse, pero no son capaces de hacerlo debido a la falta de toma de decisión colectiva.

Parte del profesor

1- Porqué Hong Kong se había convertido en una colonia Británica?
2- ¿Qué hace China el fabricante más grande del mundo el día de hoy?
3- ¿Cuál beneficio el gobierno Británico ofreció a los Hongkoneses en 1842?
4- ¿Cuál fue la polémica entre Hongkoneses y la gente de la República Popular de China?
5- ¿Porqué podría ser una amenaza nacional para el Reino Unido si la ciudadanía Británica había otorgado a todos los hongkoneses sin derechos limitados?
6- Según la historia ¿qué título podría ser mejor para la lectura de comprensión?

Reading comprehension

Ask the students to read the story. After reading, ask if they understood. When "yes" pick a student to explain what he/she understood. If "no" give them a summary of the story to explain what happened. Later double check by asking all the students if they understood the story. Then get to the teacher's final questions.

The solar system consists of the sun and the planetary system that orbits it directly or indirectly. The sun plays a very important role on our planet and without it, our planet would have been uninhabited. Its surface is about 12,000 times larger than our planet which means the sun's magnetic field is very wide to warm our atmosphere and without the sun activities around the earth, our planet will return to the icy era, as it was 500 million years ago. The sun keeps us alive and our planet warm, heating the surface, help the lakes, flowing through our wood and keep our plants flourishing in their process of development. The radiation that emits from the sun is reflected on the earth's surface and the clouds; however, we are not affected by it due to the ozone cape that protects us. Research has known five ice ages in the earth's history, the last glacial period of the Quaternary ended up approximately 11,700 years ago with the start of the Holocene epoch, base on climate proxies and the paleoclimatologists study. A million years ago, it was very difficult to survive an icy era, but actually, Mankind has developed different types of technology in order to resist any climate change whether it comes with a low or high temperature. Most of the technologies such as the panel solar and others have been created to bring artificial heat in every household on the planet. Not only when the winter comes but also if the icy era event occurs once again in our history. Our planet is not the only planet benefited from the magnetic field of the sun. Its magnetic field expands further beyond the space and has reached the planet Pluto, and this extension magnetic field has been called by the scientists Interplanetary Magnetic Field" (IMF).

Teacher's part

1- What would our planet become without the magnetic field emitted by the sun?
2- According to the passage, how long ago did our planet suffer the icy era?
3- What have scientists done to protect us in the event if an icy era occurs again?
4- What could happen if the ozone cape had not been there to protect us from the radiation?
5- Which other planet is benefited by the magnetic field of the sun?
6- What do scientists call the extension of the magnetic field of the sun?

Lectura de comprensión

Pide a los estudiantes de leer la historia. Después de leer, pregunte si entienden. Si entienden, elige un estudiante para explicar lo que él o ella entiende. Si no entienden, dé un resumen de la historia para explicar lo que pasó. Luego vuelva a comprobar si han captado la explicación de la historia. Después del debate de la historia usa las preguntas del profesor cuestionando a cada estudiante.

El sistema solar está formado por el sol y el sistema planetario que gira a su alrededor directa o indirectamente. El sol juega un papel muy importante en nuestro planeta y sin él nuestro planeta hubiera sido inhabitado. Su superficie es de aproximadamente 12.000 mil veces más grande que nuestro planeta lo que significa que el campo magnético del sol es muy amplia para calentar nuestra atmósfera y sin las actividades del sol alrededor de la tierra, nuestro planeta pudiera volver a la era de hielo, como lo fue anteriormente hace 500 millones años. El sol nos mantiene vivos y nuestro planeta caliente, calienta la superficie, ayuda a los lagos fluir a través de nuestros bosques y mantiene nuestras plantas florecentes en su proceso de desarrollo. La radiación que emite el sol se refleja en la superficie de la tierra y las nubes, sin embargo, no nos afectamos debido a la capa de ozono que nos protege. De acuerdo a investigaciones cinco edades de hielo ha sido conocido en historia de la tierra, el último período glacial cuaternario terminó hace aproximadamente11.700 años con el inicio de la época Holoceno basado en los proxis climáticos y el estudio de paleo climatólogos. Hace un millón de años, era muy difícil sobrevivir a una era glacial, actualmente, el ser humano ha desarrollado diferentes tipos de tecnología con el fin de resistir a cualquier cambio climático sin importarse que sea una temperatura baja o alta. La mayor parte de la tecnología, tal como el panel solar y otros han sido creados para traer un calor artificial en todos los hogares en el planeta. No solamente cuando llegue el invierno, pero también en el evento que vuelva a presentar una vez más una era de hielo en nuestra historia. Nuestro planeta no es el único planeta beneficiado del campo magnético del sol. Su campo magnético se expande más allá del espacio y ha llegado al planeta Plutón, la extensión a este campo magnético ha sido llamada por los científicos **"campo magnético interplanetario."**

Parte del profesor

1-¿En qué se convertirá nuestro planeta sin el campo magnético emitido por el sol?

2-¿Según el pasaje, hace cuánto tiempo nuestro planeta ha sufrido la era glacial?

3-¿Qué ha hecho los científicos para protegernos en el evento que vuelva a occurir una era glacial?

4-¿Qué pasaría si la capa de ozono no había estado allí para protegernos de la radiación?

5-¿Qué otro planeta está beneficiado por el campo magnético del sol?

6-¿Cómo los científicos llamaron la extensión del campo magnético del Sol?

Reading comprehension

Ask the students to read the story. After reading, ask if they understood. When "yes" pick a student to explain what he/she understood. If "no" give them a summary of the story to explain what happened. Later double check by asking all the students if they understood the story. Then get to the teacher's final questions.

The violation of law is a crime against any country's constitution. That crime sometimes could be a sentence to a lifetime in prison or a short period of time. Misdemeanors and felonies have been considered one of those violations. What is a misdemeanor and what is a felony? A misdemeanor is a minor crime committed in the legal law system. For instance, infractions, robberies are considered misdemeanor crimes usually punished for years in jail. In the United States people, can be released paying for a bail if they have been arrested for a misdemeanor law violation, though a person who committed this crime mostly is on probation passing a time doing community service after incarceration. The United States Supreme Court has made no exception of age, adults, and minors can be judged and sentenced for a long time depending on the gravity of their crimes. A felony is a federal violation mostly considered a high crime, sometimes sentenced to the death penalty depending on the state law in the United States. An example of this violation is if someone crossed the United States border with no prior authorization by the U.S government repetively after being arrested, this will be a federal violation. Both misdemeanors and felonies can have a severe impact on someone's life at a professional level. If somebody is guilty of any of this crime, that person can't work either for the government or at any private companies, unless that person has his own business. There are many online records set up to check on people's personal background to know whether or not they have been victimized by either misdemeanor or felony. Among those links we count the vinelink. Once somebody is put into that system it will pursue him for the rest of his life and there is no way that can be deleted. A country's law is always different from another, in certain sub-developing countries government has no access to that information unless it has been sent to them by another country in order to search for a fugitive and that information can't be accessed by the public but only by the foreign government in concern.

Teacher's part

1- According to the story, define what is a misdemeanor and a felony?
2- How can a misdemeanor and a felony affects our lives?
3- What caution should be taken to avoid this and protect our professional lives?
4- What is the advantage and disadvantage of a developing and sub-developing country?
5- At what social level are people in jail?
6- According to the story, what title would be appropriate for the text?

Lectura de comprensión

Pide a los estudiantes de leer la historia. Después de leer, pregunte si entienden. Si entienden, elige un estudiante para explicar lo que él o ella entiende. Si no entienden, dé un resumen de la historia para explicar lo que pasó. Luego vuelva a comprobar si han captado la explicación de la historia. Después del debate de la historia usa las preguntas del profesor cuestionando a cada estudiante.

La violación de la ley es un crimen frente a la constitución de cualquier país. Este crimen a veces podría ser sentenciado de por vida en prisión o en un corto período. Delitos menores y delitos graves han sido considerados como uno de esas violaciónes. ¿Qué es un misdemeanor y qué es un felony? Un misdemeanor es un delito menor cometido en el sistema de derecho legal en los Estados Unidos. Por ejemplo, las infracciones, los robos se consideran como delitos menores por lo general castigado por años, en los Estados Unidos las personas, pueden ponerse en libertad pagando una fianza si han sido detenidos por Misdemeanor, así que si una persona comete este crimen debe pasar un tiempo en aprobación haciendo un servicio comunitario después de su encarcelamiento. Es decir el Tribunal Supremo de los Estados Unidos no ha hecho ninguna excepción de edad, los adultos y los menores pueden ser juzgados y condenados por un largo tiempo dependiendo de la gravedad de sus delitos. Un felony es una violación federal sobre todo considerado como un crimen de alta gravedad, a veces condenado por pena de muerte dependiendo de la ley del Estado en los Estados Unidos. Un ejemplo de esta violación si alguien cruzó la frontera de los Estados Unidos repetivamente después de ser arestado sin la autorización previa por parte del gobierno, esto será considerado como una violación federal. Tanto el delito Misdemeanor y Felony puede tener un grave impacto en la vida de alguien a nivel profesional. Una persona culpable de cualquiera de estos crímenes no puede trabajar ni por el gobierno ni por cualquier empresa, al menos que esa persona sea dueño de su propio negocio, hay muchos registros en línea creados para permitir a cualquier persona checar los antecedentes personales de otras, VINELink es uno de ellos. Una vez que alguien se pone en ese sistema eso lo perseguirá por el resto de su vida y no hay manera de eliminarlo. La ley de un país es siempre diferente de otro, en algunos países sub desarrollados el gobierno no tiene acceso a esa información al menos que haya sido enviado con el fin de buscar una persona furgitiva y esta información no puede ser visto por el público, sino solamente por el gobierno en respeto.

Parte del profesor

1- ¿De acuerdo con la historia define lo que es misdemeanor y felony?
2- ¿Cómo misdemeanor y felony puede afectar toda nuestra vida?
3- ¿Qué precaución debemos tomar para evitar esto y proteger nuestra vida profesional?
4- ¿Cuál es la ventaja y desventaja de un país desarrollado y un país sub desarrollado?
5- ¿A qué nivel social está la gente en la cárcel?
6- Según la historia ¿qué título podría ser mejor para esta lectura de comprensión?

Reading comprehension

Ask the students to read the story. After reading, ask if they understood. When "yes" pick a student to explain what he/she understood. If "no"give them a summary of the story to explain what happened. Later double check by asking all the students if they understood the story. Then get to the teacher's final questions.

Marriage is a sacred union build by society where both men and women vow to love, respect, protect each other until death sets them apart. On the other hand, polygamy has been considered a controversy against marriage. Polygamy is the practice or condition of having more than one husband and wife.In our modern time, it's been viewed as a sin by religious beliefs and has been declaring an act of immorality. Back in the day it was a norm in Arab tribes, having two or three wives was a noble thing to do. Research has shown that polygamy comes in three different ways: **polygyny (a man has the right to have more than two wives at the same time), polyandry (a woman has the right to have more than one husband).** Thousand of years ago, it was practiced in the West African continent, as in India, and ancient Greece. That practice took place as well in the early years of Christian church. The Native American Indian has adopted it as well, but this ceased in 1890-1899 with President Wilford Woodruff. That time all polygamous members had been considered a threat, and rejected by their own church. Lately, this practice has been voted and permitted in China in 1949. What drew people to practice polygamy? Back in time researchers have never been interested in finding what causes this subject due to lack of information. Today this subject has been considered taboo in our modern society; still there are other countries with this ideology.

Teacher's part

1- According to the text, what is the controversy between marriage and polygamy?
2- Why polygamy has been considered a threat to marriage?
3- What is the difference between polygyny and polyandry?
4- If you had to take a side between polygamy and marriage, which would, you take?
5- Considering the story, what is your point of view about polygamy?
6- According to the story, what title would be appropriate for the text?

Lectura de comprensión

Pide a los estudiantes de leer la historia. Después de leer, pregunte si entienden. Si entienden, elige un estudiante para explicar lo que él o ella entiende. Si no entienden, de un resumen de la historia para explicar lo que pasó. Luego vuelva a comprobar si han captado la explicación de la historia. Después del debate de la historia usa las preguntas del profesor cuestionando a cada estudiante.

El matrimonio es una unión sagrada construido por la sociedad en el que tanto los hombres y las mujeres se comprometieron de amarse, respetarse, protegerse uno a otro hasta que la muerte les separe. Por otro lado, la poligamia ha sido considerada como una controversia en contra el matrimonio. La poligamia es la práctica o condición de tener más de un marido y mujer. En nuestra época se ha considerado como pecado por las creencias religiosas y ha sido declarada un acto de inmoralidad. Hace tiempo en las tribus árabes, tener dos o tres esposas era una norma y algo noble. Investigación ha demostrado que la poligamia se presenta en tres formas diferentes: la poliginia, un hombre tiene derecho de tener más de dos esposas al mismo tiempo, la poliandria, una mujer tiene el derecho de tener más de un marido. Hace mil años, esa norma se ha practicado en el continente de África Occidental como en la India y la antigua Grecia. Esa práctica se llevó a cabo, también en los primeros años de la historia de la iglesia Cristiana. El nativo indio americano lo ha adoptado también, pero esto se ha dejado en 1890 al 1899 con el presidente Wilford Woodruff, en ese tiempo todos los miembros polígamos han sido considerados como una amenaza y rechazado por su propia iglesia. Últimamente, esta práctica se ha votado y permitido en China en el año 1949. ¿Qué atrajo a la gente a practicar la poligamia? Tiempo atrás los investigadores nunca han estado interesados en la búsqueda de las causas de este tema debido a la falta de información. Hoy este tema ha sido considerado tabú en nuestra sociedad moderna, sin embargo todavía hay otros países con esta ideología.

Parte del profesor

1- De acuerdo con el texto, ¿cuál es la controversia entre el matrimonio y la poligamia?
2- Porqué la poligamia ha sido considerado como una amenaza al institución de matrimonio?
3- ¿Cuál es la diferencia entre la poligamia y la poliandria?
4- Si tuvieras que tomar un voto entre la poligamia y el matrimonio, ¿qué lado tomarías?
5- De acuerdo a la historia ¿cuál es su punto de vista acerca de la poligamia?
6- Según la historia ¿qué título podría ser mejor para esta lectura de comprensión?

Reading comprehension

Ask the students to read the story. After reading, ask if they understood. When "yes" pick a student to explain what he/she understood. If "no" give them a summary of the story to explain what happened. Later double check by asking all the students if they understood the story. Then get to the teacher's final questions.

Lately, social media such as the internet and television have become almost indispensable in a person's life. With the signal of the satellite it is easier now to communicate anywhere in the world, where there is internet connection. Almost everything can be found on the internet when it comes to searching for information related to business or any other questionable issues. As the internet can have a positive impact on our lives it can also bring a negative effect on us and that negative effect can mostly affect children. Research has proven that seventy five and ninety(75 &90%) percent of teenagers use the internet to send instant messages and they are curious to explore other malicious subjects in it. They also became addicted to online video games neglect their school tasks. The majority of people spend more time on the internet chatting instead of giving more attention directly to their love ones and that has created the loss of the human touch According to the American Psychological Association spending a lot of time on the web can have both negative and positive effects on young people. On the other hand, television has had a potential reaction not only on adults but children as well as young people. From the 19th to the 20th century, today's news is more accessible to be informed about what is really happening in the world, thanks to the invention of the television. Television has been used as home entertainment for everyone to be enjoyed during their spare time. It gives us quick learning about things, however, expert analysis proved that too much television is not good for our mind and health. It can entertain us and it can be at times damaging and harmful for adults, young people and especially for children, whose brain is in process of growing. Watching too mucho television with them will decline their creativity or imagination and make it hard for them to think on their own. Besides, violent movies will not be appropriate for them as they might lead toward a bad direction that will end up with violence. Whatsoever the cons and the pros, internet and television might present, the world would not become what it is today without the advance of technology.

Teacher's part

1- What are the pros and cons about television and the internet usage?
2- How does television and the internet impact people's lives?
3- Why is not recommended for children to watch too much t.v?
4- What are the risks that the internet represents for children?
5- What is the percentage of teenagers in the U.S that used the internet to chat?
6- According to the story, what title would be appropriate for the text?

Lectura de comprensión

Pide a los estudiantes de leer la historia. Después de leer, pregunte si entienden. Si entienden, elige un estudiante para explicar lo que él o ella entiende. Si no entienden, dé un resumen de la historia para explicar lo que pasó. Luego vuelva a comprobar si han captado la explicación de la historia. Después del debate de la historia usa las preguntas del profesor cuestionando a cada estudiante.

Últimamente, los medios sociales tales como el internet y la televisión se han vuelto casi indispensables en la vida de una persona. Con la señal del satélite es más fácil ahora comunicarse con alguien en cualquier parte del mundo, donde haya conexión de internet. Casi todo se puede encontrar a través de internet a la hora de buscar información relacionada a los negocios o cualquier otro asunto. Mientras que el internet puede tener un impacto positivo en nuestras vidas también nos puede traer un efecto negativo y este efecto negativo puede afectar principalmente a los niños. Las investigaciones han demostrado que el 75 y 90 por ciento de los adolescentes utilizan internet para enviar mensajes instantáneos y explorar otro asunto malicioso. También los videos juegos se convierten en adicción y les hacen desatender sus tareas escolares. La mayoría de la gente tiene más tiempo absorbente en el chat en vez de dar más atención dirigida a su a sus seres queridos y eso ha creado una pérdida de contacto humano. Según la Asociación Americana de Psicología pasar mucho tiempo en el web puede tener efectos tantos negativos como positivos en los jóvenes. Por otro lado, la televisión ha tenido una reacción potencial no sólo en los adultos, pero también en los niños y los jóvenes, después de su invención del siglo 19 al 20, la noticia de hoy es más accesible para saber lo que está pasando en el mundo gracias a la invención de la televisión. La televisión ha sido utilizado como un entretenimiento en el hogar para todo el mundo en tiempo libre y nos da un rápido aprendizaje acerca de las cosas, sin embargo, el análisis de expertos demostraron que el exceso de ver televisión no es bueno para la mente y la salud, ya que puede ser a veces dañinos y perjudiciales para los adultos, los jóvenes y en especial para los niños, cuyo cerebro está en proceso de crecimiento. Ver demasiada televisión con ellos disminuirá su creatividad e imaginación y hacer que sea difícil para ellos pensar por sí mismos. A parte, las películas violentas no serán apropiadas para ellos, ya que les dirigirían a la violencia. A pesar del por y contra que presenta el internet y la televisión, el mundo no se convertiría en lo que es el día de hoy sin el avance de la tecnología.

Parte del profesor

1- ¿Cuál es el lado positivo y negativo del uso de la televisión y del internet?
2- ¿Cómo la televisión y el internet impactan la vida de las personas?
3- ¿Por qué no se recomienda a los niños ver demasiada televisión?
4- ¿Cuáles son los riesgos que representan el internet para los niños?
5- ¿Qué porcentaje de adolescentes en Estados Unidos utilizan el internet para chatear?
6- Según la historia ¿qué título podría ser mejor para la lectura de comprensión?

COMMON IRREGULAR VERBS IN SPANISH

VERBOS IREGULARES COMÚNES EN ESPAÑOL

To want	querrer	To play	jugar
To follow	perder	To discover	descubrir
To return	volver	To repeat	repetir
To request/ask for	pedir	To show/demonstrate	demostrar
To remember/remind	recordar	To move	mover
To obtain	conseguir	To close	cerrar
To start	comenzar	To stop	detener
To serve	servir	To refer	referir
To maintain	mantener	To elect/choose	elegir
To open	abrir	To propose	proponer
To convert/ to change	convertir	To walk	andar
To recognize	reconocer	To disappear	desaparecer
To offer	ofrecer	To establish	establecer
To deny/refuse	negar	To include	incluir
To solve/resolve/settle	resolver	To prevent	prevenir
To impose/enforce	imponer	To deserve/to merit	merecer
To warn	advertir	To cover	cubrir
To verify/check	comprobar	To construct	construir
To extend	extender	To defend	defender
To intervern	intervenir	To express	expresar
To stay/remain	pertenecer	To save/to rescue	salvar,rescatar
To expose	exponer	To observe	observar
To advise	aconsejar	To notice	notificar,darse cuenta

REGULAR VERBS
VERBOS REGULARES

PRESENT SIMPLE/TIEMPO PRESENTE	PAST SIMPLE/TIEMPO PASADO
Abandon(abandon) abandonar Adapt(adapt) adaptar	Abandoned(abandond) Adapted(adaptid)
Add(add) sumar, agregar Admire(admaier) admirar Admit(admit) admitir, confesar	Added(addid) Admired(admaierd) Admited(admitid)
Anounce(anons) anunciar Answer(enser) contestar Appear(apir) aparecer	Anounced(anonst) Answered(enserd) Appeared(apird)
Ask(asc) preguntar Ask for(asc for) pedir Attack(atac) atacar	Asked(askt) Asked for(askt for) Attacked(atact)
Attend(atend) asistir, atender Award(aword) ortogar Achieve(achiv) lograr	Attended(atendid) Awarded(awordid) Achieved(achivt)
Bake(beik) hornear Believe(biliv) creer Brush(brash) cepillar	Baked(beikt) Believed(bilivd) Brushed(brasht)
Burn(bern) quemar Call(coll) llamar Change(cheinch) cambiar	Burned(bernd) Called(cold) Changed(cheincht)
Clean(klin) limpiar Climb(claimb) escalar Close(clos) cerrar	Cleaned(klind) Climbed(claimbd) Closed(closd)
Cook(cuc) cocinar Complete(complit) completar Collect(colect) cobrar	Cooked(cuct) Completed(complitid) Collected(colectid)
Compose(compos) componer Communicate(comiunikeit) comunicar Conquere(conker) conquistar	Composed(compost) Communicated(comiunikeitid) Conquered(conkerd)
Construct(conschuorct) construir Combine(combain) combinar Cover(cover) cubrir	Constructed(conschuorctid) Combined(combaind) Covered(coverd)

PRESENT SIMPLE/TIEMPO PRESENTE	PAST SIMPLE/TIEMPO PASADO
Cross(cros) cruzar Cry(crai) llorar Copy(copi) copiar	Crossed(crost) Cried(craid) Copied(copid)
Celebrate(selebreit) celebrar Carry(kerri) cargar Color(color) colorear	Celebrated(selebreitid) Carried(kerrid) Colored(colord)
Decide(disaid) decidir Dance(dens) bailar Dress(dress) vestir	Decided(disaidid) Danced(denst) Dressed(dresst)
Divide(divaid) dividir Decorate(decoreit) decorar Deliver(deliver) entregar	Divided(divaidid) Decorated(decoreitid) Delivered(deliverd)
Defeat (difit) vencer Demonstrate(demonstrueit) demostrar Design(disaign) diseñar	Defeated(defitid) Demonstrated(demonstrueitid) Designed(desaignd)
Develop(develop) desarrollar Die(dai) morir Discuss(discas) discutir	Developed(developt) Died(daid) Discussed(discast)
Dream(drim) soñar End(end) terminar Erase(ireiss) borrar	Dreamed(drimd) Ended(endid) Erased(ireisst)
Enjoy(enyoi) disfrutar Enter(enter) ingresar Excuse(exkius) disculpar	Enjoyed(enyoid) Entered(enterd) Excused(exkiusd)
Explain(explain) explicar Exist(exist) existir Express(expres) expreasar	Explained(explaind) Existed(existid) Expressed(exprest)
Explore(exploor) explorar Fail(feil) fallar Finish(finish) terminar	Explored(explordFail ed(feild) Finished(finisht)
Fix(fix) arreglar Follow(falou) seguir Fry(frai) freir	Fixed(fixd) Followed(falod) Fried(fraid)
Face(feis) enfrentar Fill(fill) llenar Fish(fish) pescar	Faced(feisd) Filled(filld) Fished(fisht)
Figure calcular Film(film) filmar Faint(feint) desmayar	Figured Filmed(filmd) Fainted(feintid)

PRESENT SIMPLE/TIEMPO PRESENTE	PAST SIMPLE/TIEMPO PASADO
Guess(gues) adivinar	Guessed(guest)
Happen(japen) suceder	Happened(japend)
Hate(jeit) odiar	Hated(jeitid)
Help(herlp) ayudar	Helped(jelpt)
Hope(jop) esperar	Hoped(jopt)
Hug(jog) abrazar	Hugged(jogd)
Hunt(jant) cazar	Hunted(jantid)
Hurry(hori) apresurar	Hurried(horid)
Invite(invait) invitar	Invited(invaitid)
Introduce(introdus) introducir	Introduced(introdust)
Insist(insist) insistir	Insisted(insistid)
Identify(aidentifai) identificar	Identified(aidentifaid)
Imagine(imayin) imaginar	Imagined(imayind)
Inform(inform) informar	Informed(informd)
Insult(insolt) insultar	Insulted(insoltid)
Infect infectar	Infected(infectid)
Improve(impruv) mejorar	Improved(impruvd)
Invent(invent) inventar	Invented(inventid)
Investigate(investigeit) investigar	Investigated(investigeitid)
Illustrate(ilustreit) ilustrar	Illustrated(ilustreitid)
Jump(yamp) brincar	Jumped(yampt)
Joke(youk) bromear	Joked(youkt)
Justify(yostifai) justificar	Justified(yostifaid)
Kick patear	Kicked(kikt)
Kill matar	Killed(kild)
Knock(noc) tocar	Knocked
Knit(nit) tejer	Knitted(nitid)
Land(lend) aterrizar	Landed(landid)
Laugh(laf) reir	Laughed(laft)
Learn(lern) aprender	Learned(lernd)
Like(laic) gustar	Liked(laict)
Live(liv) vivir	Lived(livd)
Love(lov) amar	Loved(lovd)
Listen to(lisen tu) escuchar	Listened to(lisend tu)
Lock(lorc) cerrar con llave	Locked(lorct)
Look at(luk at) mirar	Looked at(luk tat)
Look for(luk for) buscar	Looked for(lukt for)
Liberate(libereit) liberar	Liberated(libereitid)
Marry(merri) casar	Married(merrid)

203

PRESENT SIMPLE/TIEMPO PRESENTE	PAST SIMPLE/TIEMPO PASADO
Miss(mis) extrañar Move(muv) mover Mix(mics) mezclar	Missed(mist) Moved(muvd) Mixed(micst)
Multiply(moltiplai) multiplicar Name(neim) nombrar Need(nid) necesitar	Multiplied(moltiplaid) Named(neimd) Needed(nidid)
Observe(observ) observer Offer(ofer) ofrecer Open(open) abrir	Observed(observd) Offered(oferd) Opened(opend)
Obey(obei) obedecer Organize(organais) organizar Owe(ou) adeudar	Obeyed(obeid) Organized(organaisd) Owed(oud)
Practice(practis) practicar Paint(peint) pintar Pass(pas) pasar	Practiced(practist) Painted(peintid) Passed(past)
Press(pres) presionar Pick(pick) recoger Play(pley) jugar	Pressed(prest) Picked(pickt) Played(pleyd)
Promise(promis) prometer Pull(pul) jalar Push((push) empujar	Promised(promist) Pulled(puld) Pushed(pusht)
Present(present) presentar Produce(prodius) producir Prefer(prifer) preferir	Presented(presentid) Produced(prodiust) Prefered(priferd)
Prepare(priper) preparar Pray(prey) rezar Print(print) imprimir	Prepared(priperd) Prayed(preyd) Printed(printid)
Produce(prodius) producir Receive(riciv) recibir Remember(rimember) recordar	Produced(prodiust) Received(ricivd) Remembered(rimemberd)
Repeat(ripit) repetir Rest(rest) descansar Return(ritern) regresar	Repeated(ripitid) Rested(restid) Returned(reternd)
Rain(rein) llover Raise(reis) criar Reach(rich) alcanzar	Rained(reind) Raised(reisd) Reached(richt)
Record(ricord) grabar Remind(rimaind) recordar Realize(rilais) darse cuenta	Recorded(ricordid) Reminded(rimaindid) Realized(rilaisd)

PRESENT SIMPLE/TIEMPO PRESENTE	PAST SIMPLE/TIEMPO PASADO
Repair(riper) reparar Rule(rul) regir Smile(smail) sonreir	Repaired(riperd) Ruled(ruld) Smiled(smaild)
Show mostrar Success tener exito Scream(scrim) gritar	Showed(showd) Succeeded(soksidid) Screamed(scrimd)
Shout(shut) gritar a voces Start(start) comenzar Study(stadi) estudiar	Shouted(shutid) Started(startid) Studied(stadid)
Sweat(suet) sudar Serve(serv) servir Save(seyv) ahorrar, salvar	Sweat(suet) Served(servd) Saved(seyvd)
Satisfy(satisfay) satisfacer Sail(seil) navegar Supply(soplai) proveer	Satisfied(satisfayd) Sailed(seild) Supplied(soplaid)
Surrender(surrender) ceder Surround(surraund) rodear Try(chruay) tratar	Surrendered(surrenderd) Surrounded((surraundid) Tried(chruayd)
Talk(toc) hablar Thank(tenk) agradecer Touch(toch) tocar	Talked(toct) Thanked(tenkt) Touched(tocht)
Test(test) probar Train(truen) entrenar Transfer(transfer) transferir	Tested(testid) Trained(truend) Transfered(transferd)
Travel(chruavel) viajar Turn(tern) dar vuelta Use(ius) usar	Traveled(chruavel) Turned(ternd) Used(iusd)
Underline(underlain) subrayar Visit(visit) visitar Wait(ueit) esperar	Underlined(underlaind) Visited(visitid) Waited(uetid)
Wash(wash) lavar Watch(watch) observar Work(work) trabajar	Washed(washt) Watched(watcht) Worked(workt)
Wave(weyv) ondear Wax(wax) encerar Walk(wolk) caminar	Waved(weyvd) Waxed(waxt) Walked(wolkd)
Wrinkle(rinkol) arrugar Worry(wori) preocuparse Waste(weist) desperdiciar	Wrinkled(rinkold) Worried(worid) Wasted(weistid)

IRREGULAR VERBS

VERBOS IREGULARES

PRESENT SIMPLE/TIEMPO PRESENTE	PAST SIMPLE/TIEMPO PASADO
Am, Are, Is ser o estar Become(bikom) llegar a ser Break(breik) romper Blow(blo) soplar	Was,were(uas,uer) Became(bikeim) Broke(brok) Blew(blu)
Build construir Bring traer Buy (bai) comprar	Built(bilt) Brought(brot) Bought(bot)
Can(ken) poder Choose escojer Catch(catch) atrapar	Could(culd) Chose(choss) Caught(cot)
Cut(cot) cortar Come venir Do(du) hacer	Cut(cot) Came(keim) Did(did)
Draw(dro) dibujar Drink tomar Drive conducir	Drew(dru) Drank(yuenk) Drove(drouv)
Eat(it) comer Fall(fol) caer Feed alimentar	Ate(eit) Fell(fel) Fed(fed)
Feel(fil) sentir Find encontrar Fight(fait) luchar	Felt(felt) Found(faond) Fought(fort)
Fly(flai)volar Forget olvidar Freeze(friss) congelar	Flew(flu) Forgot(forgat) Froze(fross)
Give dar Go ir Get conseguir	Gave(gueiv) Went(went) Got(gat)
Grow crecer Have(jav) tener Hear(hir) oir	Grew(gru) Had(jad) Heard(herd)

PRESENT SIMPLE/TIEMPO PRESENTE	PAST SIMPLE/TIEMPO PASADO
Hide(haid) esconder	Hid(hid)
Hit golpear	Hit(hit)
Hold sostener	Held
Hurt(hert) herir	Hurt(hert)
Keep(kip) empezar, guardar, mantener	Kept(kept)
Know(no) conocer	Knew(nu)
Lead(lid) dirigir	Led(lerd)
Let(lert) permitir	Let(lert)
Lend prestar	Lent(lent)
Lose(luss) perder	Lost(lorst)
Leave(liv) dejar, partir	Left(lerf)
Make(meik) hacer	Made(med)
Mean(min) querer decir	Meant(ment)
Meet(mit) conocer	Met
Pay(pei) pagar	Paid(peid)
Put(put) poner	Put(put)
Read(rid) leer	Read(red)
Ride(raid) aventón, pasear, paseo	Rode(roud)
Ring sonar	Rang(reng)
Run(ran) correr	Ran(ren)
Rise(reiss) subir	Rose(rouss)
Say(sei) decir	Said(seid)
See(si) ver	Saw(so)
Sing(sing) cantar	Sang(seng)
Sell(seil) vender	Sold(sold)
Send enviar	Sent(sent)
Sit sentar	Sat(sat)
Shut(shut) cerrar	Shut(shat)
Sleep(slip) domir	Slept(slerpt)
Speak(spik) hablar	Spoke(spork)
Stand(stend) pararse	Stood(stud)
Strike(straik) golpear	Struck
Slide(slaid) resbalar	Slid(slid)
Spend gastar	Spent(spent)
Sweep(suip) barrer	Swept(swept)
Swim(suim) nadar	Swam(suem)
Steal(stil) robar	Stole(storl)
Stick(stic) adherir	Stuck(stak)
Stink(stink) apestar	Stank(stenk)

PRESENT SIMPLE/TIEMPO PRESENTE	PAST SIMPLE/TIEMPO PASADO
Swear(suer) jurar Spring(spring) brincar Spread(spred) extender	Swore(sour) Sprang Spread(spred)
Take(teic) tomar Teach(tich) enseñar Tear(tir) rascar	Took(tuk) Taught Tore(tor)
Think(tenk) pensar Tell(tel) decir Understand(onderstend) comprender	Thought(tort) Told(told) Understood(onderstud)
Wear(wer) usar ropa Weep(wip) llorar Win(win) ganar(en juegos)	Wore(wor) Wept(wept) Won(won)
Write(rait) escribir Withdraw(witzdrou) retirar	Wrote(rort) Withdrew(uitzdru)

SOME COMMON VERBS TO MEMORIZE
ALGUNOS VERBOS PARA MEMORIZAR

PRESENT TENSES	PAST TENSES	FUTURE TENSES	CONDITIONAL
TO BE: SER O ESTAR			
I am - (yo) soy/estoy	I was - (yo) fui/estaba	I will be - (yo) seré/estaré	I would be - (yo) sería/estaría
You are - (tú) eres/estás	You were - (tú) fuiste/estabas	You will be - (tú) serás/estarás	You would be - (tú) serías/estarías
He is - (él) es/está	He was - (él) fue/estaba	He will be - (él) será/estará	He would be - (él) sería/estaría
She is - (ella) es/está	She was - (ella) fue/estaba	She will be - (ella) será/estará	She would be - (ella) sería/estaría
It is - (esto) es/está	It was - (esto) fue/estaba	It will be - (esto) será/estará	It would be - (esto) sería/estaría
We are - somos/estamos	We were - fuimos/estabamos	We will be - seremos/estaremos	We would be - seríamos/estaríamos
You are - (ústedes) son/están	You were - fueron/estaban	You will be - serán/estarán	You would be - serían/estarían
They are - (ellos)(as) son/están	They were - fueron/estaban	They will be - serán/estarán	They would be - serían/estarían
TO DO: HACER			
I do (du) - (yo) hago	I did - (yo) hacía	I will do - (yo) haré	I would do - (yo) haría
You do - (tú) haces	You did - (tú) hacías	You will do - (tú) harás	You would do - (tú) harías
He does - (él) hace	He did - (él) hacía	He will do - (él) hará	He would do - (él) haría
She does - (ella) hace	She did - (ella) hacía	She will do - (ella) hará	She would do - (ella) haría
It does - (esto) hace	It did - (esto) hacía	It will do - (esto) hará	It would do - (esto) haría
We do - (nosotros) hacemos	We did - (nosotros) hacíamos	We will do - (nosotros) haremos	We would do - (nosotros) hariamos
You do - (ústedes) hacen	You did - (ústedes) hacían	You will do - (ústedes) harán	You would do - (ústedes) harian
They do - (ellos o ellas) hacen	They did - (ellos as) hacían	They will do - (ellos o ellas) harán	They would do - (ello(as) harían
TO HAVE: HABER/TENER			
I have - (yo) tengo	I had - (yo) tenía	I will have - (yo) tendré	I would have - (yo) tendría
You have - (tú) tienes	You had - (tú) tenías	You will have - (tú) tendrás	You would have - (tú) tendrías
He has - (él) tiene	He had - (él) tenía	He will have - (él) tendrá	He would have - (él) tendría
She has - (ella) tiene	She had - (ella) tenía	She will have - (ella) tendrá	She would have - (ella) tendría
It has - (esto) tiene	It had - (esto) tenía	It will have - (esto) tendrá	It would have - (esto) tendría
We have - (nosotros) tenemos	We had - (nosotros) teníamos	We will have - (nosotros) tendremos	We would have - tendríamos
You have - (ústedes) tienen	You had - (ústedes) tenían	You will have - (ústedes) tendrán	You would have - tendrían
They have - (ellos)(as) tienen	They had - (ellos)(as) tenían	They will have - (ellos o ellas) tendrán	They would have - tendrían
TO ABANDON: ABANDONAR			
I abandon - (yo) abandono	I abandoned - (yo) abandonaba	I will abandon - (yo) abandonaré	I would abandon - abandonaría
You abandon - (tú) abandonas	You abandoned - (tú) abandonabas	You will abandon - (tú) abandonarás	You would abandon - abandonarías
He abandons - (él) abandona	He abandoned - abandonaba	He will abandon - (él) abandonará	He would abandon - abandonaría
She abandons - (ella) abandona	She abandoned - abandonaba	She will abandon - (ella) abandonará	She would abandon - abandonaría
It abandons - (esto) abandona	It abandoned - abandonaba	It will abandon - (esto) abandonará	It would abandon - abandonaria
We abandon - abandonamos	We abandoned - abandonabamos	We will abandon - abandonaremos	We would abandon - abandonaríamos
You abandon - abandonan	You abandoned - abandonaban	You will abandon - abandonarán	You would abandon - abandonarían
They abandon - abandonan	They abandoned - abandonaban	They will abandon - abandonarán	They would abandon - abandonarían
TO ADAPT: ADAPTAR			
I adapt - (yo) adapto	I adapted - (yo) adaptaba	I will adapt - (yo) adaptaré	I would adapt - (yo) adaptaría
You adapt - (tú) adaptas	You adapted - (tú) adaptabas	You will adapt - (tú) adaptarás	You would adapt - (tú) adaptarías
He adapts - (él) adapta	He adapted - (él) adaptaba	He will adapt - (él) adaptará	He would adapt - (él) adaptaría
She adapts - (ella) adapta	She adapted - (ella) adaptaba	She will adapt - (ella) adaptará	She would adapt - (ella) adaptaría
It adapts - (esto) adapta	It adapted - (esto) adaptaba	It will adapt - (esto) adaptará	It would adapt - (esto) adaptaría
We adapt - adaptamos	We adapted - adaptabamos	We will adapt - (nosotros) adaptaremos	We would adapt - adaptaríamos
You adapt - adaptan	You adapted - adaptaban	You will adapt - (ústedes) adaptarán	You would adapt - adaptarian
They adapt - adaptan	They adapted - adaptaban	They will adapt - (ellos as) adaptarán	They would adapt - adaptarian
TO ADD: SUMAR			
I add (add) - (yo) sumo	I added (addid) - (yo) sumaba	I will add - (yo) sumaré	I would add - (yo) sumaría
You add - (tú) sumas	You added - (tú) sumabas	You will add - (tú) sumarás	You would add - (tú) sumarias
He adds - (él) suma	He added - (él) sumaba	He will add - (él) sumará	He would add (él) sumaría
She adds - (ella) suma	She added - (ella) sumaba	She will add - (ella) sumará	She would add (ella) sumaria
It adds - (esto) suma	It added - (esto) sumaba	It will add - (esto) sumará	It would add (esto) sumaria
We add - (nosotros) sumamos	We added - sumabamos	We will add - (nosotros) sumaremos	We would add - sumaríamos
You add - (ústedes) suman	You added - sumaban	You will add - (ústedes) sumarán	You would add - sumarían
They add - (ellos)(as) suman	They added - sumaban	They will add - (ellos o ellas) sumarán	They would add - sumarían

LA MANERA MÁS FÁCIL DE APRENDER Y ENSEÑAR INGLÉS/ESPAÑOL

PRESENT TENSES

TO ANNOUNCE: ANUNCIAR
I announce - (yo)anuncio
You announce-(tú)anuncias
He announces-(él) anuncia
She announces - (ella) anuncia
It announces-(esto)anuncia
We announce - anunciamos
You announce - anuncian
They announce –anuncian

TO ANSWER: CONTESTAR
I answer(enser) - (yo) contesto
You answer - (tú) contestas
He answers - (él) contesta
She answers - (ella) contesta
It answers- (esto) contesta
We answer-contestamos
You answer - contestan
They answer - contestan

TO ASK: PREGUNTAR
I ask(asc) - (yo) pregunto
You ask - (tú) preguntas
He asks - (él) pregunta
She asks - (ella) pregunta
It asks- (esto) pregunta
We ask- preguntamos
You ask - preguntan
They ask - preguntan

TO ASK FOR: PEDIR
I ask for(asc for) - (yo) pido
You ask for- (tú) pides
He asks for - (él) pide
She asks for-(ella)pide
It asks for- (esto) pide
We ask for- pedimos
You ask for - piden
They ask for - piden

TO ATTACK: ATACAR
I attack(atac) - (yo)ataco
You attack - (tú) atacas
He attacks - (él) ataca
She attacks - (ella) ataca
It attacks-(esto) ataca
We attack - atacamos
You attack - atacan
They attack - atacan

TO ATTEND: ATENDER
I attend(atend) - (yo) asisto
You attend - (tú) asistes
He attends - (él) asiste
She attends - (ella) asiste
It attends- (esto) asiste
We attend - asistimos
You attend -asisten
They attend - asisten

TO AWARD: OTORGAR
I award(aword) - (yo) otorgo
You award - (tú) otorgas
He awards - (él) otorga
She awards - (ella) otorga
It awards-(esto) otorga
We award - otorgamos
You award - otorgan
They award - otorgan

PAST TENSES

I announced - anunciaba
You announced - anunciabas
He announced - anunciaba
She announced - anunciaba
It announced - anunciaba
We announced - anunciabamos
You announced - anunciaban
They announced - anunciaban

I answered - (yo) contestaba
You answered - contestabas
He answered - contestaba
She answered - contestaba
It answered - contestaba
We answered -contestabamos
You answered - contestaban
They answered - contestaban

I asked(askt) - (yo) preguntaba
You asked - (tú) preguntabas
He asked - (él) preguntaba
She asked - (ella) preguntaba
It asked - (esto) preguntaba
We asked - preguntabamos
You asked- preguntaban
They asked - preguntaban

I asked for- (yo) pedía
You asked for - (tú) pedías
He asked for - (él) pedía
She asked for - (ella) pedía
It asked for- (esto) pedía
We asked for- pedíamos
You asked for - pedían
They asked for - pedían

I attacked(atact) - (yo) atacaba
You attacked - (tú) atacabas
He attacked - (él) atacaba
She attacked - (ella) atacaba
It attacked - (esto) atacaba
We attacked - atacabamos
You attacked - atacaban
They attacked - atacaban

I attended - (yo) asistía
You attended - (tú) asistías
He attended - (él) asistía
She attended - (ella) asistía
It attended - (esto) asistía
We attended - asistíamos
You attended - asistían
They attended - asistian

I awarded - (yo) otorgaba
You awarded - (tú) otorgabas
He awarded - (él) otorgaba
She awarded - (ella) otorgaba
It awarded - (esto) otorgaba
We awarded -otorgabamos
You awarded - otorgaban
They awarded - otorgaban

FUTURE TENSES

I will announce - (yo)anunciaré
You will announce - (tú)anunciarás
He will announce- (él)anunciará
She will announce - (ella)anunciará
It will announce-(esto)anunciará
We will announce - anunciarémos
You will announce - anunciarán
They will announce -(ellos(a)anunciarán

I will answer - (yo) contestaré
You will answer - (tú) contestarás
He will answer - (él) contestará
She will answer - (ella) contestará
It will answer- (esto) contestará
We will answer - contestaremos
You will answer - (ústedes) contestarán
They will answer - (ellos(as) contestarán

I will ask - (yo) preguntaré
You will ask - (tú) preguntarás
He will ask- (él) preguntará
She will ask - (ella) preguntará
It will ask - (esto) preguntará
We will ask - (nosotros) preguntaremos
You will ask- (ústedes) preguntarán
They will ask- (ellos(as) preguntarán

I will ask for - (yo) pediré
You will ask for - (tú) pedirás
He will ask for- (él) pedirá
She will ask for - (ella) pedirá
It will ask for - (esto) pedirá
We will ask for - (nosotros) pediremos
You will ask for- (ústedes) pedirán
They will ask for- (ellos(as) pedirán

I will attack - (yo) atacaré
You will attack - (tú) atacarás
He will attack - (él) atacará
She will attack - (ella) atacará
It will attack - (esto) atacará
We will attack - (nosotros) atacaremos
You will attack - (ústedes) atacarán
They will attack- (ellos(as) atacarán

I will attend - (yo) asistiré
You will attend - (tú) asistirás
He will attend - (él) asistirá
She will attend - (ella) asistirá
It will attend - (esto) asistirá
We will attend - (nosotros) asistiremos
You will attend - (ústedes) asistirán
They will attend - (ellos(as) asistirán

I will award - (yo) otorgaré
You will award - (tú) otorgarás
He will award - (él) otorgará
She will award - (ella) otorgará
It will award - (esto) otorgará
We will award - (nosotros) otorgaremos
You will award- (ústedes) otorgarán
They will award - (ellos(as) otorgarán

CONDITIONAL

I would announce - (yo)anunciaría
You would announce- anunciarías
He would announce - (él)anunciaría
She would announce -(ella)anunciaría
It would announce - (esto)anunciaría
We would announce -anunciaríamos
You would announce -anunciarían
They would announce -anunciarían

I would answer - (yo) contestaría
You would answer -(tú) contestarías
He would answer- (él) contestaría
She would answer - (ella) contestaría
It would answer- (esto) contestaría
We would answer - contestaríamos
You would answer- contestarian
They would answer - contestarían

I would ask - (yo) preguntaría
You would ask - (tú) preguntarías
He would ask- (él) preguntaría
She would ask - (ella) preguntaría
It would ask- (esto) preguntaria
We would ask - preguntaríamos
You would ask - preguntarian
They would ask -preguntarian

I would ask for - (yo) pediría
You would ask for - (tú) pedirías
He would ask for - (él) pediría
She would ask for- (ella) pediría
It would ask for-(esto) pediría
We would ask for- pediriamos
You would ask for- pedirían
They would ask for - pedirian

I would attack - (yo) atacaría
You would attack - (tú) atacarías
He would attack- (él) atacaría
She would attack - (ella) atacaría
It would attack- (esto) atacaría
We would attack-atacaríamos
You would attack - atacarían
They would attack - atacarian

I would attend - (yo) asistiría
You would attend - (tú) asistirías
He would attend- (él) asistiría
She would attend- (ella) asistiría
It would attend - asistiría
We would attend - asistiriamos
You would attend - asistirían
They would attend - asistirían

I would award - (yo) otorgaría
You would award - (tú) otorgarías
He would award- (él) otorgaría
She would award - (ella) otorgaria
It would award- (esto) otorgaria
We would award-otorgaríamos
You would award - otorgarían
They would award - otorgarian

PRESENT TENSES

TO ACHIEVE: LOGRAR
I achieve(achiv) - (yo) logro
You achieve - (tú) logras
He achieves - (él) logra
She achieves - (ella) logra
It achieves - (esto) logra
We achieve - logramos
You achieve - logran
They achieve - logran

TO BAKE: HORNEAR
I bake(beik) - (yo) horneo
You bake - (tú) horneas
He bakes - (él) hornea
She bakes - (ella) hornea
It bakes - (esto) hornea
We bake - horneamos
You bake - hornean
They bake - hornean

TO BRUSH: CEPILLAR
I brush(brash) - (yo) cepillo
You brush - (tú) cepillas
He brushes - (él) cepilla
She brushes - (ella) cepilla
It brushes - (esto) cepilla
We brush - cepillamos
You brush - cepillan
They brush - cepillan

TO BURN: QUEMAR
I burn(bern) - (yo) quemo
You burn - (tú) quemas
He burns - (él) quema
She burns - (ella) quema
It burns - (esto) quema
We burn - quemamos
You burn - (ustedes) queman
They burn - (ellos(as) queman

TO CALL: LLAMAR
I call(coll) - (yo) llamo
You call - (tú) llamas
He calls - (él) llama
She calls - (ella) llama
It calls - (esto) llama
We call - (nosotros) llamamos
You call - (ústedes) llaman
They call - (ellos(as) llaman

TO CHANGE: CAMBIAR
I change - (yo) cambio
You change - (tú) cambias
He changes - (él) cambia
She changes - (ella) cambia
It changes - (esto) cambia
We change - cambiamos
You change - cambian
They change - cambian

TO CLEAN: LIMPIAR
I clean(klin) - (yo) limpio
You clean - (tú) limpias
He cleans - (él) limpia
She cleans - (ella) limpia
It cleans - (esto) limpia
We clean - limpiamos
You clean - (ústedes) limpian
They clean - (ellos(as) limpian

PAST TENSES

I achieved - (yo) lograba
You achieved - (tú) lograbas
He achieved - (él) lograba
She achieved - (ella) lograba
It achieved - (esto) lograba
We achieved - lograbamos
You achieved - lograban
They achieved - lograban

I baked(beikt) - (yo) horneaba
You baked - (tú) horneabas
He baked - (él) horneaba
She baked - (ella) horneaba
It baked - (esto) horneaba
We baked - horneabamos
You baked - horneaban
They baked - horneaban

I brushed - (yo) cepillaba
You brushed - (tú) cepillabas
He brushed - (él) cepillaba
She brushed - (ella) cepillaba
It brushed - (esto) cepillaba
We brushed - cepillabamos
You brushed - cepillaban
They brushed - cepillaban

I burned(bernd) - (yo) quemaba
You burned - (tú) quemabas
He burned - (él) quemaba
She burned - (ella) quemaba
It burned - (esto) quemaba
We burned - quemabamos
You burned - quemaban
They burned - quemaban

I called(cold) - (yo) llamaba
You called - (tú) llamabas
He called - (él) llamaba
She called - (ella) llamaba
It called - (esto) llamaba
We called - llamabamos
You called - llamaban
They called - llamaban

I changed - (yo) cambiaba
You changed - (tú) cambiabas
He changed - (él) cambiaba
She changed - (ella) cambiaba
It changed - (esto) cambiaba
We changed - cambiabamos
You changed - cambiaban
They changed - cambiaban

I cleaned(klind) - (yo) limpiaba
You cleaned - (tú) limpiabas
He cleaned - (él) limpiaba
She cleaned - (ella) limpiaba
It cleaned - (esto) limpiaba
We cleaned - limpiabamos
You cleaned - limpiaban
They cleaned - limpiaban

FUTURE TENSES

I will achieve - (yo) lograré
You will achieve - (tú) lograrás
He will achieve - (él) logrará
She will achieve - (ella) logrará
It will achieve - (esto) logrará
We will achieve - (nosotros) lograremos
You will achieve - (ústedes) lograrán
They will achieve - (ellos(as) lograrán

I will bake - (yo) hornearé
You will bake - (tú) hornearás
He will bake - (él) horneará
She will bake - (ella) horneará
It will bake - (esto) horneará
We will bake - (nosotros) hornearemos
You will bake - (ústedes) hornearán
They will bake - (ellos(as) hornearán

I will brush - (yo) cepillaré
You will brush - (tú) cepillarás
He will brush - (él) cepillará
She will brush - (ella) cepillará
It will brush - (esto) cepillará
We will brush - (nosotros) cepillaremos
You will brush - (ústedes) cepillarán
They will brush - (ellos(as) cepillarán

I will burn - (yo) quemaré
You will burn - (tú) quemarás
He will burn - (él) quemará
She will burn - (ella) quemará
It will burn - (esto) quemará
We will burn - (nosotros) quemaremos
You will burn - (ústedes) quemarán
They will burn - (ellos(as) quemarán

I will call - (yo) llamaré
You will call - (tú) llamarás
He will call - (él) llamará
She will call - (ella) llamará
It will call - (esto) llamará
We will call - (nosotros) llamaremos
You will call - (ústedes) llamarán
They will call - (ellos(as) llamarán

I will change - (yo) cambiaré
You will change - (tú) cambiarás
He will change - (él) cambiará
She will change - (ella) cambiará
It will change - (esto) cambiará
We will change - (nosotros) cambiaremos
You will change - (ústedes) cambiarán
They will change - (ellos(as) cambiarán

I will clean - (yo) limpiaré
You will clean - (tú) limpiarás
He will clean - (él) limpiará
She will clean - (ella) limpiará
It will clean - (esto) limpiará
We will clean - (nosotros) limpiaremos
You will clean - (ústedes) limpiarán
They will clean - (ellos(as) limpiarán

CONDITIONAL

I would achieve - (yo) lograría
You would achieve - (tú) lograrías
He would achieve - (él) lograría
She would achieve - (ella) lograría
It would achieve - (esto) lograría
We would achieve - lograríamos
You would achieve - lograrían
They would achieve - lograrían

I would bake - (yo) hornearía
You would bake - (tú) hornearias
He would bake - (él) hornearía
She would bake - (ella) hornearía
It would bake - (esto) hornearía
We would bake - hornearíamos
You would bake - hornearían
They would bake - hornearian

I would brush - (yo) cepillaría
You would brush - (tú) cepillarías
He would brush - (él) cepillaría
She would brush - (ella) cepillaria
It would brush - (esto) cepillaría
We would brush - cepillaríamos
You would brush - cepillarían
They would brush - cepillarían

I would burn - (yo) quemaría
You would burn - (tú) quemarias
He would burn - (él) quemaría
She would burn - (ella) quemaría
It would burn - (esto) quemaría
We would burn - quemaríamos
You would burn - quemarían
They would burn - quemarian

I would call - (yo) llamaría
You would call - (tú) llamarías
He would call - (él) llamaría
She would call - (ella) llamaria
It would call - (esto) llamaría
We would call - llamaríamos
You would call - llamarian
They would call - llamarían

I would change - (yo) cambiaría
You would change - (tú) cambiarias
He would change - (él) cambiaría
She would change - (ella) cambiaría
It would change - (esto) cambiaría
We would change - cambiaríamos
You would change - cambiarían
They would change - cambiarían

I would clean - (yo) limpiaria
You would clean - (tú) limpiarías
He would clean - (él) limpiaría
She would clean - (ella) limpiaría
It would clean - (esto) limpiaría
We would clean - limpiaríamos
You would clean - limpiarían
They would clean - limpiarían

PRESENT TENSES | PAST TENSES | FUTURE TENSES | CONDITIONAL

TO CLIMB: ESCALAR

PRESENT TENSES	PAST TENSES	FUTURE TENSES	CONDITIONAL
I climb (claimb) -(yo) escalo	I climbed -(yo) escalaba	I will climb -(yo) escalaré	I would climb -(yo) escalaria
You climb-(tú) escalas	You climbed -(tú) escalabas	You will climb-(tú) escalarás	You would climb -(tú) escalarías
He climbs -(él) escala	He climbed -(él) escalaba	He will climb-(él) escalará	He would climb-(él) escalaría
She climbs -(ella) escala	She climbed -(ella) escalaba	She will climb -(ella) escalará	She would climb -(ella) escalaría
It climbs-(esto) escala	It climbed -(esto) escalaba	It will climb -(esto) escalará	It would climb -(esto) escalaría
We climb - escalamos	We climbed - escalabamos	We will climb -(nosotros) escalaremos	We would climb -escalaríamos
You climb -(ústedes) escalan	You climbed - escalaban	You will climb-(ústedes) escalarán	You would climb -escalarían
They climb -(ellos(as) escalan	They climbed -escalaban	They will climb -(ellos(as) escalarán	They would climb -escalarían

TO CLOSE: CERRAR

PRESENT TENSES	PAST TENSES	FUTURE TENSES	CONDITIONAL
I close (clos) -(yo) cierro	I closed (closd) -(yo) cerraba	I will close -(yo) cerraré	I would close -(yo) cerraría
You close -(tú) cierras	You closed -(tú) cerrabas	You will close -(tú) cerrarás	You would close -(tú) cerrarías
He closes -(él) cierra	He closed -(él) cerraba	He will close-(él) cerrará	He would close-(él) cerraría
She closes -(ella) cierra	She closed -(ella) cerraba	She will close -(ella) cerrará	She would close -(ella) cerraría
It closes -(esto) cierra	It closed -(esto) cerraba	It will close -(esto) cerrará	It would close-(esto) cerraría
We close -(nosotros) cerramos	We closed -cerrabamos	We will close -(nosotros) cerraremos	We would close-cerraríamos
You close-(ústedes) cierran	You closed -cerraban	You will close -(ústedes) cerrarán	You would close -cerrarían
They close -(ellos(as) cierran	They closed - cerraban	They will close -(ellos(as) cerrarán	They would close -cerrarian

TO COOK: COCINAR

PRESENT TENSES	PAST TENSES	FUTURE TENSES	CONDITIONAL
I cook (cuc) -(yo) cocino	I cooked (cuct) - (yo) cocinaba	I will cook-(yo) cocinaré	I would cook - (yo) cocinaría
You cook-(tú) cocinas	You cooked - (tú) cocinabas	You will cook - (tú) cocinarás	You would cook - (tú) cocinarías
He cooks - (él) cocina	He cooked - (él) cocinaba	He will cook - (él) cocinará	He would cook - (él) cocinaría
She cooks - (ella) cocina	She cooked - (ella) cocinaba	She will cook- (ella) cocinará	She would cook - (ella) cocinaría
It cooks - (esto) cocina	It cooked - (esto) cocinaba	It will cook- (esto) cocinará	It would cook - (esto) cocinaría
We cook - cocinamos	We cooked -cocinabamos	We will cook- cocinaremos	We would cook- cocinaríamos
You cook -(ústedes) cocinan	You cooked - cocinaban	You will cook - cocinarán	You would cook - cocinarían
They cook - (ellos as) cocinan	They cooked - cocinaban	They will cook - (ellos(as) cocinarán	They would cook - cocinarían

TO COMPLETE: COMPLETAR

PRESENT TENSES	PAST TENSES	FUTURE TENSES	CONDITIONAL
I complete - (yo) completo	I completed - (yo) completaba	I will complete -(yo) completaré	I would complete -(yo) completaría
You complete - completas	You completed - completabas	You will complete -(tú) completarás	You would complete (tú)completarías
He completes - completa	He completed - completaba	He will complete -(él) completará	He would complete -(él)completaría
She completes - completa	She completed - completaba	She will complete -(ella) completará	She would complete(ella)completaría
It completes - completa	It completed - completaba	It will complete-(esto) completará	It would complete -(esto)completaría
We complete -completamos	We completed -completabamos	We will complete -completaremos	We would complete -completaríamos
You complete- completan	You completed -completaban	You will complete -completarán	You would complete-completarían
They complete - completan	They completed- completaban	They will complete -completarán	They would complete -completarían

TO COLLECT: COBRAR

PRESENT TENSES	PAST TENSES	FUTURE TENSES	CONDITIONAL
I collect (colect) -(yo) cobro	I collected - (yo) cobraba	I will collect - (yo) cobraré	I would collect - (yo) cobraría
You collect-(tú) cobrás	You collected - (tú) cobrabas	You will collect - (tú) cobrarás	You would collect - (tú) cobrarías
He collects - (él) cobra	He collected - (él) cobraba	He will collect - (él) cobrará	He would collect - (él) cobraria
She collects - (ella) cobra	She collected - (ella) cobraba	She will collect - (ella) cobrará	She would collect - (ella) cobraría
It collects - (esto) cobra	It collected - (esto) cobraba	It will collect - (esto) cobrará	It would collect - (esto) cobraría
We collect - cobramos	We collected -cobrabamos	We will collect - (nosotros) cobraremos	We would collect- cobraríamos
You collect-(ústedes) cobran	You collected - cobraban	You will collect-(ústedes) cobrarán	You would collect - cobrarían
They collect - (ellos(as) cobran	They collected - cobraban	They will collect - (ellos(as) cobrarán	They would collect - cobrarian

TO COMPOSE: COMPONER

PRESENT TENSES	PAST TENSES	FUTURE TENSES	CONDITIONAL
I compose - (yo) compongo	I composed - (yo) componía	I will compose - (yo) compondré	I would compose - (yo) compondría
You compose - (tú) compones	You composed - componías	You will compose-(tú) compondrás	You would compose - compondrías
He composes - (él) compone	He composed - componía	He will compose - (él) compondrá	He would compose - compondría
She composes - (ella) compone	She composed - componía	She will compose - (ella) compondrá	She would compose -compondría
It composes- (esto) compone	It composed -componía	It will compose- (esto) compondrá	It would compose- compondría
We compose- componemos	We composed -componíamos	We will compose-compondremos	We would compose -compondríamos
You compose - componen	You composed - componían	You will compose - compondrán	You would compose-compondrían
They compose - componen	They composed - componían	They will compose-compondrán	They would compose-compondrían

TO CONQUERE: CONQUISTAR

PRESENT TENSES	PAST TENSES	FUTURE TENSES	CONDITIONAL
I conquere -(yo)conquisto	I conquered-(yo)conquistaba	I will conquere -(yo)conquistaré	I would conquere -(yo)conquistaria
You conquere-(tú)conquistas	You conquered- conquistabas	You will conquere-(tú)conquistarás	You would conquere-(tú)conquistarias
He conqueres-(él)conquista	He conquered - conquistaba	He will conquere-(él)conquistará	He would conquere-(él)conquistaría
She conqueres-(ella)conquista	She conquered-conquistaba	She will conquere-(ella)conquistará	She would conquere-(ella)conquistaría
It conqueres-(esto)conquista	It conquered-conquistaba	It will conquere-(esto)conquistará	It would conquere-(esto)conquistaria
We conquere-conquistamos	We conquered-conquistabamos	We will conquere-conquistaremos	We would conquere-conquistaríamos
You conquere-conquistan	You conquered-conquistaban	You will conquere-conquistarán	You would conquere-conquistarían
They conquere-conquistan	They conquered-conquistaban	They will conquere-conquistarán	They would conquere-conquistarían

PRESENT TENSES	PAST TENSES	FUTURE TENSES	CONDITIONAL
TO CONSTRUCT: CONSTRUIR			
I construct-(yo)construyo	I constructed-(yo)construía	I will construct-(yo)construiré	I would construct -(yo)construiría
You construct-(tú)construyes	You constructed-(tú)construías	You will construct -(tú)construirás	You would construct-(tú)construirías
He constructs-(él)construye	He constructed-(él)construía	He will construct-(él)construirá	He would construct-(él)construiría
She constructs-(ella)construye	She constructed-(ella)construía	She will construct-(ella)construirá	She would construct-(ella)construiría
It constructs -(esto)construye	It constructed--(esto)construía	It will construct-(esto)construirá	It would construct-(esto)construiría
We construct-construimos	We constructed-construíamos	We will construct-construiremos	We would construct-construiríamos
You construct-construyen	You constructed-construían	You will construct-construirán	You would construct-construirían
They construct-construyen	They constructed-construían	They will construct-construirán	They would construct-construirían
TO COMBINE: COMBINAR			
I combine-(yo) combino	I combined-(yo) combinaba	I will combine -(yo) combinaré	I would combine -(yo) combinaría
You combine -(tú) combinas	You combined - combinabas	You will combine -(tú) combinarás	You would combine -(tú) combinarías
He combines -(él) combina	He combined - combinaba	He will combine-(él) combinará	He would combine-(él) combinaría
She combines -(ella)combina	She combined -combinaba	She will combine -(ella) combinará	She would combine -(ella) combinaría
It combines -(esto)combina	It combined - combinaba	It will combine-(esto)combinará	It would combine-(esto)combinaría
We combine - combinamos	We combined- combinabamos	We will combine- combinaremos	We would combine - combinaríamos
You combine - combinan	You combined - combinaban	You will combine - combinarán	You would combine- combinarían
They combine -combinan	They combined-combinaban	They will combine - combinarán	They would combine -combinarían
TO COVER: CUBRIR			
I cover-(yo)cubro	I covered -(yo) cubría	I will cover -(yo) cubriré	I would cover -(yo) cubriría
You cover -(tú)cubres	You covered -(tú) cubrías	You will cover -(tú) cubrirás	You would cover -(tú) cubrirías
He covers -(él) cubre	He covered -(él) cubría	He will cover -(él) cubrirá	He would cover-(él) cubriría
She covers -(ella) cubre	She covered -(ella) cubría	She will cover -(ella) cubrirá	She would cover -(ella) cubriría
It covers -(esto) cubre	It covered -(esto) cubría	It will cover -(esto) cubrirá	It would cover-(esto)cubriría
We cover -(nosotros) cubrimos	We covered - cubriamos	We will cover -(nosotros) cubriremos	We would cover - cubririamos
You cover-(ústedes)cubren	You covered -(ústedes) cubrían	You will cover-(ústedes) cubrirán	You would cover-cubrirían
They cover -(ellos(as)cubren	They covered-ellos(as)cubrían	They will cover-(ellos(as) cubrirán	They would cover - cubrirían
TO CROSS: CRUZAR			
I cross-(yo)cruzo	I crossed -(yo) cruzaba	I will cross-(yo) cruzaré	I would cross-(yo) cruzaría
You cross-(tú) cruzas	You crossed -(tú) cruzabas	You will cross-(tú)cruzarás	You would cross -(tú)cruzarías
He crosses -(él) cruza	He crossed -(él) cruzaba	He will cross-(él) cruzará	He would cross-(él) cruzaría
She crosses -(ella) cruza	She crossed -(ella) cruzaba	She will cross-(ella)cruzará	She would cross-(ella)cruzaría
It crosses-(esto)cruza	It crossed -(esto) cruzaba	It will cross-(esto)cruzará	It would cross-(esto) cruzaría
We cross -(nosotros) cruzamos	We crossed cruzabamos	We will cross-(nosotros) cruzaremos	We would cross - cruzaríamos
You cross-(ústedes) cruzan	You crossed-cruzaban	You will cross-(ústedes)cruzarán	You would cross - cruzarían
They cross-(ellos(as)cruzan	They crossed -cruzaban	They will cross-(ellos(as)cruzarán	They would cross-cruzarían
TO CRY: LLORAR			
I cry(crai)-(yo)lloro	I cried(craid) -(yo) lloraba	I will cry -(yo) lloraré	I would cry -(yo) lloraría
You cry -(tú)lloras	You cried -(tú) llorabas	You will cry -(tú) llorarás	You would cry -(tú) llorarías
He cries -(él) llora	He cried -(él) lloraba	He will cry -(él) llorará	He would cry -(él) lloraría
She cries -(ella)llora	She cried -(ella)lloraba	She will cry -(ella) llorará	She would cry -(ella) lloraría
It cries -(esto)llora	It cried -(esto) lloraba	It will cry -(esto)llorará	It would cry -(esto) lloraría
We cry -(nosotros)lloramos	We cried -llorabamos	We will cry -(nosotros) lloraremos	We would cry-llorariamos
You cry -(ustedes)lloran	You cried -(ústedes)lloraban	You will cry -(ústedes)llorarán	You would cry - llorarían
They cry -(ellos(as)lloran	They cried-(ellos(as) lloraban	They will cry -(ellos(as)llorarán	They would cry -llorarian
TO COPY: COPIAR			
I copy (copi) -(yo) copio	I copied (copid) -(yo) copiaba	I will copy -(yo) copiaré	I would copy -(yo) copiaría
You copy -(tú)copias	You copied -(tú) copiabas	You will copy -(tú) copiarás	You would copy -(tú) copiarías
He copies -(él) copia	He copied -(él) copiaba	He will copy -(él) copiará	He would copy -(él) copiaría
She copies -(ella) copia	She copied -(ella) copiaba	She will copy -(ella) copiará	She would copy -(ella) copiaría
It copies -(esto)copia	It copied -(esto) copiaba	It will copy -(esto) copiará	It would copy -(esto) copiaría
We copy -(nosotros) copiamos	We copied - copiabamos	We will copy -(nosotros) copiaremos	We would copy- copiaríamos
You copy -(ústedes) copian	You copied -(ústedes)copiaban	You will copy -(ústedes) copiarán	You would copy - copiarían
They copy -(ellos(as) copian	They copied -(ellos(as) copiaban	They will copy -(ellos(as)copiarán	They would copy - copiarían
TO CELEBRATE: CELEBRAR			
I celebrate -(yo)celebro	I celebrated-(yo)celebraba	I will celebrate -(yo) celebraré	I would celebrate-(yo) celebraría
You celebrate -(tú)celebras	You celebrated -(tú) celebrabas	You will celebrate -(tú)celebrarás	You would celebrate -(tú)celebrarías
He celebrates -(él) celebra	He celebrated -(él) celebraba	He will celebrate -(él) celebrará	He would celebrate-(él) celebraría
She celebrates -(ella) celebra	She celebrated -(ella) celebraba	She will celebrate -(ella) celebrará	She would celebrate-(ella) celebraría
It celebrates-(esto)celebra	It celebrated -(esto) celebraba	It will celebrate-(esto)celebrará	It would celebrate -(esto) celebraría
We celebrate - celebramos	We celebrated - celebrabamos	We will celebrate-celebraremos	We would celebrate -celebraríamos
You celebrate - celebran	You celebrated - celebraban	You will celebrate - celebrarán	You would celebrate-celebrarían
They celebrate-celebran	They celebrated - celebraban	They will celebrate - celebrarán	They would celebrate -celebrarian

PRESENT TENSES

TO CARRY:CARGAR

I carry(kerri) -(yo)cargo
You carry -(tú)cargas
He carries -(él) carga
She carries -(ella) carga
It carries-(esto) carga
We carry -(nosotros) cargamos
You carry -(ústedes) cargan
They carry -(ellos(as)cargan

TO DECIDE: DECIDIR

I decide (disaid) - (yo) decido
You decide - (tú) decides
He decides - (él) decide
She decides - (ella) decide
It decides - (esto) decide
We decide - (nosotros) decidimos
You decide - (ústedes) deciden
They decide - (ellos(as) deciden

TO DANCE:BAILAR

I dance (dens) -(yo) bailo
You dance -(tú) bailas
He dances-(él) baila
She dances-(ella) baila
It dances -(esto) baila
We dance -(nosotros) bailamos
You dance-(ústedes) bailan
They dance-(ellos (as) bailan

TO DIVIDE: DIVIDIR

I divide(divaid)-(yo) divido
You divide-(tú) divides
He divides-(él) divide
She divides-(ella) divide
It divides-(esto) divide
We divide-(nosotros) dividimos
You divide-(ústedes) dividen
They divide -(ellos(as) dividen

TO DECORATE:DECORAR

I decorate -(yo) decoro
You decorate-(tú) decoras
He decorates -(él) decora
She decorates -(ella) decora
It decorates -(esto) decora
We decorate-decoramos
You decorate- decoran
They decorate-decoran

TO DELIVER:ENTREGAR

I deliver - (yo) entrego
You deliver - (tú) entregas
He delivers - (él) entrega
She delivers - (ella) entrega
It delivers- (esto) entrega
We deliver-entregamos
You deliver-entregan
They deliver-entregan

TO DEFEAT:VENCER

I defeat(difit) - (yo) venzo
You defeat - (tú) vences
He defeats- (él) vence
She defeats - (ella) vence
It defeats- (esto) vence
We defeat - vencemos
You defeat- vencen
They defeat- vencen

PAST TENSES

I carried -(yo) cargaba
You carried -(tú) cargabas
He carried -(él) cargaba
She carried -(ella) cargaba
It carried -(esto) cargaba
We carried - cargabamos
You carried - cargaban
They carried - cargaban

I decided (disidid) - (yo) decidía
You decided -(tú) decidías
He decided - (él) decidía
She decided - (ella) decidía
It decided -(esto) decidía
We decided -decidiamos
You decided - decidían
They decided - decidían

I danced (deynst) -(yo) bailaba
You danced -(tú)bailabas
He danced -(él) bailaba
She danced -(ella) bailaba
It danced -(esto) bailaba
We danced -bailabamos
You danced-bailaban
They danced-bailaban

I divided(dividid) -(yo)dividía
You divided -(tú) dividías
He divided-(él) dividía
She divided-(ella) dividía
It divided -(esto) dividía
We divided - dividiamos
You divided-(ústedes) dividían
They divided-(ellos(as) dividían

I decorated- (yo) decoraba
You decorated-(tú) decoorabas
He decorated-(él) decoraba
She decorated-(ella) decoraba
It decorated-estodecoraba
We decorated- decorabamos
You decorated - decoraban
They decorated-decoraban

I delivered - (yo) entregaba
You delivered - (tú) entregabas
He delivered - (él) entregaba
She delivered - (ella) entregaba
It delivered - (esto) entregaba
We delivered-entregabamos
You delivered-entregaban
They delivered- entregaban

I defeated(defitid) - (yo) vencí
You defeated - (tú) vencíste
He defeated- él venció
She defeated-ellavenció
It defeated-esto venció
We defeated-vencimos
You defeated- vencieron
They defeated-vencieron

FUTURE TENSES

I will carry -(yo) cargaré
You will carry -(tú) cargarás
He will carry -(él) cargará
She will carry -(ella) cargará
It will carry -(esto) cargará
We will carry -(nosotros) cargaremos
You will carry -(ústedes) cargarán
They will carry -(ellos(as)cargarán

I will decide - (yo) decidiré
You will decide -(tú) decidirás
He will decide-(él) decidirá
She will decide - (ella) decidirá
It will decide - (esto) decidirá
We will decide -(nosotros)decidiremos
You will decide-(ústedes) decidirán
They will decide-(ellos(as) decidirán

I will dance -(yo)bailaré
You will dance -(tú) bailarás
He will dance-(él) bailará
She will dance-(ella) bailará
It will dance-(esto) bailará
We will dance -(nosotros) bailaremos
You will dance-(ústedes)bailarán
They will dance-(ellos(as)bailarán

I will divide-(yo) dividiré
You will divide -(tú) dividirás
He will divide--(él)dividirá
She will divide--(ella) dividirá
It will divide-(esto) dividirá
We will divide-(nosotros) dividiremos
You will divide-(ústedes) dividirán
They will divide-(ellos(as) dividirán

I will decorate- (yo) decoraré
You will decorate-(tú) decorarás
He will decorate- (él) decorará
She will decorate-(ella) decorará
It will decorate-(esto) decorará
We will decorate-decoraremos
You will decorate-decorarán
They will decorate-decorarán

I will deliver- (yo) entregaré
You will deliver-(tú) entregarás
He will deliver-(él) entregará
She will deliver - (ella) entregará
It will deliver-(esto) entregará
We will deliver-entregaremos
You will deliver- entregarán
They will deliver-entregarán

I will defeat - (yo) venceré
You will defeat -(tú) vencerás
He will defeat - (él) vencerá
She will defeat - (ella) vencerá
It will defeat-(esto) vencerá
We will defeat - venceremos
You will defeat- vencerán
They will defeat –vencerán

CONDITIONAL

I would carry -(yo) cargaría
You would carry -(tú) cargarías
He would carry -(él) cargaría
She would carry-(ella) cargaría
It would carry-(esto) cargaría
We would carry - cargaríamos
You would carry - cargarían
They would carry - cargarian

I would decide - (yo) decidiría
You would decide - decidirías
He would decide - decidiría
She would decide - decidiría
It would decide - decidiría
We would decide - decidiríamos
You would decide- decidirían
They would decide- decidirían

I would dance -(yo) bailaría
You would dance -(tú) bailarías
He would dance-(él) bailaría
She would dance-(ella) bailaría
It would dance-(esto) bailaría
We would dance - bailaríamos
You would dance-bailarían
They would dance- bailarían

I would divide -(yo) dividiría
You would divide -(tú) dividirías
He would divide-(él) dividiría
She would divide-(ella) dividiría
It would divide-(esto) dividiría
We would divide- dividiríamos
You would divide- dividirían
They would divide-dividirían

I would decorate - (yo) decoraría
You would decorate - (tú) decorarías
He would decorate-(él) decoraría
She would decorate - (ella) decoraría
It would decorate- (esto) decoraría
We would decorate - decoraríamos
You would decorate - decorarían
They would decorate- decorarían

I would deliver- (yo) entregaría
You would deliver-(tú)entregarías
He would deliver- (él)entregaría
She would deliver- (ella)entregaría
It would deliver- (esto) entregaría
We would deliver-entregaríamos
You would deliver- entregarían
They would deliver- entregarían

I would defeat - (yo) vencería
You would defeat - (tú) vencerías
He would defeat- (él) vencería
She would defeat- (ella) vencería
It would defeat- (esto) vencería
We would defeat-venceríamos
You would defeat - vencerían
They would defeat- vencerían

PRESENT TENSES

TO DEMONSTRATE: DEMOSTRAR

I demonstrate - demuestro
You demonstrate - demuestras
He demonstrates- demuestra
She demonstrates- demuestra
It demonstrates- demuestra
We demonstrate- demostramos
You demonstrate- demostran
They demonstrate-demuestran

TO DESIGN: DISEÑAR

I design - (yo) diseño
You design- (tú) diseñas
He designs- (él) diseña
She designs- (ella) diseña
It designs-diseña
We design-diseñamos
You design- diseñan
They design- diseñan

TO DEVELOP: DESARROLLAR

I develop - (yo) desarrollo
You develop-(tú)desarrollas
He develops- desarrolla
She develops- desarrolla
It develops- desarrolla
We develop- desarrollamos
You develop-desarrollan
They develop- desarrollan

TO DISCUSS: DISCUTIR

I dicuss - (yo) discuto
You dicuss-(tú)discutes
He dicusses-(él) discute
She dicusses-(ella) discute
It dicusses-(esto) discute
We dicuss-discutimos
You dicuss-discuten
They dicuss- discuten

TO DREAM:SOÑAR

I dream(drim)-(yo)sueño
You dream-(tú) sueñas
He dreams-(él) sueña
She dreams-(ella) sueña
It dreams-(esto) sueña
We dream-soñamos
You dream-sueñan
They dream-sueñan

TO ERASE:BORRAR

I erase(ireiss)-(yo)borro
You erase(tú)borras
He erases-(él) borra
She erases -(ella)borra
It erases-(esto) borra
We erase- borramos
You erase- borran
They erase-borran

PAST TENSES

I demonstrated - (yo)demostraba
You demonstrated-demostrabas
He demonstrated-demostraba
She demonstrated-demostraba
It demonstrated-demostraba
We demonstrated- demostrábamos
You demonstrated-demostraban
They demonstrated- demostraban

I designed-(yo)diseñaba
You designed-(tú)diseñabas
He designed-(él) diseñaba
She designed-(ella)diseñaba
It designed-(esto)diseñaba
We designed-diseñabamos
You designed- diseñaban
They designed- diseñaban

I developed -(yo) desarrollaba
You developed-(tú)desarrollabas
He developed- desarrollaba
She developed- desarrollaba
It developed- desarrollaba
We developed- desarrollabamos
You developed-desarrollaban
They developed- desarrollaban

I dicussed - (yo) discutía
You dicussed - (tú) discutías
He dicussed-(él) discutía
She dicussed-(ella) discutia
It dicussed-(esto)discutía
We dicussed- discutíamos
You dicussed-discutían
They dicussed- discutían

I dreamed - (yo) soñaba
You dreamed- (tú) soñabas
He dreamed- (él) soñaba
She dreamed- (ella) soñaba
It dreamed- (esto) soñaba
We dreamed-soñabamos
You dreamed-soñaban
They dreamed- soñaban

I erased (iréisst) -(yo)borraba
You erased -(tú)borrabas
He erased -(él) borraba
She erased -(ella) borraba
It erased-(esto) borraba
We erased- borrabamos
You erased-borraban
They erased- borraban

FUTURE TENSES

I will demonstrate-(yo)demostraré
You will demonstate- demostrarás
He will demonstate- (él) demostrará
She will demonstate-demostrará
It will demonstate- demostrará
We will demonstate- demostraremos
You will demonstate- demostrarán
They will demonstate- demostrarán

I will design-(yo)diseñaré
You will design-(tú) diseñarás
He will design-(él) diseñará
She will design-(ella) diseñará
It will design-(esto) diseñará
We will design-diseñaremos
You will design- diseñarán
They will design- diseñarán

I will develop-(yo) desarrollaré
You will develop-(tú)desarrollarás
He will develop- desarrollará
She will develop- desarrollará
It will develop- desarrollará
We will develop- desarrollaremos
You will develop- desarrollarán
They will develop- desarrollarán

I will discuss-(yo) discutiré
You will discuss-(tú)discutirás
He will discuss-(él) discutirá
She will discuss - (ella) discutirá
It will discuss-(esto)discutirá
We will discuss- discutiremos
You will discuss- discutirán
They will discuss- discutirán

I will dream - (yo) soñaré
You will dream-(tú) soñarás
He will dream-(él) soñará
She will dream- (ella)soñará
It will dream- (esto) soñará
We will dream-soñaremos
You will dream- (ústedes) soñarán
They will dream- soñarán

I will erase -(yo) borraré
You will erase-(tú) borrarás
He will erase-(él) borrará
She will erase-(ella) borrará
It will erase-esto borrará
We will erase- borraremos
You will erase- borrarán
They will erase-borrarán

CONDITIONAL

I would demonstrate-demostraría
You would demonstrate-demostrarías
He would demonstrate- demostraría
She would demonstrate- demostraría
It would demonstrate-demostraría
We would demonstrate-demostraríamos
You would demonstrate- demostrarían
They would demonstrate- demostrarian

I would design - (yo) diseñaría
You would design-(tú) diseñarías
He would design-(él) diseñaria
She would design-(ella) diseñaría
It would design- (esto) diseñaría
We would design- diseñaríamos
You would design- diseñarían
They would design- diseñarian

I would develop-(yo) desarrollaría
You would develop- (tú) desarrollarías
He would develop-(él) desarrollaría
She would develop-(ella) desarrollaría
It would develop- (esto) desarrollaría
We would develop- desarrollaríamos
You would develop- desarrollarían
They would develop-desarrollarían

I would discuss - (yo) discutiría
You would discuss-(tú)discutirías
He would discuss-(él) discutiría
She would discuss-(ella) discutiría
It would discuss- (esto) discutiria
We would discuss- discutiríamos
You would discuss- discutirían
They would discuss- discutirían

I would dream- (yo) soñaría
You would dream-(tú) soñarias
He would dream - (él) soñaría
She would dream- (ella) soñaría
It would dream- (esto) soñaría
We would dream- soñaríamos
You would dream- soñarian
They would dream- soñarían

I would erase -(yo) borraría
You would erase-(tú) borrarias
He would erase-(él) borraría
She would erase-(ella) borraría
It would erase-(esto)borraría
We would erase- borraríamos
You would erase- borrarian
They would erase-borrarían

PRESENT TENSES

TO ENJOY: DISFRUTAR

I enjoy -(yo) disfruto
You enjoy-(tú) disfrutas
He enjoys-(él) disfruta
She enjoys-(ella) disfruta
It enjoys-(esto) disfruta
We enjoy - disfrutamos
You enjoy- disfrutan
They enjoy-disfrutan

TO ENTER: INGRESAR

I enter(enter) -(yo) entro
You enter-(tu) entras
He enters-(él) entra
She enters-(ella) entra
It enters-(esto) entra
We enter- entramos
You enter-(ustedes) entran
They enter-ellos(as) entran

TO EXPLAIN: EXPLICAR

I explain -(yo) explico
You explain-(tú) explicas
He explains-(él) explica
She explains-(ella) explica
It explains-(esto) explica
We explain- explicamos
You explain-explican
They explain-explican

TO EXIST: EXISTIR

I exist(exist) -(yo) existo
You exist -(tú) existes
He exists-(él) existe
She exists-(ella) existe
It exists-(esto) existe
We exist- existimos
You exist-(ústedes) existen
They exist-(ellos as) existen

TO EXPRESS: EXPRESAR

I express-(yo) expreso
You express -(tú) expresas
He expresses-(él) expresa
She expresses-(ella) expresa
It expresses-(esto) expresa
We express- expresamos
You express-expresan
They express-expresan

TO EXPLORE: EXPLORAR

I explore-(yo) exploro
You explore-(tú) exploras
He explores-(él) explora
She explores-(ella) explora
It explores-(esto) explora
We explore-exploramos
You explore-exploran
They explore-exploran

TO FAIL: FALLAR

I fail(feil) -(yo) fallo
You fail-(tú) fallas
He fails-(él) falla
She fails-(ella) falla
It fails -(esto) falla
We fail -(nosotros) fallamos
You fail-(ústedes) fallan
They fail-(ellos(as) fallan

PAST TENSES

I enjoyed-(yo) disfrutaba
You enjoyed-(tú) disfrutabas
He enjoyed -(él) disfrutaba
She enjoyed -(ella) disfrutaba
It enjoyed -(esto) disfrutaba
We enjoyed- disfrutabamos
You enjoyed- disfrutaban
They enjoyed- disfrutaban

I entered(enterd) -(yo) entraba
You entered-(tu) entrabas
He entered -(él) entraba
She entered-(ella) entraba
It entered -(esto) entraba
We entered- entrabamos
You entered-entraban
They entered- entraban

I explained -(yo) explicaba
You explained-(tú) explicabas
He explained-(él) explicaba
She explained-(ella) explicaba
It explained-(esto) explicaba
We explained-explicabamos
You explained- explicaban
They explained-explicaban

I existed(existid) -(yo) existía
You existed -(tú) existías
He existed -(él) existía
She existed -(ella) existía
It existed-(esto) existía
We existed-existíamos
You existed-(ústedes) existían
They existed-ellos(as) existian

I expressed -(yo) expresaba
You expressed -(tú) expreesabas
He expressed -(él) expresaba
She expressed -(ella) expresaba
It expressed-(esto) expresaba
We expressed - expresabamos
You expressed-expresaban
They expressed- expresaban

I explored-(yo) exploraba
You explored -(tú) explorabas
He explored-(él) exploraba
She explored -(ella) exploraba
It explored -(esto) exploraba
We explored -explorabamos
You explored- exploraban
They explored- exploraban

I failed(feild) -(yo) fallaba
You failed -(tú) fallabas
He failed -(él) fallaba
She failed -(ella) fallaba
It failed -(esto) fallaba
We failed -fallabamos
You failed -(ústedes) fallaban
They failed -(ellos(as) fallaban

FUTURE TENSES

I will enjoy -(yo) disfrutaré
You will enjoy-(tú) disfrutarás
He will enjoy-(él) disfrutará
She will enjoy-(ella) disfrutará
It will enjoy-(esto) disfrutará
We will enjoy- disfrutaremos
You will enjoy - disfrutarán
They will enjoy- disfrutarán

I will enter -(yo) entraré
You will enter-(tu) entrarás
He will enter-(él) entrará
She will enter-(ella) entrará
It will enter-(esto) entrará
We will enter - entraremos
You will enter -(ustedes) entrarán
They will enter-(ellos(as) entrarán

I will explain-(yo) explicaré
You will explain-(tú) explicarás
He will explain-(él) explicará
She will explain-(ella) explicará
It will explain-(esto) explicará
We will explain-explicaremos
You will explain- explicarán
They will explain- explicarán

I will exist-(yo) existiré
You will exist-(tú) existtirás
He will exist-(él) existirá
She will exist-(ella) existirá
It will exist-(esto) existtirá
We will exist- existiremos
You will exist-(ústedes) existirán
They will exist-(ellos(as) existirán

I will express-(yo) expresaré
You will express-(tú) expresarás
He will express-(él) expresará
She will express-(ella) expresará
It will express -(esto) expresará
We will express -expresaremos
You will express-expresarán
They will express -expresarán

I will explore-(yo) exploraré
You will explore-(tú) explorarás
He will explore-(él) explorará
She will explore -(ella) explorará
It will explore-(esto) explorará
We will explore- exploraremos
You will explore- explorarán
They will explore-explorarán

I will fail -(yo) fallaré
You will fail -(tú) fallarás
He will fail-(él) fallará
She will fail -(ella) fallará
It will fail -(esto) fallará
We will fail -(nosotros) fallaremos
You will fail -(ústedes) fallarán
They will fail-(ellos(as) fallarán

CONDITIONAL

I would enjoy -(yo) disfrutaría
You would enjoy-(tú) disfrutarías
He would enjoy-(él) disfrutaría
She would enjoy-(ella) disfrutaría
It would enjoy -(esto) disfrutaría
We would enjoy-disfrutaríamos
You would enjoy-disfrutarían
They would enjoy-disfrutarían

I would enter -(yo) entraría
You would enter-(tu) entrarías
He would enter-(él) entraría
She would enter -(ella) entraría
It would enter-(esto) entraría
We would enter-entrariamos
You would enter - entrarían
They would enter - entrarían

I would explain-(yo) explicaría
You would explain-(tú) explicarías
He would explain-(él) explicaría
She would explain-(ella) explicaría
It would explain-(esto) explicaría
We would explain- explicaríamos
You would explain- explicarían
They would explain-explicarian

I would exist -(yo) existiría
You would exist-(tú) existirias
He would exist-(él) existiría
She would exist-(ella) existiría
It would exist-(esto) existiría
We would exist-existiríamos
You would exist-existirían
They would exist- existirian

I would express-(yo) expresaría
You would express-(tú) expresarías
He would express-(él) expresaría
She would express-(ella) expresaría
It would express-(esto) expresaría
We would express-expresaríamos
You would express- expresarían
They would express-expresarían

I would explore-(yo) exploraría
You would explore-(tú) explorarías
He would explore-(él) exploraría
She would explore-(ella) exploraría
It would explore-(esto) exploraría
We would explore-exploraríamos
You would explore- explorarían
They would explore- explorarian

I would fail-(yo) fallaría
You would fail -(tú) fallarías
He would fail -(él) fallaría
She would fail -(ella) fallaría
It would fail -(esto) fallaría
We would fail -(nosotros) fallaríamos
You would fail -(ústedes) fallarían
They would fail-(ellos(as) fallarían

PRESENT TENSES

TO FINISH: TERMINAR
I finish -(yo)termino
You finish-(tú)terminas
He finishes -(él)termina
She finishes -(ella)termina
It finishes-(esto)termina
We finish- terminamos
You finish -terminan
They finish - terminan

TO FIX: ARREGLAR
I fix (fix) -(yo) arreglo
You fix -(tú) arreglas
He fixes -(él) arregla
She fixes -(ella) arregla
It fixes-(esto) arregla
We fix - arreglamos
You fix -(ústedes) arreglan
They fix -(ellos(as) arreglan

TO FOLLOW: SEGUIR
I follow (falo)-(yo) sigo
You follow -(tú) sigues
He follows -(él) sigue
She follows -(ella) sigue
It follows-(esto) sigue
We follow- seguimos
You follow - siguen
They follow - siguen

TO FRY: FREIR
I fry(frai) -(yo) frio
You fry - (tú) fries
He fries - (él) frie
She fries-ella frie
It fries-(esto) frie
We fry - (nosotros) freimos
You fry -(ústedes) frien
They fry - (ellos(as) frien

TO FACE: ENFRENTAR
I face(feis) -(yo) enfrento
You face - (tú) enfrentas
He faces - (él) enfrenta
She faces-ella enfrenta
It faces - (esto) enfrenta
We face - enfrentamos
You face -enfrentan
They face -enfrentan

TO FILL: LLENAR
I fill(fill) -(yo)lleno
You fill -(tú) llenas
He fills-(él) llena
She fills-ella llena
It fills-(esto) llena
We fill - (nosotros) llenamos
You fill -(ústedes) llenan
They fill -(ellos(as) llenan

TO FISH: PESCAR
I fish(fish) -(yo) pezco
You fish - (tú) pezcas
He fishes -(él) pezca
She fishes - (ella) pezca
It fishes - (esto) pezca
We fish - pezcamos
You fish - pezcan
They fish - pezcan

PAST TENSES

I finished -(yo)terminaba
You finished -(tú)terminabas
He finished -(él)terminaba
She finished -(ella)terminaba
It finished -(esto)terminaba
We finished-terminabamos
You finished-terminaban
They finished-terminaban

I fixed -(yo) arreglaba
You fixed -(tú) arreglabas
He fixed -(él) arreglaba
She fixed -(ella) arreglaba
It fixed -(esto) arreglaba
We fixed - arreglabamos
You fixed - arreglaban
They fixed -arreglaban

I followed (falod)-(yo) seguía
You followed -(tú) seguías
He followed -(él) seguía
She followed -(ella) seguía
It followed -(esto) seguía
We followed - seguíamos
You followed - seguían
They followed- seguían

I fried (fraid) - (yo) freía
You fried -(tú) freías
He fried - (él) freía
She fried-ella freía
It fried - (esto) freía
We fried - (nosotros) freíamos
You fried - (ústedes) freían
They fried - (ellos(as) freían

I faced (feisd) - (yo) enfrentaba
You faced - (tú)enfrentabas
He faced - (él) enfrentaba
She faced - (ella) enfrentaba
It faced - (esto) enfrentaba
We faced - enfrentabamos
You faced - enfrentaban
They faced -enfrentaban

I filled(filld) - (yo) llenaba
You filled - (tú) llenabas
He filled - (él) llenaba
She filled - (ella) llenaba
It filled - (esto) llenaba
We filled -llenabamos
You filled - llenaban
They filled -llenaban

I fished(fisht) - (yo) pezcaba
You fished - (tú) pezcabas
He fished - (él) pezcaba
She fished - (ella) pezcaba
It fished - (esto) pezcaba
We fished - pezcabamos
You fished - pezcaban
They fished -pezcaban

FUTURE TENSES

I will finish -(yo)terminaré
You will finish -(tú)terminarás
He will finish -(él)terminará
She will finish -(ella)terminará
It will finish-(esto)terminará
We will finish-terminaremos
You will finish- terminarán
They will finish- terminarán

I will fix -(yo) arreglaré
You will fix -(tú) arreglarás
He will fix-(él) arreglará
She will fix -(ella) arreglará
It will fix-(esto) arreglará
We will fix - arreglaremos
You will fix -(ústedes) arreglarán
They will fix -(ellos(as) arreglarán

I will follow -(yo) seguiré
You will follow -(tú) seguirás
He will follow -(él) seguirá
She will follow -(ella) seguirá
It will follow-(esto) seguirá
We will follow-seguiremos
You will follow-(ústedes)seguirán
They will follow – (ellos(as)seguirán

I will fry -(yo) freiré
You will fry - (tú) freirás
He will fry - (él) freirá
She will fry - (ella) freirá
It will fry - (esto) freirá
We will fry -(nosotros) freiremos
You will fry - (ústedes) freirán
They will fry - (ellos(as) freirán

I will face - (yo) enfrentaré
You will face - (tú) enfrentarás
He will face-(él) enfrentará
She will face - (ella) enfrentará
It will face-(esto) enfrentará
We will face- enfrentaremos
You will face- enfrentarán
They will face-enfrentarán

I will fill-(yo)llenaré
You will fill - (tú) llenarás
He will fill - (él) llenará
She will fill - (ella) llenará
It will fill - (esto)llenará
We will fill-llenaremos
You will fill - llenarán
They will fill-llenarán

I will fish - (yo) pezcaré
You will fish - (tú) pezcarás
He will fish - (él) pezcará
She will fish - (ella) pezcará
It will fish-(esto) pezcará
We will fish- pezcaremos
You will fish - pezcarán
They will fish-pezcarán

CONDITIONAL

I would finish-(yo)terminaría
You would finish-(tú)terminarías
He would finish-(él)terminaria
She would finish-(ella)terminaría
It would finish-(esto)terminaria
We would finish- terminaríamos
You would finish-terminarían
They would finish-terminarían

I would fix -(yo) arreglaria
You would fix -(tú) arreglarías
He would fix-(él) arreglaría
She would fix-(ella) arreglaría
It would fix-(esto) arreglaría
We would fix - arreglaríamos
You would fix - arreglarian
They would fix-arreglarian

I would follow -(yo) seguiria
You would follow -(tú) seguirías
He would follow-(él) seguiria
She would follow-(ella) seguiría
It would follow-(esto) seguiria
We would follow - seguiríamos
You would follow - seguirian
They would follow -seguirían

I would fry - (yo) freiría
You would fry - (tú) freirías
He would fry - (él) freiría
She would fry - (ella) freiría
It would fry - (esto) freiría
We would fry - freiríamos
You would fry - freirían
They would fry - freirian

I would face - (yo) enfrentaría
You would face - (tú) enfrentarías
He would face-(él) enfrentaría
She would face - (ella) enfrentaría
It would face- (esto) enfrentaria
We would face-enfrentaríamos
You would face- enfrentarian
They would face - enfrentarian

I would fill - (yo) llenaría
You would fill - (tú) llenarías
He would fill-(él)llenaría
She would fill - (ella) llenaría
It would fill - (esto) llenaría
We would fill-llenaríamos
You would fill - llenarian
They would fill-llenarían

I would fish - (yo) pezcaría
You would fish - (tú) pezcarías
He would fish- (él) pezcaría
She would fish - (ella) pezcaría
It would fish-(esto) pezcaria
We would fish- pezcaríamos
You would fish- pezcarían
They would fish-pezcarían

PRESENT TENSES

TO FIGURE:CALCULAR
I figure - (yo) calculo
You figure - (tú) calculas
He figures - (él) calcula
She figures - (ella) calcula
It figures - (esto) calcula
We figure - calculamos
You figure - calculan
They figure - calculan

TO FILM:FILMAR
I film (film) - (yo) filmo
You film - (tú) filmas
He films - (él) filma
She films - (ella) filma
It films - (esto) filma
We film - filmamos
You film - filman
They film - filman

TO GUESS: ADIVINAR
I guess(gues) - (yo) adivino
You guess - (tú) adivinas
He guesses - (él) adivina
She guesses - (ella) adivina
It guesses - (esto) adivina
We guess - adivinamos
You guess - adivinan
They guess - adivinan

TO HATE: ODIAR
I hate (jeit) - (yo) odio
You hate - (tú) odías
He hates - (él) odia
She hates - ella odia
It hates - (esto) odia
We hate - odiamos
You hate - odian
They hate - odian

TO HELP:AYUDAR
I help (herlp) - (yo) ayudo
You help - (tú) ayudas
He helps - (él) ayuda
She helps - (ella) ayuda
It helps - (esto) ayuda
We help - ayudamos
You help - ayudan
They help - ayudan

TO HOPE:ESPERAR
I hope (jop) - (yo) espero
You hope - (tú) esperas
He hopes - (él) espera
She hopes - (ella) espera
It hopes - (esto) espera
We hope - esperamos
You hope - esperan
They hope - esperan

TO HUG:ABRAZAR
I hug (jog) - (yo) abrazo
You hug - (tú) abrazas
He hugs - (él) abraza
She hugs - (ella) abraza
It hugs - (esto) abraza
We hug - abrazamos
You hug - abrazan
They hug - abrazan

PAST TENSES

I figured - (yo) calculaba
You figured - (tú) calculabas
He figured - (él) calculaba
She figured - (ella) calculaba
It figured - (esto) calculaba
We figured - calculabamos
You figured - calculaban
They figured - calculaban

I filmed (filmd) - (yo) filmaba
You filmed - (tú) filmabas
He filmed - (él) filmaba
She filmed - (ella) filmaba
It filmed - (esto) filmaba
We filmed - filmabamos
You filmed - filmaban
They filmed - filmaban

I guessed - (yo) adivinaba
You guessed - (tú) adivinabas
He guessed - (él) adivinaba
She guessed - (ella) adivinaba
It guessed - (esto) adivinaba
We guessed - adivinabamos
You guessed - adivinaban
They guessed - adivinaban

I hated(jeitid) - (yo) odiaba
You hated - (tú) odiabas
He hated - (él) odiaba
She hated - (ella) odiaba
It hated - (esto) odiaba
We hated - odiabamos
You hated - odiaban
They hated - odiaban

I helped (jelpt) - (yo) ayudaba
You helped - (tú) ayudabas
He helped - (él) ayudaba
She helped - (ella) ayudaba
It helped - esto ayudaba
We helped - ayudabamos
You helped - ayudaban
They helped - ayudaban

I hoped (jopt) - (yo) esperaba
You hoped - (tú) esperabas
He hoped - (él) esperaba
She hoped - (ella) esperaba
It hoped - (esto) esperaba
We hoped - esperabamos
You hoped - esperaban
They hoped - esperaban

I hugged (jogd) - (yo) abrazaba
You hugged - (tú) abrazabas
He hugged - (él) abrazaba
She hugged - (ella) abrazaba
It hugged - (esto) abrazaba
We hugged - abrazabamos
You hugged - abrazaban
They hugged - abrazaban

FUTURE TENSES

I will figure - (yo) calcularé
You will figure - (tú) calcularás
He will figure - (él) calculará
She will figure - (ella) calculará
It will figure - (esto) calculará
We will figure - calcularemos
You will figure - calcularán
They will figure - calcularán

I will film - (yo) filmaré
You will film - (tú) filmarás
He will film - (él) filmará
She will film - (ella) filmará
It will film - (esto) filmará
We will film - filmaremos
You will film - filmarán
They will film - filmarán

I will guess - (yo) adivinaré
You will guess - (tú) adivinarás
He will guess - (él) adivinará
She will guess - (ella) adivinará
It will guess - (esto) adivinará
We will guess - adivinaremos
You will guess - adivinarán
They will guess - adivinarán

I will hate - (yo) odiaré
You will hate - (tú) odiarás
He will hate - (él) odiará
She will hate - (ella) odiará
It will hate - (esto) odiará
We will hate - odiaremos
You will hate - odiarán
They will hate - odiarán

I will help - (yo) ayudaré
You will help - (tú) ayudarás
He will help - (él) ayudará
She will help - (ella) ayudará
It will help - (esto) ayudará
We will help - ayudaremos
You will help - ayudarán
They will help - ayudarán

I will hope - (yo) esperaré
You will hope - (tú) esperarás
He will hope - (él) esperará
She will hope - (ella) esperará
It will hope - (esto) esperará
We will hope - esperaremos
You will hope - esperarán
They will hope - esperarán

I will hug - (yo) abrazaré
You will hug - (tú) abrazarás
He will hug - (él) abrazará
She will hug - (ella) abrazará
It will hug - (esto) abrazará
We will hug - abrazaremos
You will hug - abrazarán
They will hug - abrazarán

CONDITIONAL

I would figure - (yo) calcularía
You would figure - (tú) calcularías
He would figure - (él) calcularía
She would figure - (ella) calcularía
It would figure - (esto) calcularía
We would figure - calcularíamos
You would figure - calcularían
They would figure - calcularian

I would film - (yo) filmaría
You would film - (tú) filmarías
He would film - (él) filmaría
She would film - (ella) filmaría
It would film - (esto) filmaría
We would film - filmaríamos
You would film - filmarían
They would film - filmarían

I would guess - (yo) adivinaría
You would guess - (tú) adivinarías
He would guess - (él) adivinaría
She would guess - (ella) adivinaría
It would guess - (esto) adivinaría
We would guess - adivinaríamos
You would guess - adivinarían
They would guess - adivinarían

I would hate - (yo) odiaría
You would hate - (tú) odiarías
He would hate - (él) odiaría
She would hate - (ella) odiaría
It would hate - (esto) odiaría
We would hate - odiaríamos
You would hate - odiarían
They would hate - odiarian

I would help - (yo) ayudaría
You would help - (tú) ayudarias
He would help - (él) ayudaría
She would help - (ella) ayudaría
It would help - (esto) ayudaría
We would help - ayudariamos
You would help - ayudarían
They would help - ayudarían

I would hope - (yo) esperaría
You would hope - (tú) esperarias
He would hope - (él) esperaría
She would hope - (ella) esperaría
It would hope - (esto) esperaría
We would hope - esperaríamos
You would hope - esperarían
They would hope - esperarían

I would hug - (yo) abrazaría
You would hug - (tú) abrazarías
He would hug - (él) abrazaría
She would hug - (ella) abrazaria
It would hug - (esto) abrazaría
We would hug - abrazaríamos
You would hug - abrazarían
They would hug - abrazarían

PRESENT TENSES

TO WALK:CAMINAR
I walk **(wolk)** - (yo) camino
You walk - (tú) caminas
He walks - (él) camina
She walks - (ella) camina
It walks - (esto) camina
We walk - caminamos
You walk - caminan
They walk - caminan

TO BELIEVE: CREER
I believe **(biliv)** - (yo) creo
You believe - (tú) crees
He believes - (él) cree
She believes - (ella) cree
It believes - (esto) cree
We believe - creemos
You believe - creen
They believe - creen

TO NEED: NECESITAR
I need **(nid)** - (yo) necesito
You need - (tú) necesitas
He needs - (él) necesita
She needs - (ella) necesita
It needs - (esto) necesita
We need - necesitamos
You need - necesitan
They need - necesitan

TO READ: LEER
I read (rid) - (yo) leo
You read - (tú) lees
He reads - (él) lee
She reads - ella lee
It reads - esto lee
We read - (nosotros) leemos
You read - (ústedes) leen
They read - (ellos (as) leen

TO LIVE: VIVIR
I live (liv) - (yo) vivo
You live - (tú) vives
He lives - (él) vive
She lives - (ella) vive
It lives - (esto) vive
We live - (nosotros) vivimos
You live - (ústedes) viven
They live – (ellos (as) viven

TO GO: IR
I go - (yo) voy
You go - (tú) vas
He goes - (él) va
She goes - (ella) va
It goes - (esto) va
We go – nosotros vamos
You go - (ústedes) van
They go - (ellos (as) van

PAST TENSES

I walked - (yo) caminaba
You walked - (tú) caminabas
He walked - (él) caminaba
She walksed - (ella) caminaba
It walked - (esto) caminaba
We walked - caminabamos
You walked - caminaban
They walked - caminaban

I believed **(bilivd)** - (yo) creía
You believed - (tú) creías
He believed - (él) creía
She believed - (ella) creía
It believed - (esto) creía
We believed - creíamos
You believed - creyeron
They believed - creyeron

I needed - (yo) necesitaba
You needed - (tú) necesitabas
He needed - (él) necesitaba
She needed - (ella) necesitaba
It needed - (esto) necesitaba
We needed - necesitabamos
You needed - necesitaban
They needed - necesitaban

I read (red) - (yo) leía
You read - (tú) leías
He read - (él) leía
She read - ella leía
It read - (esto) leía
We read - (nosotros) leíamos
You read - (ústedes) leían
They read - (ellos (as) leían

I lived (livd) - (yo) vivía
You lived - (tú) vivías
He lived - (él) vivía
She lived - (ella) vivía
It lived - (esto) vivía
We lived - (nosotros) vivíamos
You lived - (ústedes) vivían
They lived - (ellos (as) vivían

I went - (yo) iba/yo fui
You went - (tú) ibas/tu fuiste
He went - (él) iba/él fue
She went - (ella) iba/ella fue
It went - (esto) iba/ fue
We went - ibamos/fuimos
You went - iban/fueron
They went - iban/fueron

FUTURE TENSES

I will walk - (yo) caminaré
You will walk - (tu) caminarás
He will walk - (él) caminará
She will walk - (ella) caminará
It will walk - (esto) caminará
We will walk - caminaremos
You will walk - caminarán
They will walk - caminarán

I will believe - (yo) creeré
You will believe - (tú) creerás
He will believe - (él) creerá
She will believe - (ella) creerá
It will believe - (esto) creerá
We will believe - creeremos
You will believe - creerán
They will believe - creerán

I will need - (yo) necesitaré
You will need - (tú) necesitarás
He will need - (él) necesitará
She will need - (ella) necesitará
It will need - (esto) necesitará
We will need - necesitaremos
You will need - necesitarán
They will need - necesitarán

I will read (rid) - (yo) leeré
You will read - (tú) leerás
He will read - (él) leerá
She will read - (ella) leerá
It will read - (esto) leerá
We will read - (nosotros) leeremos
You will read - (ústedes) leerán
They will read - (ellos (as) leerán

I will live - (yo) viviré
You will live - (tú) vivirás
He will live - (él) vivirá
She will live - (ella) vivirá
It will live - (esto) vivirá
We will live - (nosotros) viviremos
You will live - (ústedes) vivirán
They will live - (ellos (as) vivirán

I will go - (yo) iré
You will go - (tú) irás
He will go - (él) irá
She will go - (ella) irá
It will go - (esto) irá
We will go - (nosotros) iremos
You will go - (ústedes) irán
They will go - (ellos (as) irán

CONDITIONAL

I would walk - (yo) caminaría
You would walk - (tú) caminarías
He would walk - (él) caminaría
She would walk - (ella) caminaría
It would walk - (esto) caminaría
We would walk - caminaríamos
You will walk - caminarían
They will walk - caminarían

I would believe - (yo) creería
You would believe - (tú) creerías
He would believe - (él) creería
She would believe - (ella) creería
It would believe - (esto) creería
We would believe - creeríamos
You would believe - creerían
They would belive - creerían

I would need - (yo) necesitaría
You would need - (tú) necesitarías
He would need - (él) necesitaría
She would need - (ella) necesitaría
It would need - (esto) necesitaría
We would need - necesitaríamos
You would need - necesitarían
They would need - necesitarían

I would read (rid) - (yo) leería
You would read - (tú) leerías
He would read - (él) leería
She would read - (ella) leería
It would read - (esto) leería
We would read - (nosotros) leeríamos
You would read - (ústedes) leerían
They would read - (ellos (as) leerían

I would live - (yo) viviría
You would live - (tú) vivirías
He would live - (él) viviría
She would live - (ella) viviría
It would live - (esto) viviría
We would live - (nosotros) viviríamos
You would live - (ústedes) vivirian
They would live - (ellos (as) vivirían

I would go - (yo) iría
You would go - (tú) irías
He would go - (él) iría
She would go - (él) iría
It would go - (esto) iría
We would go - (nosotros) iríamos
You would go - (ústedes) irían
They would go - (ellos (as) irían

Made in the USA
Las Vegas, NV
10 June 2025

23471413R00131